UNITED NATIONS PEACEKEEPING IN THE POST-COLD WAR ERA

This study examines whether peacekeeping fundamentally changed between the Cold War and post-Cold War periods, focusing on contrasting case studies of the Congo, Cyprus, Somalia and Angola, as well as more recent operations in Sierra Leone and East Timor. The authors conclude that most peacekeeping operations – whether in the Cold War or post-Cold War periods – were flawed due to the failure of the UN member states to agree upon achievable objectives, the precise nature of the operations and provision of the necessary resources, and unrealistic post-1989 expectations that UN peacekeeping operations could be adapted to the changed international circumstances. The study concludes by looking at the Brahimi reforms, questions whether these were realistically achievable and looks at their impact on contemporary peace operations in Sierra Leone, East Timor and elsewhere.

John Terence O'Neill is a former Colonel in the Irish Defence Forces, who served on UN missions in the Congo, Lebanon and Angola, and is a research associate, Department of Modern History at Trinity College Dublin.

Nicholas Rees is Dean of Graduate Studies and Jean Monnet Professor of European Institutions and International Relations at the University of Limerick.

THE CASS SERIES ON PEACEKEEPING
ISSN 1367–9880
General Editor: Michael Pugh

This series examines all aspects of peacekeeping, from the political, operational and legal dimensions to the developmental and humanitarian issues that must be dealt with by all those involved with peacekeeping in the world today.

1. *Beyond the Emergency: Development within UN Missions*
edited by Jeremy Ginifer

2. *The UN, Peace and Force*
edited by Michael Pugh

3. *Mediating in Cyprus: The Cypriot Communities and the United Nations*
by Oliver P. Richmond

4. *Peacekeeping and the UN Agencies*
edited by Jim Whitman

5. *Peacekeeping and Public Information: Caught in the Crossfire*
by Ingrid A. Lehman

6. *US Peacekeeping Policy under Clinton: A Fairweather Friend?*
by Michael MacKinnon

7. *Peacebuilding and Police Reform*
edited by Tor Tanke Holm and Espen Barth Eide

8. *Peacekeeping and Conflict Resolution*
edited by Oliver Ramsbotham and Tom Woodhouse

9. *Managing Armed Conflicts in the 21st Century*
edited by Adekeye Adebajo and Chandra Lekha Sriram

10. *Women and International Peacekeeping*
edited by Louise Olsson and Torunn L. Tryggestad

11. *Recovering from Civil Conflict: Reconciliation, Peace and Development*
edited by Edward Newman and Albrecht Schnabel

12. *Mitigating Conflict: The Role of NGOs*
edited by Henry F. Carey and Oliver P. Richmond

13. *Ireland and International Peacekeeping 1960–2000: A Study of Irish Motivation*
Katsumi Ishizuka

14. *Peace Operations after September 11, 2001*
edited by Thierry Tardy

15. *Confronting Past Human Rights Violations: Justice vs. Peace in Times of Transition*
Chandra Lekha Sriram

16. *A UN 'Legion': Between Utopia and Reality*
Stephen Kinloch-Pichat

17. *The Politics of Peacekeeping in the Post-Cold War Era*
edited by David S. Sorensen and Pia Christina Wood

18. *United Nations Peacekeeping in the Post-Cold War Era*
John Terence O'Neill and Nicholas Rees

UNITED NATIONS PEACEKEEPING IN THE POST-COLD WAR ERA

John Terence O'Neill
and Nicholas Rees

Routledge
Taylor & Francis Group

LONDON AND NEW YORK

First published 2005
by Routledge
2 Park Square, Milton Park, Abingdon, Oxon, OX14 4RN

Simultaneously published in the USA and Canada
by Routledge
270 Madison Ave, New York NY 10016

Routledge is an imprint of the Taylor & Francis Group

Transferred to Digital Printing 2007

© 2005 John Terence O'Neill and Nicholas Rees

Typeset in Times New Roman by
Keystroke, Jacaranda Lodge, Wolverhampton

British Library Cataloguing in Publication Data
A catalogue record for this book is available from the British Library

Library of Congress Cataloging in Publication Data

ISBN 0–714–65597–X (hbk)
ISBN 0–714–68489–9 (pbk)

Publisher's Note
The publisher has gone to great lengths to ensure the quality
of this reprint but points out that some imperfections in the
original may be apparent

Printed and bound by CPI Antony Rowe, Eastbourne

CONTENTS

LIST OF ILLUSTRATIONS

Figures

Maps

Plate

Tables

NOTE ON CONTRIBUTORS

John Terence O'Neill is a former Colonel in the Irish Defence Forces. He has served on UN missions in the Congo (1961), Lebanon (1982–3) and Angola (1993) and holds a Ph.D. from Trinity College, Dublin. Terry O'Neill has published articles in *Irish Studies in International Affairs* and *International Peacekeeping*. He is currently working on a study of the UN's role in Liberia, with Nicholas Rees.

Nicholas Rees is Dean of Graduate Studies and Jean Monnet Professor of European Institutions and International Relations at the University of Limerick. He researches and writes on the European Union, international relations and peacekeeping, and is a former editor of *Irish Political Studies*, is co-author of *Ireland's Poor Relations: Irish Foreign Policy towards the Third World* (Gill and Macmillan) and writes an annual review of Irish foreign policy for *Irish Studies in International Affairs*.

ACKNOWLEDGEMENTS

We would like to thank Lt General William O'Callaghan, DSM (former Force Commander UNIFIL), Jan Risvik and Tore Gustavsson of Norsk Utenrikspolitisk Institutt (Norway), and the many other military and civilian personnel involved in UN peacekeeping, who were interviewed and gave generously of their time over the years. An especial thanks to Professors Patrick Keatinge, Michael Marsh, Eunan O'Halpin (Trinity College Dublin), Dr Ray Murphy (National University of Ireland Galway), Professor Edward Moxon-Browne (University of Limerick), and Mr Noel Dorr, (former Secretary, Department of Foreign Affairs, Ireland) for their helpful comments.

Our thanks to our respective families, for their support and encouragement, in the completion of this project.

Terry O'Neill
Nick Rees
Summer 2004

1

INTRODUCTION

The main aim of this study is to examine those activities carried out by the UN in the period 1946 to 2003 employing military and police personnel and coming under the rubric 'UN Peacekeeping'. In particular, it seeks to ascertain whether those operations which took place in the period following the improvement of relations between East and West in the late 1980s were markedly different in terms of their nature and objectives from those which had gone before, and the impact upon operations of the changes in the international system post-Cold War. Certainly, the late 1980s witnessed a number of successes in peacekeeping, including the successful resolution of conflicts in Central America, Africa and the Middle East, while the early 1990s were marked by a significant increase in the number of authorisations of new missions. The diversity of missions and the range of new requirements seemed to fundamentally change the nature of peacekeeping; yet was this actually the case, or are many commentators guilty of over-simplifying the type of operations undertaken in the past while assuming new operations were of a more complex nature? Did the end of the Cold War explain the transformation of peacekeeping, or are there broader developments associated with globalisation that help to account for the growing demand for peacekeeping.[1]

During the Cold War, the UN's ability to engage in collective action was seen to have been impeded by East–West divisions which effectively limited the possibility of cooperation in the UN Security Council. The end of the Cold War was to have introduced an era of peace with an emphasis on the rights and privileges of human rights.[2] However, expectations of more effective peacekeeping post-Cold War proved misplaced. As early as 1994, Adam Roberts described UN peacekeeping as 'in crisis'.[3] Tried and tested principles and practices had been modified or abandoned and the distinction between peacekeeping and various enforcement activities had become blurred. UN efforts in Bosnia had exposed the organisation to accusations of weakness and the initially successful UN operation in Angola had been followed by resumption of warfare. The UN role in these states seemed to do little to address the underlying causes of conflict. These problems and failures had arisen at a time when, Roberts claimed, there was a widespread feeling of optimism that the UN could have a more central role in international security and that peacekeeping could tackle a wide range of international problems.

1

'The international community now wants the UN to demarcate boundaries, control and eliminate heavy weapons, quell anarchy and guarantee the delivery of humanitarian aid. There are increasing demands that the UN now enforce the peace as originally envisaged in the UN Charter.'[4]

John Mackinlay also writing in 1994, presented the situation in starker terms. There were, he maintained, signs that the fashion to promote peacekeeping was now over.[5] Peacekeeping, a concept that was successful during the Cold War, was now being used in contingencies for which it was not designed. Why was this the case and what led the UN to engage in such a range of new operations? The very visual images of suffering in conflict situations certainly led to a call for 'international action' and the CNN factor was undoubtedly important in understanding why there was felt to be a need to act. In Washington and the capitals of Europe, however, there was disenchantment and a growing reluctance to become involved in further peace-supporting activities. The visual failure of the UN in Somalia, Bosnia and Rwanda, as well as the increasing risk of casualties, left the US and many European states reluctant to participate in operations that might be prolonged and likely to lead to loss of life. As an issue this was less prevalent among developing states, who for a mix of motives were still willing to commit forces to such operations, but often found themselves in situations for which they had not been adequately prepared and trained, as seems to have been the case in Sierra Leone. Nevertheless, the UN also had its limited successes in the late 1990s, in East Timor, Bosnia and Herzegovina, and Afghanistan, suggesting that the UN's approach might be a factor in helping to resolve the immediate conflict and assist the transition to a state of more permanent peace.

As a part of the broader objective of this study we are concerned with looking at whether the UN has adapted as a system to meet the increasing expectations of it as a force for peace in the post-Cold War era. In particular, although our choice of case studies is by necessity selective, we are interested in comparing the cases, as well as looking at all other instances of peacekeeping, with a view to determining to what extent the UN has learnt lessons from its past failures. Again, commentary from two recent Secretaries-General, has tended to suggest that the UN has been slow to learn from its own mistakes, whether made in New York, or at an operational level in the field. Those involved in operations often express the view that much of what they have learnt is seldom listened to in New York and many valuable lessons are not adequately recorded back at UN headquarters. In this context, has much changed in the post-Cold War period, and have the attempts at change and reform in the administrative structure and management of UN peacekeeping in New York addressed these questions?

The impact of September 11, Afghanistan and Iraq on the UN

The events of September 11, the US response in Afghanistan and the American-led coalition attack on Iraq, all seem to suggest that the search for security, and by extension peace, remain core to any attempt to understand global politics and the role of the UN. The nature of the threat, whether it is international terrorism or the defiance of a rogue state, is far from new and in some ways is more normal than it might initially appear. The world did not change after September 11, and the attack on America was reflective of an anti-American feeling in many Islamic states. The US responded to the attacks by launching 'a war on terrorism' and tightening its own 'defence of the homeland'.[6] In so doing there was an initial rapprochement between the US, Russia and the EU, all of whom were committed to opposing terrorism and adopting tougher new measures to confront terrorist organisations and their activities.

The US response in Afghanistan and Iraq has been predictable and consistent with the increasingly unilateralist and militaristic policy pursued by the Bush Administration (e.g. note US rejection of the International Criminal Court, the Kyoto Protocol and the Comprehensive Test Ban Treaty). Such an approach does not bode well for the UN and suggests that the consensus that existed in the Security Council in the early 1990s is over. In Afghanistan the US administration sought to pursue its military objective of defeating the Taliban regime and al-Qaida and replacing it with a government favourable to the US by employing its military might. Following the end of the military phase of the campaign, the American government supported the authorisation by the UN of small, armed force, the International Security Assistance Force (ISAF), for deployment under UK command in Kabul. The US, however, was reluctant to take a leading role in the force. Notably, in July 2002 the US threatened to block all UN-mandated peace-keeping operations if the rules of the International Criminal Court were applied to the US.

The US-led attack on Iraq in 2003, seemed to undermine the role of the UN, again suggesting that the US was willing to take independent action without UN authorisation, with the objective of securing its own security interests. American policy towards Iraq typified the Bush Administration's militaristic and more unilateral approach to opponents and those seen to be a threat to the US. As the military action in Iraq declined, it became increasingly evident that the US, through its appointment of a former US military commander, Jay Garner, would shape the establishment of a new administration in Iraq. The US sought to keep the UN at arm's length, preferring instead to pursue it own solutions in Iraq rather than reverting to the UN. Such an approach seems to further undermine the role of the UN, something that the US administration had already done in its initial decision to go to war, but which was further reinforced by its approach in post-war Iraq. The long-term impact of US actions on the UN's peacekeeping role has yet to be seen, but certainly American policy under Bush is not supportive of the UN, and has once again fragmented consensus in the Security Council.

Collective security, peacekeeping and the UN system

In standing back from recent events, much has been written about the collective security and the role of the United Nations in peacekeeping from a variety of different perspectives involving academics, UN officials and those involved in peacekeeping operations. The present study seeks to examine by means of case studies, as well as by reference to the overall role of the UN in peacekeeping, whether the UN's role in peacekeeping did change in the post-Cold War environment. The literature on peacekeeping includes case studies of either single operations[7] or comparisons of different cases, often of successes and failures.[8] Other studies focus on the history and evolution of peacekeeping.[9] There are also a range of broader studies that look at the UN as a political and administrative organisation, focusing on UN reform, leadership, and institutional issues, as well as placing the UN in a broader context.[10] A relatively small number of studies have focused on the UN from a theoretical perspective.[11] Following the end of the Cold War and the growth in the number of peacekeeping operations, many of the new studies focused on the changing nature of peacekeeping, operational issues and the changing international system.[12]

At a theoretical level the logic of collective security rests on the assumptions that the interest of sovereign nations is in maintaining peace, and that they are willing and able to collectively respond to threats to the peace. In instances where threats to peace occur the states must be willing to respond in an organised and collective way so as to ensure that peace is either maintained or restored. An initial attempt was made to incorporate such an approach into the Covenant of the League of Nations, under Articles 10 and 11.

> The Members of the League undertake to respect and preserve as against external aggression the territorial integrity and existing political independence of all Members of the League.
>
> Any war or threat of war, whether immediately affecting any of the Members of the League or not, is hereby declared a matter of concern to the whole League, and the League shall take any action that may be deemed wise and effectual to safeguard the peace of nations.

These provisions were supported by the possibility of sanctions, although in practice they were not applied when Japan invaded Manchuria in 1931, were used with limited effect against Italy following its attack on Ethiopia in 1935–6, and not at all against Germany in 1936. In light of these experiences, the commitment to collective security in the UN Charter was unlikely to provide a particularly good basis for ensuring peace. Article 1 of the UN Charter states that the purposes of the United Nations are:

> To maintain international peace and security, and to that end: to take effective collective measures for the prevention and removal of threats to

4

the peace, and for the suppression of acts of aggression or other breaches of the peace, and to bring about by peaceful means, and in conformity with the principles of justice and international law, adjustment or settlement of international disputes or situations which might lead to a breach of the peace.

The Charter places the main responsibility for the maintenance of peace on the Security Council (Article 24). The Charter offered two possible routes, with Chapter VI focused on the 'pacific settlement of disputes', and Chapter VII, 'action with respect to threats to the peace, breaches of the peace, and acts of aggression'. In practice, the development of peacekeeping in relation to Chapter VI and VII differed considerably from the idea of collective security as envisaged, in so much as the objective has not been to defeat an aggressor, but to prevent violence, maintain a ceasefire and act as a buffer between parties to a conflict.[13] In many instances the UN has gone beyond Chapter VI, but have stopped short of peace enforcement, leading commentators to dub these operations 'Chapter Six and One-half'.

The term 'peacekeeping' has never been given a fixed and detailed meaning (and is not mentioned in the UN Charter), and many of the terms used by politicians and commentators to describe various UN activities lack a precise and universally accepted definition. It is the word 'peace' and the associated plethora of terms such as peacekeeping, peacekeepers, peace-enforcement, peace-making, peace-building, peace-maintenance that demands particular attention. Overall, it is also necessary to examine not only the language and terminology, but the context and years in which they are used. The idea of peacekeeping has changed and definitions in the early twenty-first century differ from those of UN activities undertaken in the 1950s, or even from activities undertaken by the League of Nations.

In the *Peacekeepers Handbook* the International Peace Academy (1984) defined peacekeeping as:

> The prevention, containment, moderation, and termination of hostilities between or within states, through the medium of a peaceful third party intervention organised and directed internally, using multinational forces of soldiers, police and civilians to restore and maintain peace. (1984)

One notable commentator uses the term:[14]

> To refer to any international effort involving an operational component to promote the termination of armed conflict or the resolution of long standing disputes. (1993)

Boutros-Ghali defined the term in *An Agenda for Peace* (1992) in the following manner:

> Peacekeeping is the deployment of a United Nations presence in the field, hitherto with the consent of all the parties concerned, normally involving

5

United Nations military and/or police personnel and frequently civilians as well. Peacekeeping is a technique that expands the possibilities for both the prevention of conflict and the making of peace.

In looking at peacekeeping he suggested that the UN was engaged in four main activities aimed at controlling conflict:

- *Preventive diplomacy*: aimed at taking action to prevent conflicts from arising in both violent and non-violent situations
- *Peacemaking*: aimed at bringing hostile parties together by peaceful means as determined in Chapter VI of the UN Charter
- *Peacekeeping*: the deployment of a UN presence in the field, with the consent of the parties, to stop conflicts and preserve peace once established
- *Peace-building*: post-conflict action aimed at ensuring that violence does not reoccur and to identify and support structures that will strengthen the peace.

The emphasis on the broader activities associated with peacekeeping reflected the realisation on the part of Boutros-Ghali that simply preventing or halting a conflict was insufficient, and that there needed to be a greater emphasis on peace-making and building processes to ensure longer term success. In an attempt to move beyond the traditional principles of peacekeeping, Boutros-Ghali argued the requirement of consent might be relaxed, so as to allow peacekeeping operations to be deployed in such situations where the warring parties had not agreed to UN intervention. Boutros-Ghali's assessment has been supported by a range of academic studies, many of which note that the UN has had limited short-term success in such conflict situations.[15] Some even go so far as to suggest that the UN may prolong conflict and limit the likelihood of resolution, as in may cases it does not address the root causes of the conflict.

There are, as we have argued, no clear cut definitions of peacekeeping, and even reference to Chapter VI (pacific settlement of disputes) and Chapter VII (peace-enforcement) operations is far from clear cut. There is a tendency on the part of contributors to the literature on peacekeeping to categorise operations under convenient but somewhat misleading labels. Even the general categories of 'Cold War', and 'post-Cold War' operations can be misleading. The Congo operation (ONUC 1960–4) did not fit neatly into the pattern of 'Cold War operations' and Paul Diehl notes that it is something of a misnomer to classify all peacekeeping operations since 1989 as if there were little distinction between them.[16] Moreover, a peacekeeping operation as demonstrated in the Congo, Somalia, and Angola, may attempt to perform more than one mission either simultaneously or sequentially. Categorisation can lead to ONUC, an operation of the early 1960s and with uncertain objectives, being described as an attempt at state/nation building,[17] a concept of the mid-1990s. Categorisation also creates the impression that operations had clear, specific objectives when in reality mandates were, and are, in the main vague, and objectives uncertain. This categorisation has also been extended to peacekeepers themselves. Masashi Nishihara, for instance, refers to (1) full fledged peacekeepers, (2) self-restrained peacekeepers, and (3) peace-enforcers. However, Irish troops were, by Nishihara's definition,[18] at different times in category (1) in Cyprus, category (2) in Somalia, and category (3) if one accepts ONUC as a case of peace enforcement. All of this would suggest that 'categorisation' has to be treated with great care.

The term 'UN peacekeeping' is used in this study to refer to those operations conducted by the UN from its foundation to the present day which involved international military, police and civilian personnel, and had as their general objective, the restoration and maintenance of international peace and security (see Chapter 2). 'Peacekeeping' may appear an optimistic term, given that in many cases, there was no peace to keep and that even when peace did exist, the UN forces had neither the authority nor the means to 'keep' it. Lacking any clearer definition than this it is worth noting that the underlying principles of traditional peacekeeping usually involved a mix of consent and cooperation by the parties affected, the impartiality of the UN, the non-use of military force (e.g. arms used only is self-defence), a UN mandate, and the deployment of a multinational force.[19] In many instances, there are examples where these principles have not guided peacekeeping, especially (but not always) in the post-Cold War world. For example, was the operation in the Congo in the 1960s impartial, or the participation of French and American contingents in Beirut in 1983?[20] Similarly, operations in Somalia and Bosnia-Herzegovina did not conform to traditional notions of peacekeeping. In some cases operations have been undertaken by bodies other than the UN, such as groupings of states, and regional organisations, such as in the EU in former Yugloslavia and Macedonia (2003–).

The UN as an organisation

The 'UN' referred to in much of the literature is an organisation which has undergone considerable change in terms of membership, and character during the period under 'examination'.[21] Membership has been gradually increased by the granting of independence to former colonies and by the break-up of former members, most notably the Soviet Union and Yugoslavia. The United Nations now has some 191 member states. Also, the political orientation and attitudes of member states has been changed by strategic, regional and internal developments. Most writers distinguish between the Cold War and post-Cold War period when examining the United Nations, with many studies of the early 1990s[22] noting and predicting that the continuing thaw in East–West relations would lead to a greater demand for peacekeeping operations.

In relation to peacekeeping operations, an increasing importance was attached to the development of greater cooperation among the permanent members of the Security Council. It was argued that changes in the international system, notably the break-up of the Soviet Union, economic reform in China, the re-emergence of a united Germany, greater European integration, and a benign American role, provided an important backdrop to improved cooperation and partnership. It was assumed by liberal international theorists that such conditions, in the context of a globalism and increased regionalism, would provide an opportunity to fulfil the original UN Charter objective of international peace and security. The reality, however, was very different from this view of the role of the UN in the post-Cold War environment. The politics of the Security Council, and the motives of its members, in promoting a far more active role in peacekeeping, have been far more complex reflecting as ever the national interests and vagaries of the Great Powers.

During the Cold War, China (Taiwan) had largely abstained on Security Council votes but had used its veto in 1965 to block (temporarily) the admission of Mongolia to the UN. By late 1968, Peking saw the US as providing a counterweight to Soviet[23] expansionist tendencies, opening doors to Japanese and Western European governments and facilitating replacement of Taiwan in the Council.[24] France under de Gaulle adopted the attitude 'Do not take initiatives. If somebody else does, say that the action contemplated is illegal or at least improper, but do not vote against it.'[25] Like the Soviet Union, it had sided with the Arabs in the 1967 and 1973 wars; it had no major objection to dealing with Marxist governments and Mitterrand told Reagan that poverty not Russia was the father of revolution.[26] Yet it had sided with the US in Security Council efforts to censure South Africa. Britain's role in Suez had put it at odds with the US and, like the Soviet Union, it had supplied arms to the Nigerian government during the civil war in that country. The Soviet Union, while less than supportive of UN peacekeeping efforts generally, had joined the US in supporting UNTEA and Indonesia's claim to West Guinea.[27] It had joined the other members of the Council in demanding a ceasefire between India and Pakistan; engaged in efforts to end the Middle East War in 1973; and toiled with the US to bring Iran to accept an end to the Iran–Iraq war.[28] In 1985, Gorbachev had argued that the problems threatening human survival were best settled through organisations such as the UN.[29] Meanwhile, US attitude to the UN and its peace-keeping efforts had been inconsistent. It had met the bulk of the costs of ONUC and supported the ONUC and UNEF operations. But having sought the presence of UN peacekeepers in Lebanon in 1978 (UNIFIL), it then made fulfilment of that Force's mandate impossible through its unstinting support for Israel. Kissinger sought to exclude the UN from his negotiations on the Middle East[30] and Reagan had even talked of withdrawal from the UN.[31] Puchala summed up US attitudes with the question: 'Do we get our money's worth from the UN?'[32] Vietnam, although one of the major conflicts of the Cold War, was not on the Council's agenda except in 1964 and both superpowers had not wanted the UN to meddle in their adventures in South East Asia.[33]

Immediately in the post-Cold War era, Russian foreign policy was at odds with its military policy. The military believed Russia should act as a force counter-ing what it saw as US aspirations to global dominance.[34] However, Russia was largely preoccupied with terrorism and conflicts within the former Soviet Union. It perceived no conflict of interests between it and the major Western powers and saw the sending of a battalion to UNPROFOR as making it a 'normal' European power.[35] The US would talk of preventing the world going up in flames but argue that while Bosnia was a human tragedy, it did 'not affect our vital national interests'.[36] Having suffered humiliation in Somalia, its President (Clinton) would accept an unpalatable compromise in Sierra Leone to avoid commitment of men and resources.[37] China remained concerned about US intentions seeing that power's role in Kosovo as manifestation of 'a desire to become Lord of the Earth'.[38] Of late it had shown a greater degree of flexibility, modifying its former rigid views on respect for state sovereignty[39] and demonstrating concern about developments within its geographical proximity such as East Timor.[40] In 1997, it agreed in principle to participate in UN DPKO's standby arrangements pledging to supply military observers and support service personnel.[41]

Underlying all of this, the UN system and the role of the UN Secretary-General have been increasingly challenged to respond to more demands for UN intervention in a range of roles as a peacekeeper. As Rivlin notes, in terms of the UN Charter the UN Secretary-General is both 'chief administrative officer' and able to pursue an autonomous political role through the Secretariat.[42] (See Article 9, UN Charter.) The UN Secretary-General plays a central and active role in UN peacekeeping using his good offices to act as a go-between, mediator and organiser of peace-keeping efforts. The role that the Secretary-General can play in peacekeeping is, of course, very much affected by and in some ways dependent on the support the individual enjoys in the Security Council. The overall effectiveness of the Secretary-General is affected by many factors, including the international environment in which he is operating, but also the ability and background of the individual is an important factor, as well as his general standing with the Great Powers (see Table 1.1). For example, many commentators credit Dag Hammarskjöld, as the second Secretary-General with considerably developing and expanding the role of the office and of its independence. His successors, up to and including Javier Pérez de Cuéllar, were seen as providing less high profile leadership. In the 1990s Boutros-Ghali when appointed enjoyed a high level of support among the member states, but was quickly the subject of controversy, accused of being outspoken, lacking in political judgement and a poor administrator. Whereas, Kofi Annan, has been seen by many commentators as a far more diplomatic figure, with over forty years experience in the UN system, including having been Assistant Secretary-General for Peacekeeping Operations (1992–3) and Under Secretary-General (1993–7).[43]

The role (and expectations) of the Secretary-General in peacekeeping was considerably enhanced as a result of the January 1992 request by the Security Council to Boutros-Ghali that he prepare within six months 'his analysis and recommendations on ways of strengthening and making more efficient within the framework of the Charter the capacity of the United Nations for preventive diplomacy, for peacemaking and peacekeeping'. The final outcome of the deliberations of the high-level group, *An Agenda for Peace*, will be explored in Chapter 7, but suffice to say that the report highlights the increasing expectations of the Secretary-General and of peacekeeping.

Table 1.1 Past UN Secretaries-General

Secretary-General	Country	Date
Trygve Lie	Norway	1946–52
Dag Hammarskjöld	Sweden	1953–61
U Thant	Burma	1961–71
Kurt Waldheim	Austria	1972–81
Javier Pérez de Cuéllar	Peru	1982–91
Boutros Boutros-Ghali	Egypt	1992–6
Kofi Annan	Ghana	1997–2006

Source: www.un.org/depts/dpko

Administration of peacekeeping

Looking at the procedures around the authorisation of peacekeeping, the UN Security Council usually decides in a first resolution to establish a peacekeeping operation.[44] It requests the Secretary-General to present a report to it outlining a detailed plan of operation including the overall approach, type of operation and number and type of personnel required. In drawing up the report, often within 48 hours, the Secretary-General usually consults with the Permanent Members of the Security Council, and with the Department of Peacekeeping Operations, who are responsible for considering the type of operation needed and the planning of the operational detail.[45] Following the publication of the Secretary-General's report a second resolution is normally passed by the Security Council authorising the operation.[46]

In considering the practicalities of how the administration of peacekeeping is organised in the Secretariat, the Department of Peacekeeping Operations (DPKO) is primarily responsible for peacekeeping operations (see Figure 1.1). The department is headed up by the Under-Secretary-General responsible for peace-keeping, and comprises the Office of Operations (including the Situation Centre, the Asia–Middle East Division, the Africa Division and the Europe and Latin America Division), the Military and Civilian Police Divisions and the Office of Mission Support (including the Logistics Support Division and Administration Support Division). Attached to the office is the Mine Action Service and the Best Practices Unit.[47] DPKO's mission 'is to plan, prepare, manage and direct UN peacekeeping operations, so that they can effectively fulfil their mandates under the overall authority of the Security Council and General Assembly, and under the command vested in the Secretary-General'.[48]

Following authorisation of a mission, the Secretariat is responsible for the implementation of the operation, discussing it with the concerned parties and liaising with the potential troop-contributing countries. In most cases, the Force Commander is selected from one of the force-contributing countries, and is a much sought after position. The operation is also usually overseen by a special representative of the Secretary-General (SRSG), who is a civilian, and may be either a senior UN

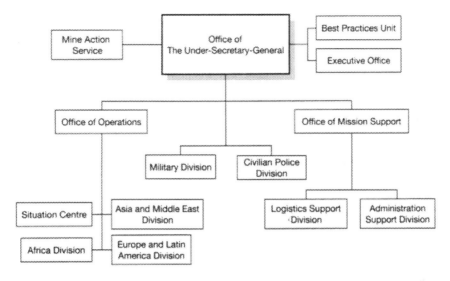

Figure 1.1 Organisational chart of UN Department of Peacekeeping Operations
Source: www.un.org/depts/dpko

official or person of high standing from outside the UN. In recent years, the role of the SRSG has grown more important on some operations, with the person appointed, having overall control of both military and civilian aspects of the operation. In tandem with this process, planning logistics and budgets must be worked out by the various offices within the DPKO. Notably the establishment of a standby arrangement system in 1994, whereby 70 states have agreed to make 100,000 personnel available for such operations, has meant that the UN can react more quickly to crises, although member states must themselves still approve such force contributions to an operation and the arrangement remains voluntary.

In 2000 the Brahimi Report (UN 2000) commissioned by Secretary-General Kofi Annan, has examined the underlying approach and the practicalities of peace-keeping, and made a number of recommendations. The decision to commission such a report arose out of a fundamental concern that a number of peace operations undertaken in the 1990s failed and opportunities were seen as having been missed. In some instances it is claimed that the presence of UN personnel may have even prolonged conflicts and led to more violence, some of it being aimed at UN personnel serving in the field. Equally disasters in Somalia and Rwanda were followed by further problems in Sierra Leone, raising questions as to whether the UN was learning anything from its practical experience on the ground. While the proposed Brahimi reforms are discussed in detail in Chapter 7, it is worth noting some of the more significant recommendations, as they reflect underlying problems in the current administration of peacekeeping and resonate with the case studies examined in Chapters 1–6:

- The establishment of Integrated Mission Taskforces (IMTFs) for each operation bringing together staff from the DPKO, the Department of Political Affairs, other agencies and departments affected by the operation in the UN system; such an approach reinforces coordination being undertaken at the executive level.
- The establishment of an ECPS Information and Strategic Analysis Secretariat to support all departments engaged in peacekeeping operations.
- A need to strengthen and refine existing standby arrangements to ensure a more rapid response (30 days for ceasefire monitoring and 90 days for complex operations).
- The creation of a roster of future SRSGs, force commanders, police commissioners and other civilian personnel.
- The delegation of budgetary authority for such operations to DKPO and field operation.
- The strengthening of DKPO staff and financial resources

A number of these recommendations reflect underlying problems that beset peacekeeping in both the Cold and post-Cold War periods, but were partly aggravated by the growth in the number and range of operations in the 1990s, leading to crisis situations in a number of peacekeeping operations.

Approach

The approach in this study is to focus on four case studies of peacekeeping, two in the Cold War period (Congo and Cyprus) and two in the post-Cold War era (Angola and Somalia). The framework employed for analysis focuses on the following key elements that may determine whether a mission succeeds or fails:

- *the nature of the conflict*;
- *the political base of the operations*: the role of external actors, such as the Great Powers, the mandate and the positions of the actors;
- *the operational base*: the role of the Secretary-General, Force Commander, Special Representative of the Secretary-General, tactical capabilities, communications and equipment.

Because the operations had a shared objective and were generally conducted according to certain recognised principles, can we assume that they were similar? Not so. Each was substantially different in nature and once launched, acquired a distinctive character of its own. While almost all sought to address the problem of conflict or its aftermath, the nature and scale of conflict were different in each case, as also were the particular tasks assigned to each force, the resources and support provided, and the degree of influence exerted by prevailing international circumstances.

A major difficulty associated with all the operations was the uncertainty as to their precise purpose. Did they constitute mere stopgap measures or were they perceived as providing solutions to the problems in question? The UN always faced the challenge of trying to engage in effective action while observing respect for state sovereignty, of trying to help without being seen to impose its will. In all operations, the underlying question has been whether the UN, an organisation embracing many cultures and values, can agree on how a problem should be addressed and at a practical level whether the resources provided by member states can be employed in an organised and efficient manner.

In order to see how UN peacekeeping operations functioned during and after the Cold War, four case studies have been chosen. They are ONUC (Congo 1960–4), UNFICYP (Cyprus 1964–), UNOSOM (Somalia 1992–5), and UNAVEM (Angola 1991–). Why these particular operations? Since two were launched during the Cold War and two subsequently, they provide an opportunity for comparison to see whether changes in the international system created a more favourable environment for international action and whether a more harmonious Security Council provided greater leadership and authority.

The operations represent attempts by the UN to address very different problems: the collapse of state authority (ONUC), ethnic rivalry (UNFICYP), famine-linked civil conflict (UNOSOM), and civil war (UNAVEM). They indicate the extent to which the UN succeeded in reaching agreement on objectives and how far it adapted its approach to each set of circumstances. Since the period from the first (1960) to the last (1992) covers a wide span of UN peacekeeping operations, they should illustrate the lessons which emerged; whether these were heeded; the extent to which the nature of operations changed with the easing of tension between the former ideological enemies (US and Soviet Union) and whether greater resources were available and employed.

ONUC, with approximately 16,000 troops, was the first major operation of the Cold War period. UNOSOM was one of the first major operations post-Cold War. Both started with peacekeeping and ended in open warfare with citizens of the host state, and can usefully be compared. The armed conflicts raise the question of how the UN justified such action and how effective was the attempt to convert peacekeepers into combat troops. ONUC is chosen for several other reasons. It was conducted during an extraordinarily tense period in the Cold War and was a test of the UN's ability and will to overcome divisions in the face of major crisis; also, the force represented an unusually wide international 'spread'. Most importantly, it represented a major change in the nature of operations – away from the passive observer or buffer-type to positive, if uncertain, action. It was in effect the UN's first attempt to 'do something' in response to widespread appeals for action, particularly in the early 1990s. UNFICYP is chosen because it demonstrates the difficulty of determining when 'peace' is seen to have been achieved.

Each of the four involved forces are of markedly different international composition and, therefore, provide an opportunity to observe how effectively such forces can function. Since ONUC and UNAVEM were predominantly African bodies operating in Africa, they provide a test of the theory that African operations are best left to Africans. UNAVEM also represents a test of the UN's ability to

13

combine peacekeeping with the provision of humanitarian assistance. Both demonstrate the problems posed for UN personnel in situations where the parties in dispute are, or become, unwilling to cooperate with the peacekeepers. They raise the question of whether mandates which are found impracticable should be changed, and if so, how effective such changes have been. UNAVEM is considered particularly worthy of examination because of the discrepancy between the scale of death[49] and destruction and the UN's response. Was it an example of skewed priorities or a demonstration of UN helplessness when faced with the problem of large scale civil war?

There are other reasons which justify the choice of case studies. ONUC was the first UN mission on which Irish troops were engaged, while Irish personnel were involved to a significant degree on the others. One of the authors, who served with ONUC and UNAVEM, therefore had first-hand experience of the workings of these operations and access to the thoughts, opinions and experiences of Irish and other nationals serving on these and various other UN operations. This empirical evidence will be employed to build up a picture of the realities of peacekeeping, to reveal the difficulties encountered and to help explain why many if not most operations fell far short of achieving the objectives set out in their original mandates. The sheer impracticability of some mandates is best demonstrated in the case of UNFICYP which since 1964 was supposed to be restoring 'normal' conditions. However, the operation did in one notable incident demonstrate the potential power of UN peacekeepers to limit the spread of violence.

It might be argued that the operations chosen represent in the main the UN's failures and it is not disputed that some operations such as that in Cambodia (UNTAC) Namibia (UNTAG), and Central America (ONUCA) did achieve a certain measure of success. However, the dominant question in the 1990s, and in 2000, with the debacle in Sierra Leone, was, and is, why, despite greater international interest and apparent goodwill, UN operations over the last decade have been less than successful. The accent is, therefore, on what went wrong and whether any lessons were or can be learned.

In dealing with operations as 'Cold War' or 'post-Cold War', the year 1989 is seen as particularly significant. While the Cold War did not specifically end on any particular date, the removal of the Berlin Wall in 1989 is generally seen as marking a dramatic change in East–West relations. This development reduced the prospect of states or elements within them being provided with arms and political support from the former rivals. A new more cooperative frame of mind appeared to have emerged during the Paris Conference on Cambodia in August 1989 leading to agreement in 1990 on a comprehensive political settlement of the Cambodian conflict.[50] Also in 1989 the UN appeared to be making progress in dealing with problems in Africa, America, and Asia. As part of the settlement of the Namibian problem, South African troops were to be withdrawn from that country and elections held: in neighbouring Angola, plans provided for the departure of Cuban troops as one stage of an overall settlement (see Case Study D). In 1987, UN efforts to settle disputes in Central America began and in 1989 were bearing fruit, particularly with the signing of an accord between the Sandanistas and Contras in Nicaragua establishing terms for the conduct of national elections.[51] By late 1988, it was clear that Soviet foreign policy had changed as Moscow pulled out of regional conflicts in Asia and Africa. The change of Administration in Washington in the winter of 1988–9 also brought a new pragmatism and flexibility to US foreign policy. In general, 1989 could be seen as a year of hope that international relations had improved, that conflict no longer fuelled by the Cold War, was less likely and that the UN was now better equipped to deal with any problems which might emerge. The operations are examined under four broad headings: 'Nature of conflict', 'Political base of operations', 'Operational base of operations', and 'Analysis'. This plan is employed in order to familiarise the reader with the details of the operation, to consider the conduct of the operation in some depth by approaching it from various angles, and finally to analyse results. It is hoped that this formula will provide helpful comparisons.

Nature of conflict

This section gives an introductory outline of each operation's purpose, highlighting its particular problems. Since the operations were intended to help resolve conflict, 'historical background' explains the origin of the violence, illustrating its nature and scale. In the case of the Congo, it deals with the phenomenon of African nationalism; in Cyprus, the origins of the ethnic confrontation; in Somalia, the unusual phenomenon of 'clan' as distinct from 'ethnic' dispute; in Angola, the origins of the bitter civil war. It introduces the major local players in each situation, referring to the external as well as internal factors which influenced the development of the conflict. The narrative then outlines the circumstances which led directly to UN intervention, events immediately following the arrival of the peacekeepers, and the reaction of the various concerned parties to their presence. Subsequent developments are then outlined, highlighting the role of the UN personnel, their problems and achievements, their influence on events generally, and the impact upon the mission of changing local and international circumstances. Reference is made to the changing nature of the operations and any efforts by the Security Council or Secretariat to help resolve the problems. In the cases of ONUC and UNFICYP, there are references to Phases 'One' and 'Two'. This is because in these operations, there was a perceived turning point at which the mission experienced a significant change of character. In the case of UNOSOM and UNAVEM, this was unnecessary because in each case there was an overlap between stages in the overall venture.

Political base of operations

Because the operations were authorised by and to a greater or lesser extent influenced by members of the Security Council, this section deals with the role and activities of the Great Powers, both before and during the operations under various headings. 'Prior involvement of the Great Powers' examines the connection between the permanent members of the Security Council and the country/region in question. In each case, one or more of the Great Powers had a particular interest in the country/ region, either through historical links or because of ideological or strategic considerations. There is, therefore, the question of the extent to which these links either directly or indirectly helped create or fuel the conflict and how the individual powers controlled or influenced the local players.

The 'Initial position of the Great Powers' in the case of Cold War operations looks at the impact of East–West rivalry upon the formulation of the enabling Security Council resolutions and at the conduct of the operations during the formative period. It looks at the way in which resolutions reflected not only compromise, but allowed the powers to interpret resolutions in a manner which suited their own purpose. It shows how this kind of rivalry created confusion as to the direction of the mission. In the case of post-Cold War operations, it looks in particular at the attitude of the US to the UN and its perception of its role as the remaining superpower.

'The Mandate' considers the tasks assigned to the international forces.[52] It asks whether the tasks were clear and commensurate with the authority and resources provided. Did the mandate reflect a serious intent on the part of the UN to address the problems or was it purely aspirational? In situations where the mandate was shown to be unsatisfactory or unworkable, did the Security Council revise or amend it and if not, why? In cases where it was changed, did this prove satisfactory?

'Political manoeuvres of the Great Powers' looks at the activities of the various powers as the mission progressed. It asks: to what extent did their efforts indicate a desire to produce a resolution of the conflict?; did they bring pressure to bear on the parties?; did they continue to support parties with whom they had earlier forged links?; how much did their off-stage activities and confrontations impinge on the efforts of the operation?

Operational base

This section examines how the respective Security Council resolutions were implemented through the operation of the chain of command running from the Secretary General through the Force Commander to the troops on the ground. 'Secretary General' looks at how the various office holders perceived and discharged their responsibilities. It considers the relationship between the Secretary-General and the Security Council, and how this relationship affected the mission. Did the office holder adopt a 'hands-on' approach and if so, to what effect? Did he provide ongoing guidance to the Force Commander or allow the mission to drift? In cases where he delegated to a Special Representative, how effective was this device in preserving the link between New York and 'the field'? What was the relationship between civilian elements involved in the operation and the military forces?

'Force Commander' looks at the role and influence of the military commander. As the person charged with implementing the mandate, he obviously occupied a critical position. We have to ask: How well briefed was he in relation to the nature of the operation? Did he enjoy the trust and support of the Secretary General? What authority did he enjoy and how did he exercise it? What was his relationship with contingent commanders and with the peacekeepers generally? In the case of the UNOSOM operation, which involved American troops, how did the structure of command cater for the presence of US personnel?

'Tactical Capabilities' is a sub-section which examines the mechanics of operations. The first of these elements is 'Contingents'. Since it is argued that the success of peacekeeping depends ultimately upon the soldier at the checkpoint, this looks at some of the various national forces involved, their ability to function in harmony with other contingents, and their relationship with the local population. It considers the extent and consequences of national governments' influence upon the conduct of operations in general and especially those involving American forces. It considers the problems arising in forces composed of personnel of diverse cultures and different values.

'Communications' looks at the importance of communications in various forms to the successful conduct of operations. It looks at the problem s created by the lack or loss of contact, not only between elements in the field, but between 'the field' and UN Headquarters. It refers to the problems arising from the inability of many contingents to converse in languages other than their own, and the consequences of this problem for joint operations. It considers the matter of communication between the peacekeepers and the local authorities and population, and alludes to the issue of intelligence-gathering which the military personnel consider critical to their work.

'Equipment' highlights the fact that peacekeeping forces are largely dependent upon equipment provided by the contingent-contributing states. It looks at the problems faced by the failure of many states to provide their troops with necessary resources, particularly vehicles, plant, and suitable clothing. It considers how UN policy in relation to armament proved particularly unfortunate in situations such as in the Congo and Somalia where lightly armed peacekeepers were suddenly expected to perform in a role for which they were not prepared, and it examines the consequential damage to performance and morale.

Since it is impossible to know what might have happened had the operation(s) not taken place, this does not attempt to present missions in terms of 'success' or 'failure'. However, in seeking to assess performance, recourse is made to criteria employed by Duane Bratt in assessing success.[53] These are listed below.

- '*Mandate performance*' considers the extent to which the operation succeeded in performing the tasks assigned. It reflects upon the immediate and long-term outcome of the peacekeepers' efforts.
- '*Facilitating conflict resolution*', asks whether, given that the purpose of the UN intervention was to help resolve conflict, peacekeepers alone could ever achieve this objective.
- '*Conflict containment*' relates largely to the Cold War preventive deployment

role of the forces. It looks at the question: was it the UN presence alone which prevented local conflict becoming regional or global?

- '*Assessment*' sums up the operation, reviewing the attitude and response of the UN and international community to the problem within its midst. It looks at whether the operation succeeded in upholding perceived international norms and the extent of states' ability and commitment to engage in collective action. It also seeks to draw lessons from the particular venture.

Sources

A range of secondary material on peacekeeping was examined along with UN documents, whether originating in UN Headquarters, New York, Force Headquarters or local HQs. Some material was gathered from documents either obtained by Terry O'Neill while employed on operations, or passed on by participants in other operations. Amongst other sources consulted were a wide variety of journals, Irish and British newspapers and, in the case of Angola, the daily reports from the leading national newspaper, *Jornal de Angola* provided for personnel serving in UNAVEM. Much material was also obtained from the Irish Army Military Archives, Dublin.

Material was also gained from interviews with military personnel of various ranks and from many countries who participated in the peacekeeping operations, which form the basis of the four case studies. Some of the interviews occurred during the course of operations, however the majority were arranged and conducted at locations in Ireland, the Netherlands and Scandinavia. The choice of many Irish sources was made not merely because of ease of access, but because the individuals chosen were known to have occupied key posts on one or more missions and to have acquired considerable and valuable experience. There were several reasons for turning to Scandinavia for other source material. Scandinavians have been associated with peacekeeping from its inception and there have been few operations that did not involve personnel from the Nordic countries. The Scandinavians have moreover made a detailed study of peacekeeping and amassed much material on the subject.

Organisation of the study

In order to achieve its aim, the research is carried out at two levels, theoretical and empirical. It begins by looking at the ways in which peacekeeping has been understood in the literature and broadly looking at peacekeeping over time. The substantive chapters consider an operation conducted during the Cold War period (1946–89) and particular operations conducted since 1989. The concluding analysis reviews the peacekeeping experience over the entire period of such operations, considers what lessons have been learnt and changes made, and draws some conclusions.

In order to provide an understanding of why UN peacekeeping operations were launched, Chapter 2 is an overview of peacekeeping operations, looks at whether and how peacekeeping changed, considers the changing role of the superpowers, and the implications of such change for peacekeeping. In particular, the chapter also looks at the way peacekeeping was perceived to have developed during the Cold War comparing the perception with the reality. It considers how the evolution of peacekeeping over a succession of operations led to the acceptance of certain practices and procedures and how these practices influenced operations, particularly in regard to the implementation of mandates. It examines the issue of how peacekeeping techniques developed within the constraints imposed by the Cold War, were relevant to later actions. The latter part of the chapter looks at how the ending of the bipolar system raised hopes that the UN and the Security Council in particular could begin to function more effectively. It considers the emergence of the US as the only remaining superpower and it examines the activity of the media in drawing attention to assorted crises.

Chapters 3 and 4 focus respectively on Congo (ONUC 1960–1964), and the operation in Cyprus (UNFICYP 1964–). Chapters 5 and 6 consist of two further case studies, UNOSOM (Somalia 1992–5) and UNAVEM (Angola 1991–9) which are treated along similar lines as those considered earlier. However, in these cases, greater emphasis is laid on such matters as the role of the US in the UN operations, the use of force in the pursuit of peace, and the issue of whether the nature of peacekeeping changed. The penultimate chapter looks first at the challenges to peacekeeping identified by the UN Secretary-General in 1996.[54] It then considers two recent (2000) major reports issued by the Secretariat[55] which deal with operational problems and certain recommendations for dealing with challenges ahead. The concluding chapter looks at changes which have been made since the Brahimi report was published in 2000, summarises the research findings and considers the options for improving UN response and effectiveness and concludes by making recommendations.

Notes

1 Peter Viggo Jakobsen, 'The Transformation of United Nations Peace Operations in the 1990s, *Cooperation and Conflict*, Vol. 37, No. 3, 2002, p. 268

2 Francis Kofi Abiew and Tom Keating, 'Outside Agents and the Politics of Peacebuilding and Reconciliation', *International Journal*, winter 1999–2000, p. 80

3 Adam Roberts, 'The Crisis in UN Peacekeeping', *Survival*, Vol. 36, No. 3, 1994, p. 93

4 Ibid., p. 104

5 John Mackinlay, 'Improving Multifunctional Forces', *Survival*, Vol. 36, No. 3 1994, p. 149

6 Nicole Gnesotto, 'Reacting to America', *Survival* Vol. 44, No 4, 2002, pp. 99–106

7 Examples of this type of literature include John Mackinlay, *The Peacekeepers: An Assessment of Peacekeeping Operations at the Arab–Israeli Interface*, London, Unwin Hyman Ltd, 1989; Alan James, *Britain and the Congo Crisis 1960–63*, London, Macmillan Press Ltd, 1996; Wolfgang Biermann and Martin, Vadset (ed.), *UN*

Peacekeeping in Trouble: Lessons Learned from the Former Yugoslavia, Aldershot, Ashgate Publishing Ltd, 1998

8 William J. Durch, (ed.) *The Evolution of UN Peacekeeping*, London, Macmillan Press, 1993; James Mayall, *The New Interventionism 1991–1994*, Cambridge, Cambridge University Press, 1996

9 Rosalyn Higgins, *United Nations Peacekeeping 1946–1976: Documents and Commentary, Vol. 3 Africa*, Oxford, Oxford University Press, 1980; Rosalyn Higgins, *United Nations Peacekeeping: Documents and Commentary* Vol. 4: Europe, Oxford, Oxford University Press, 1981; Alan James, *Peacekeeping in International Politics*, London, Macmillan Academic and Professional Ltd, 1990; Anthony Parsons, *From Cold War to Hot Peace: UN Interventions 1947–1994*, London, Michael Joseph, 1995

10 Alan James, *The Politics of Peacekeeping*, London: Chatto and Windus Ltd, 1969; Dimitris Bourantonis and Jarrod Wiener (eds), *The United Nations in the New World Order*, Basingstoke, Hants: Macmillan, 1995; Thomas Weiss, David P. Forsythe and Roger A. Coate *The United Nations and Changing World Politics*, Boulder, Colorado, Westview Press, 1997

11 For example, Inis L. Claude, *Swords into Plowshares*, London, University of London Press, 1965; Roland Paris, 'Peacebuilding and the Limits of Liberal Internationalism', *International Security*, Vol. 22, No. 2, 1997, pp. 54–89

12 Mayall, *The New Interventionism*; Steven R. Ratner, *The New UN Peacekeeping*, London, Macmillan Press Ltd, 1997; David Malone and Karin Wermester, 'Boom and Burst? The Changing Nature of UN Peacekeeping', *International Peacekeeping*, Vol. 7, No. 4, 2000, pp. 37–54; Margaret Karns and Karen Mingst, 'Peacekeeping and the Changing Role of the United Nations: Four Dilemmas', in Thakur, Ramesh and Albrecht Schnabel (eds), *United Nations Peacekeeping Operations*, New York, UN University Press, 2001, pp. 215–37; Birthe Hansen and Heurlin, *The New World Order*, London, Macmillan, 2000; Ramesh Thakur and Albrecht Schnabel (eds), *United Nations Peacekeeping Operations*, New York, UN University Press, 2001

13 A. Leroy Bennett, *International Organisations: Principles and Issues*, Englewood Cliffs, New Jersey, Prentice-Hall International, Inc., 1988, p. 145

14 Diehl, Paul, *International Peacekeeping*, Baltimore/London, Johns Hopkins University Press, 1993

15 Diehl, Paul, Jennifer Reifschneider and Paul Hensel, 'United Nations Intervention and Recurring Conflict', *International Organisation*, Vol. 40, No. 4, 1996, pp. 683–700

16 Paul Diehl, 'Forks in the Road: Theoretical and Policy Concepts for 21st Century Peacekeeping', *Global Society*, Vol. 14, No. 3, 2000, p. 338

17 Ibid., p. 359

18 Masashi Nishihara, 'Trilateral Country Roles: Challenges and Opportunities', in *Keeping the Peace in the Post-Cold War Era: Strengthening Multilateral Peacekeeping*, New York, Trilateral Commission, 1993, pp. 51–9

19 Alan James, 'UN Peacekeeping: Recent Developments and Current Problems', in Dimitris Bourantonis and Jarrod Wiener (eds), *The United Nations in the New World Order: The World Organisation at Fifty*, Basingstoke, Macmillan, 1995, pp. 105–23

20 Ibid, p. 108

21 Thomas Weiss, David P. Forsythe and Roger A. Coate *The United Nations and Changing World Politics* Boulder, Colorado, Westview Press, 1997

22 Voronkov, Lev 'International Peace and Security: New Challenges to the UN' in Dimitris Bourantonis and Jarrod Wiener (eds), *The United Nations in the New World Order: The World Organisation at Fifty*, Basingstoke, Hants., Macmillan, 1995, pp. 1–18; Alan James 'UN Peacekeeping: Recent Developments and Current Problems' in Dimitris

Bourantonis and Jarrod Wiener (eds), *The United Nations in the New World Order: The World Organisation at Fifty*, Basingstoke, Hants., Macmillan, 1995, pp. 105–23

23 Andrew Boyd, *Fifteen Men on a Powder Keg*, London, Macmillan & Co. Ltd, 1971, p. 60

24 Michael Oksenberg, 'A Decade of Sino-American Relations: Politics in the World Arena' in Steven L. Spiegel (ed.), *At Issue*, New York, St Martin's Press, 1984, p. 234

25 Andrew Boyd, *Fifteen Men on a Powder Keg*, pp. 29–30

26 James O. Goldsborough, 'The Roots of Western Disunity' in *At Issue*, (see n. 24 above), p. 234

27 William J. Durch, 'Getting Involved: Political-Military Context', in William J. Durch (ed), *The Evolution of UN Peacekeeping*, London, Macmillan Press Ltd, 1993, p. 23

28 Efraim Karsh, 'Cold War, Post Cold-War: Does It Make a Difference for the Middle East?', in Efraim Inbar and Gabriel Sheffer (eds), *The National Security of Small States*, London, Frank Cass, 1997, p. 80

29 Parsons, *From Cold War to Hot Peace*, p. 118

30 Ibid., p. 26

31 Ibid., p. 23

32 Donald Puchala, 'The United Nations Today: Reflections on a Dangerous and Fragmented World', *At Issue*, p. 427

33 Parsons, *From Cold War to Hot Peace*, p. 160

34 Pavel Baev, *The Russian Army in a Time of Trouble*, Oslo, Norsk Utenrikspolitisk Institutt, 1996, p. 29

35 Ibid., p. 156

36 Mats Berdal, 'Fateful Encounter: The United States and UN Peacekeeping', *Survival*, spring 1994, p. 37

37 William Reno, 'War and the Failure of Peacekeeping in Sierra Leone', *SIPRI Yearbook 2001*, pp. 153–4

38 Bates, Gill and James Reilly, 'Sovereignty, Intervention and Peacekeeping: The View from Beijing', *Survival*, autumn 2000, p. 48

39 Ibid., pp. 42–3

40 Ibid., p. 50

41 Ibid., p. 52

42 Rivlin, 1995, pp. 81–2; also James 1993

43 Ibid., p. 84

44 Hisako Shimura, 'The Role of the UN Secretariat in Organising Peacekeeping', in Ramesh Thakur and Albrecht Schnabel (eds), *United Nations Peacekeeping Operations*, New York, UN University Press, 2001, pp. 45–6

45 Ibid., p. 45

46 Ibid.

47 See UN Department of Peacekeeping Operations: www.un.org/depts/dpko

48 Ibid.

49 1,000 per day. Margaret Anstee, *Orphan of the Cold War*, London, Macmillan, 1996, p. 505

50 Parsons, *From Cold War to Hot Peace*, p. 163

51 Brien D. Smith and William J. Durch, 'United Nations Central America Observer Group', in William J. Durch (ed.), *The Evolution of UN Peacekeeping*, pp. 442–4

52 For past UN Resolutions, see: http://www.un.org/documents

53 Duane Bratt, 'Assessing the Success of UN Peacekeeping Operations', in Michael Pugh (ed.), *The UN, Peace and Force*, London, Frank Cass, 1997, pp. 67–9

54 Kofi Annan, 'Challenges of the New Peacekeeping', in Olara Otunnu and Michael W.

Doyle (eds), *Peacemaking and Peacekeeping in the New Century*, Maryland, US, Rowman and Littleford Inc., 1996, p. 172

55 (a) Comprehensive Review of the Whole Question of Peacekeeping Operations in All Their Aspects, 21 August 2000; (b) Multidisciplinary Peacekeeping: Lessons From Recent Experience, 9 August, 2000

2

PEACEKEEPING IN THE COLD WAR/POST-COLD WAR

In this chapter we examine peacekeeping generally, comparing the Cold War and post-Cold War periods, considering what, if anything has changed between these two periods. The chapter begins with an overview of peacekeeping operations, from the earliest identified operations up to the present day. We proceed then to consider how interpretations of peacekeeping have been changing, looking at both traditional peacekeeping operations and the growth in 'robust' operations, as well as the employment of multi-component missions. Again, an examination of the changing role of the superpowers in the UN Security Council provides a further basis for understanding how and in what ways peacekeeping has been seen as changing.

An overview of peacekeeping operations

In looking at the period between 1947 and 1985, it is important to recognise that the UN undertook only thirteen peacekeeping operations in total (see Table 2.1).[1] The types of operations were 'unarmed' or 'armed', the former consisting of unarmed observers, the latter involving lightly armed troops. While the first explicitly labelled 'peacekeeping' operation was the UN Emergency Force (UNEF I) dispatched to the Sinai Peninsula following the Suez crisis of 1956,[2] the official view of the UN is that the UN Truce Supervisory Organisation, UNTSO, was the first peacekeeping operation. It consisted of unarmed military observers who were sent to Palestine in June 1948 to supervise a truce negotiated by Count Bernadotte of Sweden in the first war between Israel and its Arab neighbours.[3] A similar group – UN Military Observer Group in India and Pakistan (UNMOGIP) was dispatched a few months later in 1949. These operations provided the working models and administrative practices for future operations and were the subject of Dag Hammarskjöld's 1958 report known as 'The Summary Report' in which he outlined the role of the Secretariat in peacekeeping operations. While these and the other observer operations are seen as having performed a useful function, it was the 'armed' operations of the period which presented the greatest challenge to the UN and which are considered most worthy of critical examination.

Table 2.1 UN peacekeeping operations during the Cold War

Continent	Operation	Date
Africa	ONUC – Congo	1960–4
Americas	DOMREP – Dominican Republic	1965–6
Asia	UNIPOM – India/Pakistan	1965–6
	UNSF – West New Guinea	1962–3
	UNMOGIP – India/Pakistan	1949–present
Europe	UNFICYP – Cyprus	1964–present
Middle East	UNTSO – Middle East	1948–present
	UNOGIL – Lebanon	1958
	UNEF I – Middle East	1956–67
	UNEF II – Middle East	1973–9
	UNYOM – Yemen	1963–4
	UNFIL – Lebanon	1978–present

Source: www.un.org/depts/dpko/home.html

Arguably, the list in Table 2.1 might also include the United Nations Security Force which served as part of the United Nations Temporary Executive Authority in West Irian (West New Guinea) (1963–4) and the United Nations Disengagement Force on the Golan Heights (1974), as both forces included armed military troops.

Notably, during the Cold War period the permanent members of the UN Security Council, and especially the two superpowers did not play a significant operational role in peacekeeping. The main countries contributing to peacekeeping during the Cold War included Australia, Austria, Canada, Denmark, Fiji, Finland, Ghana, India, Ireland, Italy, Nepal, New Zealand, Norway, Pakistan, Senegal, Sweden and the Netherlands. The levels of commitment, the overall training of military personnel, the availability of equipment and the preparedness of such contingents for peacekeeping varied considerably, with some countries developing both good and poor reputations for their contributions. Moreover, the size of such operations varied quite significantly in the Cold War period, with only UNEF I and II, ONUC, UNFICYP and UNIFIL exceeding 3,000 personnel. The largest operation was that carried out in the Congo, which involved some 15,000–20,000 from 34 states over most of the period of the operation.

Much UN peacekeeping during the Cold War rather than being deliberately planned and properly resourced operations were little more than hastily organised responses to various crises, that often seemed to lack clear objectives, leadership and guidance. Most of these operations were aimed at monitoring ceasefires, except in the cases of the Congo and UNTEA in Western Irian. Such forces were also usually used to maintain buffer zones, undertake border patrols, and observation of ceasefire lines. There was no 'government' pursuing its agenda, no military high command controlling and reacting. Unlike conventional military operations, there were no templates to apply and therefore no matching of resources to task. Once on the ground, the international forces were, to all intents and purposes, left to

24

function as best they could. They were frequently denied freedom of movement and had little say in the matter of their deployment. For example, in Lebanon, it was not the UN but Israel, the state whose aggression had led to the UN presence, which dictated exactly where the 'front-line' peacekeepers would deploy.[4]

As demonstrated by UNIFIL in particular, little consideration was given by those planning and directing operations to compatibility or acceptability of contingents, while uneven standards of training and in the case of some contingents lack of equipment, added to the problems created by placing troops in hostile climatic environments. In Lebanon, 'non-white' troops were resented by the local population and cultural differences led to considerable hostility between these elements of the Force.[5] For instance, when Fijian and Ghanaian troops met in numbers as at sports events, weapons frequently had to be impounded to avoid the possibility of open warfare between these contingents.[6] Inadequately equipped contingents such as the Nepalese, created problems for other contingents who were forced to share their limited resources in the interests of the operation.[7] The poor standard of training of some Third World contingents impacted on operational efficiency, causing friction within the Force and consequential accusations of racism. Operational efficiency was also impaired by the clear unsuitability of African troops for service in the hills of South Lebanon during the severe winters. Nigerian and Ghanaian troops were incapable of functioning effectively in the ankle-deep snow or of dealing with icy roads. Within two years of arrival in Lebanon, all 18 of the Ghanaian armoured personnel carriers (APCs) were severely damaged and effectively unserviceable.[8] Such problems, some or all of which would feature in other missions, were never addressed by the Secretariat.

The particular crises passed, missions were allowed to drift. Overshadowed by Cold War developments, operations quickly passed from public notice. UN peacekeeping became something of a curiosity of interest only to those directly involved and a number of academics. Within the Secretariat, lessons in relation to clarity of mandate and availability of resources from successive operations went largely ignored. In subsequent reviews of Cold War operations, officials at the UN headquarters in New York would choose to highlight the achievements rather than the limitations. It was they who would have been expected to observe operations with a critical eye, identify shortcomings, draw lessons and make recommendations for improvement.

Marrack Goulding, former Under Secretary for UN Peacekeeping Operations, described the period from 1956 to 1974 during which the UN established ten of its thirteen Cold War missions as 'the golden age' of United Nations peacekeeping.[9] He also credited the operations established during the Cold War with fostering the gradual evolution of a body of principles, practices and procedures for peace-keeping and with constituting a body of core law and customary practice which he held was, by and large, accepted by all.[10] This latter claim is undoubtedly true; but were peacekeeping operations conducted during this period, which he saw as 'helping resolve as well as control armed conflict',[11] unqualified successes? He accepted that UNIFIL (United Nations Interim Force in Lebanon 1978–) had been unable to carry out its mandate, but noted that its presence had brought succour to the people of South Lebanon. This is indisputable, but was this the primary purpose of peacekeeping? He acknowledged that the problems of Cyprus remained unresolved but argued that the long-standing peacekeeping operations such as UNFICYP may sometimes be the least bad option available to the community. ONUC, he claimed, had succeeded in its objectives but added that achievement of these objectives had only been possible through what he saw as a transition from peacekeeping to peace enforcement. This was to present a rather flattering picture of ONUC and the way it had been conducted. And how were other operations of this period viewed in UN Headquarters?

Brian Urquhart, former UN Under-Secretary-General for Political Affairs, described UNEF (United Nations Emergency Force, later called UNEF I 1956–67) as an 'immensely successful operation',[12] and F.T. Liu, former UN Assistant Secretary General for Special Political Affairs, described that mission as 'a resounding success and as a model for subsequent forces'.[13] But was it really a success and a suitable model? UNEF I's tasks were (1) supervision of the post-Suez 1956 ceasefire and withdrawal of foreign forces from Egypt, and (2) provision of an informal buffer.[14] That it succeeded in accomplishing task (1) is undoubted. However, it clearly failed to accomplish task (2). This was due to a number of reasons but in particular three which were to bedevil many other operations: (1) lack of a clearly stated objective, understood and accepted by all parties; (2) lack of necessary resources; (3) reliance on consent of the host state. Egyptian consent to the entry, presence and functioning of the UN force was a direct result of the interpretations given by and negotiations concluded with Hammarskjöld. The essence of exchanges between the Secretary-General and the Egyptian government centred on the latter's anxiety to clarify its position with regard to the duration of UNEF's stay on its territory. Hammarskjöld was less than specific as to the task and duration of the Force linking them to the 'liquidation of the crisis'. Egypt's leader, General Nasser, however maintained that UNEF I's presence was not to resolve any question or settle any problem, but to put an end to the presence of invading forces on Egyptian territory.[15] With the withdrawal of Israeli forces in March 1957, that task was, as far as Egypt was concerned, accomplished, but UNEF I stayed on ostensibly to prevent the passage of raiding parties, a task which it was incapable of fulfilling.[16] This was largely due to a lack of resources.

The UNEF I Force Commander, General Burns of Canada, believed the task of providing a buffer required the employment of a divisional size force equipped with a brigade of tanks and fighter aircraft.[17] Given the size of the area involved, this would have appeared the minimum force required. However, he was given only 6,000 men, a number which quickly dwindled to 3,400.[18] This small force was designed to stand between the disputants but once one of them pushed it away, the whole object of the exercise was nullified. The Force's continued presence was, the Secretary-General accepted, rendered useless, its position untenable, and its withdrawal inevitable.[19] As Egypt in May 1967 prepared to attack Israel, the host state withdrew its consent to the UN presence and the Secretary-General ordered a pullout. However, UNEF I's days were already numbered. Many governments were concerned about the Force's presence and functions, and such concerns proved justified.[20] It had barely begun its withdrawal when hostilities broke out, fifteen UN soldiers being killed.[21] The operation provided an excellent example of the obstructive possibilities open to the UN but highlighted the limitations which attend its activities in the field. It could not create peaceful conditions but merely reflect and assist a mutual and transitory desire of the parties to live in peace. Its achievements were not insignificant but it could not accurately be described as successful. It manifestly failed in the preventive role and its ending had been inglorious. The collapse of the operation exposed the fragile basis of 'traditional' peacekeeping. It also had serious effects on the Middle East situation. UNEF I's withdrawal showed that Israel could never rely on the UN for its safety.

UNEF II (1973–9) established after the October 1973 war between Israel and its Arab neighbours, was described by Urquhart as 'especially successful' in pinning down the original ceasefire and in monitoring and managing the successive disagreements.[22] However, its perceived success was due largely to the fact that it enjoyed particularly favourable conditions for a peacekeeping operation. It had the unanimous support of the Security Council and was readily accepted by the belligerents. Egypt had quickly recognised Israel's superiority and had accepted its position as hopeless. Israel, its morale severely dented and having suffered greater losses than on any previous occasion, recognised that it could not face a costly war of attrition.[23] Thus, it was the parties' cooperation which was the basis for the mission's perceived success. But for the peacekeeping troops, there were major problems, operational and otherwise.

The Force Commander, General Ensio Siilasvuo of Finland, upon whose efforts the outcome of the related peace conference in Geneva hinged, complained that not only had he no experience of international negotiations, but that no one could clearly define his task.[24] There were serious deficiencies of staff at Force HQ and contingents also had to solve supply problems themselves largely through support from their home countries or through procurement in Egypt and Israel.[25] Thus, the Force was largely dependent upon the conflict parties. The Irish Battalion was deployed on the Israeli 'side' and since Ireland had not established diplomatic relations with Israel, the Irish became 'hostages' in the hands of the Israelis.[26] This dependence also affected operations. The lightly armed troops could not prevent armed attacks and when Swedish troops attempted to stop Israeli tanks, they were threatened with being 'mangled'. In the interests of continuing cooperation, the Israelis had to be let through.[27] Failure to prevent incursions of which there were many, left the Force open to accusations of partiality but for it to have engaged in armed confrontation, would have been suicidal. Even without direct engagement, Force losses on this 'successful' operation were extraordinarily high – in three years about 40 UN soldiers were killed by mines or in car accidents.[28] UNEF II was successful not because it constituted an effective buffer, but because Egypt and Israel at this stage genuinely wanted peace.

'A remarkable achievement because it does its job so well' was Marrack Goulding's description of UNDOF (United Nations Disengagement Observer Force 1974–) located on the Golan Heights.[29] F.T. Liu however, cites the Force as a further example of how effectiveness was contingent upon the cooperation of the parties concerned.[30] James also saw UNDOF as doing an extremely valuable job in helping the parties to avoid an unsought war but recognised that the Force had no responsibility at all for making the peace between Israel and Syria. Neither party was particularly happy with the UN force. Syria was not well disposed towards the idea of a UN force patrolling a buffer zone and wanted only observers. Israel, while given to regarding UN peacekeepers as rather tiresome bodies, wanted a real buffer zone and organised military units amounting to not less than 3,000. The compromise was the agreed figure of 1,250.[31] Despite the joint acceptance of the Force, both sides showed a readiness to exploit the UN's dependence upon consent. Threats by Syria to reject renewal (in 1976) required intense negotiation by the Secretary-General. When Israel, weary of Syria's tactics at renewal, suggested that it (Israel) no longer needed the Force, the renewal problem effectively ended.[32] Both parties toyed with the UN force in other ways. Although one of UNDOF's tasks was to verify that the limitation of weapons was adhered to, the Force was not allowed to enter certain places. When UNDOF sought to have these restrictions lifted, it was told by both sides that 'there should be some secrets' and that the 'threat of war was not immediate'.[33] UNDOF was successful in the sense that calm had been continually maintained between the two states whom its buffer zone divided. However, its achievement was possible essentially because local conditions in terms of a desire by both parties for peace could hardly have been better.

UNTAG (Namibia 1989–90) was also acclaimed a 'success' by Goulding,[34] with some justification. But it has been argued that the Force was largely unnecessary since it was unable to prevent South African activities in Namibia and was not needed to supervise South African withdrawal once it was negotiated.[35] Even those negotiations were not entirely UN-brokered but were pursued concurrently by the Secretary-General and a five nation 'Contact Group',[36] which exerted considerable political leverage on South Africa.[37] Moreover, when members of the South West African Peoples' Organisation (SWAPO) infiltrated into Namibia in violation of ceasefire terms, UN representatives authorised or at least tolerated a South African use of force to stop this infiltration. The judgement of many of those involved was that this use of force (by the very South African forces that were at the time the subject of a UN arms embargo) was a necessary precondition for the successful completion of UNTAG's peacekeeping and election-monitoring operations.[38]

Since preventing escalation of the original crises could be regarded as a major achievement and since many mandates were unclear, vague or impossible, it is not surprising that UN officials should laud certain ventures in peace restoration. However, by describing as 'successful' operations which failed to achieve their stated objectives or by rationalising failure as in the case of UNIFIL, such influential officials/commentators helped foster a false impression of what UN peacekeeping could achieve. Implicitly they also suggested that peacekeeping techniques constituted a full set of tools for addressing virtually any problem.

As demonstrated by the various Cold War operations, the proclaimed principles of consent, impartiality and non-use of force was in practice a mixed blessing, their strict application being frequently inimical to the successful implementation of mandates. The consent principle had been shown to be one of peacekeeping's major weaknesses. As demonstrated by UNEF I, consent once given could later be withdrawn, thereby negating all the efforts of the peacekeepers. Equally, as demonstrated in Cyprus (see Chapter 4), consent to the presence of a UN force was of limited value only, if freedom of movement was denied. Dependence on consent, it was clear, was a major impediment to effective UN action within states. In effect, it was the state in question not the UN which determined what would happen and whether the operation would 'succeed'. The UN's initial impartiality in the dispute between the Congolese government and Katanga had contributed in a major way to erosion of what little authority the fledgeling government possessed. This situation made defiance by dissident elements and the associated possibility of civil war ever more likely. The UN's impartiality, therefore, appeared to make resolution of the problem all the more difficult. Impartiality in Cyprus had meant that the situation created by the initial aggression of the Greek Cypriots and the subsequent invasion by the Turks were not reversed. As a result, the mandate rather than being implemented had become meaningless. By failing to take action against the PLO in Lebanon in 1978, the UN provided Israel with an apparently legitimate reason to remain in its South Lebanon 'security zone'. By failing to take action against Israel, the UN provided the PLO and later the Hizbollah with an excuse for action which merely perpetuated the vicious circle of violence.

It was, however, the issue of force, or its perceived non-use, which created greatest confusion about how Cold War peacekeeping was conducted. On the question of how much armament peacekeepers should possess, John Holst referred to 'the ultimate ambiguity' – the theory that forces should be 'as powerful as possible but not necessarily very powerful'.[39] During the Cold War operations, what exactly constituted 'powerful' was not defined, so forces though composed of soldiers were never proper military bodies. To talk of the 'use of minimal force' as if it represented an option was to indicate ignorance of the reality that peace-keepers were obliged through the limitations of their arms and equipment to act purely defensively. That UNEF I or II might have been employed against the armies of Egypt, Israel or Syria or even the militias of South Lebanon was unthinkable. Equally unthinkable was the possibility that UNFICYP could have taken direct action against the Greek or Turkish Cypriots.

The technique of peacekeeping developed during the Cold War was a com-promise born out of a divided UN Security Council. Peacekeepers were enjoined to establish their authority in the conflict zones but their powers and abilities were extremely limited. Theirs was a largely passive role and there was no concept for the progressive escalation of their activities to the eventual use of force. Rather than 'keeping' the peace, their role was limited to observing it. Perhaps, Ratner notes, peacekeeping was supposed to create the conditions for peace but rarely did this appear to happen. Indeed, the UN's presence may well have prolonged the underlying conflict by removing any incentives to settle it.[40] The development of peacekeeping during the UN's first four decades was, in Roberts' opinion, 'impressive' but he argues it would be wrong to depict it as a 'golden age'.[41] As Mats Berdal observes, the principles and practices of Cold War peacekeeping were wholly inadequate as a basis for initiating and sustaining the kind of large multi-component missions which would be attempted in the post-Cold War period.[42] Such operations were to be a consequence of a newly emerging international system.

In contrast to the earlier period, in the post-Cold War era the UN Security Council authorised some 42 operations, of which 33 have been completed, and 9 remain in operation in 2003, alongside 5 existing Cold War operations (see Tables 2.2 and 2.3). What is remarkable is not only the three-fold increase in the number of operations, but that so many of these were authorised in a relatively short period of time in the mid-1990s. It is also noticeable that the geographic focus of operations has shifted from the Middle East to Africa and Europe, as well as to a lesser extent Central America and Asia.

Such figures, of course, tell us only a limited amount about the operations authorised during this period, and we need to look more substantively at what happened during this period to understand how this affected peacekeeping on the ground. In essence, there were increases in all of the types of operations undertaken under Chapters VI and VII of the UN Charter ranging from traditional peace-keeping, as described below, to more complex operations, whether conducted by the UN or delegated. Nevertheless, there was an increased tendency for the UN to place peace forces in situations where conflicts were still ongoing and in which personnel were allowed to use military force to achieve mission goals. The emphasis also shifted from preventing violence to peace-building, including supporting civil society, institutional development and democracy as in the cases of East Timor and Bosnia and Herzegovina. The demands, therefore, being made on the UN and its members increased and diversified. Notably, in 2002 the UN was involved in 15 peacekeeping operations, but was also active in 13 political and peace-building missions. Some 44,000 military personnel and civilian police were involved in these operations, alongside in excess of 10,500 international and local civilian staff.[43]

Has peacekeeping changed?

Some commentators differentiate between 'traditional' peacekeeping, associated with the Cold War period, and 'new', post-Cold War operations. Inis Claude, in 1965, described preventive diplomacy as aiming, not to threaten an expansionist state with defeat, but to offer the promise of assistance to competing states or blocs in limiting the scope of their competition. Helping all states to avoid war rather than helping the states to resist attack was for him the theme of preventive

Table 2.2 Peacekeeping operations completed, post-Cold War

Continent	Operation	Date
Africa	UNAVEM I – Angola	1988–91
	UNAVEM II – Angola	1991–5
	UNAVEM III – Angola	1995–7
	MONUA – Angola	1997–9
	MINURCA – Central African Rep.	1998–2000
	UNASOG – Chad/Libya	1994
	UNOMIL – Liberia	1993–7
	ONUMOZ – Mozambique	1992–4
	UNTAG – Namibia	1989–90
	UNAMIR – Rwanda	1993–6
	UNOMUR – Rwanda/Uganda	1993–4
	UNOMSIL – Sierra Leone	1998–9
	UNOSOM I – Somalia	1992–3
	UNOSOM II – Somalia	1993–5
Americas	ONUCA – Central America	1989–92
	ONUSAL – El Salvador	1991–5
	MINUGUA – Guatemala	1997
	UNMIH – Haiti	1993–6
	UNSMIH – Haiti	1996–7
	UNTMIH – Haiti	1997
	MIPONUH – Haiti	1997–2000
Asia	UNGOMA – Afghanistan/Pakistan	1988–90
	UNAMIC – Cambodia	1991–2
	UNTAC – Cambodia	1992–3
	UNTAET – East Timor	1999–2002
	UNMOT – Tajikistan	1994–2000
Europe	UNCRO – Croatia	1995–6
	UNTAES – Croatia	1996–8
	UNPSG – Croatia	1998
	UNPROFOR – Former Yugoslavia	1992–5
	UNPREDEP – FY Macedonia	1995–6
	UNMIBH – Bosnia and Herzegovina	1995–2002
Middle East	UNIIMOG – Iran/Iraq	1988–91

Source: www.un.org

diplomacy, and he referred to the rationalisation and interpretation of the UN mission in the Congo as being 'cast predominantly in the new terminology'.[44] As employed in that case, and in the earlier so-called 'traditional peacekeeping' missions, the UN preventive action initiated by UN Secretary-General Dag Hammarskjöld was intended to forestall action from any of the major parties, the initiative for which might be taken for preventive purposes but which might, in turn, lead to counter-action from the other side. Some of the operations, for example United Nations Emergency Force (UNEF I), also had a distinctly

31

Table 2.3 Ongoing peacekeeping operations, post-Cold War

Africa	MONUC – Congo	1999–
	UNMEE – Ethiopia/Eritrea	2000–
	UNAMSIL – Sierra Leone	1999–
	MINURSO – Western Sahara	1991–
Asia	UNMISET – East Timor	2002–
Europe	UNOMIG – Georgia	1993–
	UNMIK – Kosovo	1999–
	UNMOP – Prevlaka Peninsula	1996–
Middle East	UNIKOM – Iraq/Kuwait	1991–

Source: www.un.org/depts/dpko/dpko/home.html

diplomatic element. The compromise activity introduced by the UN was preferable to total inaction. But the employment of military forces, albeit lightly armed, was certain to create confusion as to the powers and possible purposes of personnel described as 'peacekeepers'. This confusion was to be particularly evident in the case of the UN operation in the Congo. It would also account for much of the disappointment expressed at the UN's efforts to resolve many post-Cold War crises.

The term 'peacekeeping' was first used after the UN operations in Egypt (1956–67), Congo (1960–4), and Cyprus (1974–). James differentiates the new procedures from the earlier somewhat discredited aspirations of collective security.[45] The 'compromise' involved would be reflected in one definition of peace-keeping as 'any military or paramilitary operations that are organised under pressure of necessity where it is impossible to put into effect the mechanisms of Article 43, that is, in the absence of special agreements aimed at making armed forces available to the organisation'.[46] The new activities were particularly congenial to the growing number of non-aligned UN states, who were repelled by collective security because of its reliance on armed force, and the Cold War connotations, which it had attracted in the UN's first decade. UN peacekeeping would come to be more fully defined as 'Field operations established by the United Nations with the consent of the parties concerned, to help control and resolve disputes between them under UN command and control at the expense collectively of the member states and with the military and other personnel and equipment provided voluntarily by them acting impartially between the parties and using force to the minimal extent necessary.'[47]

In terms of the Security Council's competence in the area of peacekeeping, Nigel White makes two points. First, there are the general powers granted to the Council under Article 24 (1) to maintain or restore international peace and security; second, an examination of the specific powers granted to the Council indicates that peacekeeping falls somewhere between Chapter VI 'Pacific Settlement of Disputes' and Chapter VII 'Action Taken with Respect to Threats to the Peace, Breaches of the Peace, and Acts of Aggression'. Peacekeeping constitutes a concrete military presence and therefore does not simply consist of mere recommendations for settlement or basic fact-finding missions as provided for in Chapter VI. However, peacekeeping is not pure military enforcement as envisaged in Chapter VII. Peacekeeping is frequently linked to or closer to Article 36 (1) of Chapter VI which provides that 'the Security Council may at any stage of a dispute . . . recommend appropriate procedures or methods of adjustment'.[48] These methods of adjustment would, in time, involve the employment of international troops at any one or more of the phases of conflict, namely (1) initially, (2) pre-violence, (3) during conflict, (4) after a ceasefire or following a peace agreement.

Traditionally, peacekeepers were perceived as representing moral authority rather than the force of arms. In their composition, they in some measure represented the universality of the organisation but conventionally did not include members of the Security Council. They were deployed with the consent and cooperation of the parties involved, were impartial and functioned in as much as it was possible without prejudice to the rights and aspirations of any side. They did not use force or the threat of force, except in self-defence, nor did they seek to impose their will on any one of the parties. The basic objective of any peacekeeping force was seen as assisting and reinforcing a broad political process towards the effective containment and, ultimately, resolution of a conflict. The ideal peacekeeping operation was seen as one in which the parties wanted to maintain or restore peace but could not establish the necessary mutual confidence without an outside agent. Three pre-requisites were therefore associated with UN peacekeeping, namely, impartiality, consent and minimum use of force.[49] How did these impact on the conduct of operations?

It was not clear exactly how 'impartiality' should be defined. The general purpose of impartiality might be to show that the UN is an honest broker with no interest other than that of assisting the warring parties towards a resolution of the conflict. However, in some operations, impartiality could be regarded as meaning not impartiality between the belligerents, but impartiality in carrying out the Security Council decisions. For example in the cases of UNIFIL (Lebanon) and ONUC (Congo), the Council Resolutions dealing with the forces' tasks showed a distinct bias against one of the parties in dispute. Impartiality would come to be defined by Jarat Chopra as 'the objectivity with which the mandate was executed rather than the degree of submission to the will of the parties in conflict'.[50]

A particular problem for the peacekeeper would always be a widespread lack of understanding of his role and capabilities. However warm the initial welcome, in time, one party to the conflict would inevitably accuse him of partiality for failing to take action against the other. Equally, media-led demands that the UN take action against one of the parties would take little account of the vulnerability of the peacekeepers and their reliance on the consent of the host state. For example, in the former Yugoslavia, the UN-declared 'safe areas' and the people inside them, including the peacekeepers, could only be fed, supplied and maintained through Serb territory and with Serb consent, yet the world cried for the UN to attack the Serbs for every transgression, a course of action which would end the cooperation without which the safe areas could not be maintained.[51]

33

Impartiality would therefore be seen as essential to the presence and well-being of UN personnel, but strict observance also created serious operational difficulties. Prevented from regarding any party as 'enemy', traditionally peacekeepers were officially prevented from intelligence gathering. This 'policy' had two major consequences: (1) it denied the military personnel access to what they regarded as one of the essential 'tools of the trade', placing them at a severe disadvantage in dangerous environments, and (2) it convinced those 'on the ground' that their masters in New York were out of touch with the realities of 'the field'. The folly of this policy would be acknowledged by the Secretary-General's statement in 1996 that intelligence was essential to the conduct of any future operations.[52] And this opinion would be re-emphasised in the 'Lessons Report' and 'Comprehensive Review' which would make clear that intelligence could greatly assist a peace-keeping operation[53] and that to retain credibility, the UN could no longer ignore the recalcitrance of one party in some operations.[54]

Consent to the peacekeeping process and the presence of the UN force was traditionally sustained in the operation area by state agreement, but this consent could be grudging and conditional. Linked to impartiality and consent was the issue of force. More than half the peacekeeping operations launched during the Cold War consisted of unarmed military observers. However, where peacekeepers were armed, it became an established principle that they should use force to the minimum extent, opening fire only in 'self-defence'. From 1973 onwards, self-defence was deemed to include situations in which peacekeepers were being prevented from fulfilling their mandate. A peacekeeper could for example, return fire if UN installations or personnel were attacked. This broad guideline would in the event be interpreted in a variety of ways, depending upon the disposition and culture of contingents.[55] However, in the main, commanders in the field would be reluctant to open fire because of their reliance on the continued cooperation of the parties and the consideration that although technically armed, UN forces would almost inevitably be heavily out-gunned as well as out-numbered.

UN rules on the use of force would at all times be less than clear. The UN efforts to end the secession of Katanga (in the Congo), would involve military action taken in 'self-defence'. The much later Chapter VII operation in Somalia would also involve lightly armed troops, highlighting the ongoing uncertainty about whether or not force should be employed. During the Cold War, the Secretariat had decided that peacekeeping operations should not be endowed with offensive capabilities. It was argued that the real strength of a peacekeeping operation lay not in its capacity to use force, but precisely in its not using force.[56] Peacekeepers were supposed to be instruments of diplomacy, not war. But peacekeepers were and are in the main military forces. The question arising, therefore, is why employ those whose training is directed towards the use of force?

There was, from the outset, a certain paradox in deploying a military force to establish peace since the classical use of force was to destroy the enemy. There were however several perceived good reasons for drawing peacekeepers from those who had military training. Such people were available for immediate dispatch to trouble spots, and they were in theory acceptable to the local military with whom they were likely to have dealings. Tight discipline would be required in such a sensitive role and the authoritative approach which military officers could assume was considered a further advantage.[57]

It could be argued that in situations where the task was that of helping restore law and order, police would have been more suited to the role than troops. Also, police would arguably be seen as presenting less of a threat to sovereignty and involve less likelihood of a misunderstanding of UN intent (see Chapter 3). Civilian police would play an important role in Cyprus and in the effective functioning of UNTAG (Namibia) which involved the presence of 1,500 police monitors.[58] Police would be increasingly employed in post-Cold War activities whether in election monitoring (UNTAC, UNAVEM) or peace-building (UNTAET and UNTAC). By February 2000, the UN would employ 5,712 police on a range of operations.[59] However, the sometimes-sensitive nature of police work – dealing directly with the local authorities and population – would require that personnel be well-trained, diplomatic and disciplined. Experience would show that national background would have a major impact upon performance of civilian police in various international operations, particularly in the 'peace-building' role.[60]

The ending of the Cold War saw a significant change in attitude to the use of force, accompanied by the associated development of what became known as 'wider peacekeeping' (also referred to as 'multidimensional' peacekeeping') in more complex situations. Since 1990, UN member states became increasingly prepared to authorise the use of force under Chapter VII of the Charter. There are several reasons for this including euphoria after the successful use of force in the Gulf Crisis, Secretary-General Boutros-Ghali's efforts to activate the role of the Security Council, states' and particularly the US's, recognition that it was safer and more convenient to use a UN 'fig-leaf' in conducting military interventions, and finally public pressure amplified by media efforts.[61]

Attention also shifted from discussions about peacekeeping to 'peace-enforcement', defined by *The British Army Field Manual* as 'operations carried out to restore peace between belligerents who do not all consent to intervention and who may be engaged in combat activities'.[62] But while this definition appears straightforward, the term 'peace-enforcement' raises a number of important issues. First, there is the question of what is to be understood by 'peace', how it is to be restored, and when it is seen to exist. There is also a major difficulty with the word 'enforcement', how and by whom it is to be employed. 'Enforcement', according to John Ruggie, is employed 'when a specific act of aggression or a more general set of hostile actions are collectively identified as a threat to international peace and security and the aggressor state is subjected to an array of sanctions until violence is reversed'.[63] Further, 'collective enforcement' (implicitly international action) is defined by Paul Diehl as 'a large-scale military operation designed to defend the victims of international aggression and restore peace and security by the defeat of the aggressor's forces'. He cites the multinational operations in Korea in the 1960s and in Kuwait in 1991 as fitting this purpose.[64] Enforcement

35

is, therefore, in Sanderson words, 'war by another name'.[65] James Mayall supports these views, describing 'Operation Desert Storm' (Kuwait) as a demonstration of peace-enforcement.[66]

However, Marrack Goulding, former Under Secretary for UN Peacekeeping Operations, muddies the waters by describing the actions in Korea and Kuwait as 'peace-enforcement',[67] while speaking of 'a transition from peacekeeping to peace-enforcement in the Congo'.[68] Also, Sally Morphet observes that some have argued that authorisation of 'use of force' moved ONUC from peacekeeping to peace-enforcement.[69] Further confusion is caused by Gareth Evans's reference to UNOSOM II as a 'peace-enforcement' operation.[70] However, there was a clear and significant difference between these two sets of operations. The Korean and Kuwait operations would be widely referred to as 'wars' fought by 'armies' and the conduct of each had been delegated to US command. The Congo and Somalia operations featured only limited and sporadic conflict; the UN forces were equipped for peacekeeping (see Chapters 3 and 5), and command was not delegated. The Korea and Kuwait operations were intended to reverse international aggression and the peace to be attained was that which existed prior to hostilities. In the case of the Congo and Somalia, the conflict was internal and there was marked disagreement as to what form of peace was contemplated.

That 'peace enforcement' is open to a variety of interpretations is shown by Anthony Francis's assertion that UNIFIL was not a peacekeeping force but 'a Peace-Enforcement Force' because its mandate required it to assist the Lebanese government to restore order.[71] But as a small lightly armed force, UNIFIL had/ has no enforcement capacity whatsoever. Peace enforcement, if taken literally, would require a clear conception of the peace being sought; a clear plan of action understood and accepted by all participants in the operation; unlimited resources and a determination on the part of those involved to see the venture through. While some of these conditions might have been present in Korea and Kuwait, none was ever evident in the other UN operations. Peace-enforcement might for many simply mean UN 'getting tough'. However, this raises the questions 'how tough', with precisely whom, with what means, and to what end? The lack of conceptual clarity is recognised by Shashi Thoroor who notes that, 'the term "peace enforcement" appears to be used to cover the desire to go to war without making the hard political and military choices that war requires'.[72]

The writings of Morphet, Evans and Goulding reflect some of the confusion surrounding the term 'peace-enforcement'. More importantly, they indicate the existence of a significant body of people who regard peacekeeping and peace-enforcement as elements in a continuum; one wherein peacekeepers could merely by the invocation of Chapter VII, be transformed into armed forces capable of waging war. The extent to which this idea prevailed within the higher echelons of the UN was evident, not only in Goulding's remark, but in the military tasks assigned to peacekeepers post-Cold War, most notably in Somalia, and later in Sierra Leone. Reference to Chapter VII and robust rules of engagement[73] was, in Sierra Leone, both meaningless and dangerous since the well-armed RUF, numbering 15,000,[74] outnumbered and outgunned a UN force (10,500) that was poorly armed and uncoordinated.

As the major powers worked reasonably closely together during the 1990s it became procedurally easier to adopt more resolutions under Chapter VII.[75] This movement towards more 'positive' peacekeeping was linked to the concept of 'wider peacekeeping' and involved the search for a third category of international operation somewhere between peacekeeping and large-scale enforcement. As Dobbie observes, peacekeeping and enforcement are mutually exclusive activities that cannot be mixed – one can be a peacekeeper or an enforcer, but not both.[76] 'Wider peacekeeping' operations are perceived as likely to take place in environments that display some or all of the following characteristics: numerous parties to a conflict, undisciplined factions not responsive to their own controlling authorities, an ineffective ceasefire, the absence of law and order, the risk of local armed opposition to UN forces, the presence and involvement of a large number of civilians, and an undefined area of objectives. Such operations are therefore likely to occur in environments that bear the characteristics of civil war or insurgency. Therefore, we need to distinguish between the approaches to 'traditional' and 'new' style operations.

Secretary-General Boutros-Ghali's 1992 definition of preventive diplomacy as 'action to prevent existing disputes from escalating into conflicts and to limit the spread of the latter when they occur'[77] would appear to describe the activities originally envisaged by Hammarskjöld, albeit there might no longer be a Cold War factor as primary incentive for these activities. Now however, the emphasis would seem to be less on the 'preventive' and more on the 'diplomacy'. Boutros-Ghali describes the most efficient employment of diplomacy as being to ease tensions before they result in conflict. Preventive diplomacy he saw as being performed by the Secretary-General personally, or by the Security Council, General Assembly or regional organisation in cooperation with the UN.[78] Gareth Evans defined the term as referring to the full range of methods described in Article 33 of the UN Charter, namely negotiation, mediation, enquiry, conciliation, arbitration, judicial settlement, resort to regional agencies or arrangements or other peaceful means, which he sees as applied 'before a dispute has crossed the threshold into armed conflict'.[79] Evans also subdivided preventive diplomacy into 'early' and 'late'. 'Early' preventive diplomacy, he saw as involving the provision of skilled assistance through good offices and mediation. 'Late preventive diplomacy' referred to attempts, often involving the Secretary-General, to persuade parties to desist when armed conflict seems imminent.[80]

The employment of troops in such situations was envisaged through the linking of preventive diplomacy with preventive deployment, which was defined as 'the employment of military or police and possible civilian personnel with the intention of preventing a dispute or in some cases emerging threat, escalating into armed conflict. Such deployments could occur on one side of a border only at the request of the state feeling threatened, or on both sides of the border at the request of both parties'.[81] Boutros-Ghali, in *An Agenda for Peace* (paragraph 29), considered that in conditions of crisis within a country when the government requests or all parties consent, preventive deployment could help in a number of ways to alleviate suffering and to limit or control violence.[82]

One preventive deployment operation, that in the former Yugoslav Republic of Macedonia in 1993, resulted from fears that if conflict erupted in Serbia's Albanian-majority province of Kosovo, the fighting would spill over into Macedonia. The operation had a particular 'preventive' character in that prior to its commencement, no major violence had occurred in the precise area of operation. The 'deterrent' role however did not extend to actually defending these borders but to interposing between forces which might otherwise clash. Defence of Macedonia from aggression remained the task of the Macedonian army.[83] The preventive role of this new style force was, it appeared, not significantly different from that of UNEF. The nature of this mission raised the question: what if anything had changed?

The major difference between the operations of the 1990s and UNEF I is the marked change in the international political environment and the greater focus on peacekeeping as a means of dealing with conflict. Increased demands for peace-keeping operations in the late 1980s and early 1990s (20 new missions between May 1988 and October 1993)[84] indicated their widespread acceptance as a means of addressing conflict. After 1988, operations came to include a remarkably wide variety of activities. These include monitoring and even running elections, for example in Angola, protecting inhabitants of a region from threat or use of force, as in Iraq, protecting disputed safe areas or ensuring the partial demilitarisation of particular areas such as in Bosnia, ensuring the delivery of humanitarian relief supplies and other humanitarian tasks, as in Somalia, assisting in the reconstruction of governmental or police functions after civil war as in El Salvador, and reporting violations of international law by belligerents.[85]

The increase in the number of operations has largely to do with the increased capacity of the UN Security Council to agree on action in particular crises, as opposed to any dramatic change arising out of the end of the Cold War.[86] While there has been much discussion of ethnic conflict, reinforced by images from Kosovo, Rwanda and elsewhere, such conflicts did not rise dramatically in the early 1990s and even declined during the latter part of the 1990s. The UN Security Council, however, largely freed from ideological deadlock, was in a stronger position to mount more operations. As Jakobsen notes, the superpowers were able to use such operations to disengage themselves from Cold War conflicts, share the burden with others, delegate to coalitions of the willing, and gain legitimacy for operations led by the permanent members.[87] The European states were also in a stronger position to support such operations, with more resources available to them, arising out of the end of the Cold War. There was also increased optimism that the UN could play a more central role in international security and preventing conflict, supporting the development of democracy and human rights.[88] The UN increasingly found itself facing situations where media interest in a particular crisis generated a public expectation that the UN would step in to solve the problem. This was especially true in a number of humanitarian crises, as well as in instances where instability undermined democratic governments. There was also an expectation that operations would not only be better resourced, but more importantly, operate with greater authority. With superpower strategic interests no longer an impediment to collective action, everything seemed possible.

The superpowers and changes in peacekeeping

During the Cold War period the superpowers within the UN system and, particularly in the Security Council, were largely in opposition to each other and therefore there was little or no cooperation amongst them. Notably, restraint was the dominant pattern of superpower behaviour during all crises in the Middle East during the Cold War, the scene of much of the UN's peacekeeping activities. In spite of keen rivalry, tacit rules for crisis management emerged and governed superpower behaviour. During the peaks of successive crises, each superpower showed determination to protect its own interests but exercised restraint with regard to encroaching on the interests of the other. Both were prepared to supply their clients with arms and to make bellicose noises and gestures, but were not prepared to give 'blank cheques' to their allies. At different times, each expressed concern about or sought to restrain their allies, the US checking the Israelis during the 1967 war, the Soviets discouraging the Syrians on their ventures into Jordan 1970 and Lebanon in 1982. The outcome was successful crisis management and avoidance of escalation to a point which would make direct superpower confrontation inevitable.[89]

Given this determination to control crises by a certain degree of brinkmanship, it was extremely unlikely that the superpowers would be willing to place great reliance upon the UN to keep the peace. However, the option in international crises would have been for the powers to assume the role of police themselves. They were, therefore, placed in a dilemma, afraid on the one hand to tolerate too much international disorder, reluctant on the other to sanction the growth of a peacekeeping authority with an independent competence of its own. They wanted a UN capable of acting reasonably effectively but at the same time, not too effectively. They wanted a police force which would be competent but whose authority would be strictly controlled.[90] This unease about the role of the UN in dealing with conflict was shared by other members of the Security Council. Britain was on the whole a supporter of the UN, but like France, was uncomfortable about the pressures for decolonisation from the US, Soviet Union and the Third World.[91] China, represented in the early years by Taiwan, was only technically 'a major power' until 1971. This lack of agreement between members prevented the Security Council from taking anything other than nominal action to contain or resolve conflicts.

There were, moreover, distinct East–West differences in attitudes to peacekeeping. Such operations often served the West's interests in regional stability.[92] In contrast, the Soviet Union's interest was to foster instability which might in turn lead to regional change. Soviet fears of UN activity were based on the action in Korea. It had further grounds for distrust when, after the outbreak of that war,

Western states tried to strengthen the General Assembly in order that it be able to act when the Soviet veto prevented the Council from acting. Soviet fears were reinforced by the creation of UNEF. It recognised the establishment of the force, but refused to pay its assessment.[93] UN operations in Cyprus (UNFICYP 1964–) and Lebanon (UNIFIL 1978–) could be seen as representing US concern at developments during the Cold War. America's suggestion that a NATO force be sent to Cyprus reflected concern at possible conflict between Greece and Turkey, two NATO members. Also, it was US concern at the threat to ongoing peace negotiations between Egypt and Israel which led to the creation of UNIFIL.[94] That the UN came increasingly to be used and controlled by the US was hardly surprising. As Donald Puchala observed: 'little of substance can happen in the UN system without American cooperation and little happens without American resources'.[95] If the UN could not work for the US, it could not work without it or against it.[96]

The post-Cold War hyperactivity of the Security Council reflected not only a more open attitude on the part of the former Soviets, but US belief in what Madeleine Albright (then US Ambassador to the UN) called the 'need to bring pressure to bear on the belligerents of the post-Cold War world'.[97] However, translating this commitment into effective action was far from simple. Post-Cold War, the US attitude to UN peacekeeping was distinguished by the fact that while it was willing to see UN authorisation for military actions in which it was involved, it was not always willing to have them placed under UN command and control. It also found involvement in peace operations, such as Somalia, difficult to domestically sustain when things went wrong and American troops lost their lives. Meanwhile, the Soviet attitude changed. With the Red Army bogged down in Afghanistan, Moscow came to the conclusion that UN conflict management was not so bad after all.[98]

The change in Soviet attitudes prompted some positive responses from the US, including behind-the-scenes cooperation over regional conflicts. The only Soviet veto in the Council post 1990 was in relation to the financial burden of the UN operation in Cyprus.[99] However, the Security Council would continue to practise imprecision as to the Charter basis for its action,[100] and despite the hugely improved relations between the US and Russia, mandates would continue to reflect a measure of political compromise. Moreover, the ambiguity of mandates reflected a failure on the part of the permanent five to examine the role of the UN, particularly in relation to internal conflict.

Failure to resolve internal conflicts in the early to mid-1990s revealed that the ending of superpower rivalry did not of itself guarantee more successful operations. Between 1 January 1987 and 31 January 1996, the Security Council passed at least 105 resolutions, under Chapter VII in nine cases. Four of these, Somalia, Liberia, Angola and Rwanda concerned civil wars, albeit with international ramifications.[101] However, China and Third World members of the Council were less than happy with the move towards 'forcible peacekeeping'. China was also uneasy about the Council taking up (in 1991) the question of violations by the Iraqi government of human rights of Iraqi Kurds, believing the Council transgressed the limits of its jurisdiction. It took a similar line during Council debates (in November 1992) on human rights abuses in Yugoslavia.[102] Western states also lost some of their enthusiasm, especially with regard to large intrusive operations.[103] They appeared less concerned with the legal and more with practical limits on Security Council activism in the international system. Many governments that had willingly provided soldiers for peacekeeping could no longer be counted on to send troops to real or potential combat situations. More than ever, potential participant states became concerned with the content and clarity of peacekeeping mandates.

The implications of change for peacekeeping operations

The decline in superpower rivalry, alongside the changing nature of peace operations, has challenged the UN in terms of how it carries out its operations, but has it sufficiently learnt from its past experiences and has this affected the conduct of operations in the post-Cold War period? The evidence provided so far suggests that the UN became increasingly active in a diverse range of operations in selective areas in the early post-Cold War period, often in response to international media exposure, but also on the demand of members of the UN Security Council who have had particular interest in different conflicts (e.g. the US in Haiti, France in Rwanda, Australia in East Timor and Italy in Albania). The demand that the UN 'do something' in the face of a crisis may not have always provided the best reasoning for becoming involved in conflicts where the parties have not agreed to the UN's intervention and in which humanitarian motives are predominant. Such an approach ignored what was possible and could be achieved by those placed as peacekeepers in such conflicts and therefore ran the risk of reducing the likelihood of a successful outcome.

In the following chapters we turn to look at whether peace operations during the Cold War period in the Congo and Cyprus differed from peace operations in Somalia and Angola during the post-Cold War era. Has the UN learnt lessons from its past experiences and is there any evidence that such lessons have affected the conduct of more recent operations? And, has the way in which the UN manages peace operations changed to reflect the changing nature of peace operations and the demands being made of those who must carry out the operations on the ground?

Notes

1   A fourteenth United Nations Transition Assistance Group – UNTAG which ran from 1989 to 1990, is treated as 'Cold War', since it was conceived in 1978. See William Durch, (ed.), *The Evolution of UN Peacekeeping*, London, Macmillan, p. 7 and p. 353
2   Ibid., p. 7
3   Marrack Goulding, 'The Evolution of United Nations Peacekeeping', *International Affairs*, Vol. 69, No. 3, 1993, p. 452
4   Col. Eiver O Hanlon (Irish Contingent), interview with Terry O'Neill, 30 May 1997, Athlone

5   Marianne Heiberg, *Observations on UN Peacekeeping in Lebanon*, Oslo, Norsk Utenrikspolitisk Institutt, 1994, p. 26
6   Lt Col. Colman Goggin (Irish Contingent), interview with Terry O'Neill, 28 December 1996, Athlone
7   The Nepalese had also arrived in UNEF II lacking essential equipment. Such was their reputation, that in time the Norwegian Army came to provide its peacekeeping forces with 15 per cent extra equipment to cater for the 'Nepalese factor'. Col. Sven Stromberg, (Royal Norwegian Army UN School), interview with Terry O'Neill, 28 August 1995, Akershus, Norway
8   Col. William Young (Irish Contingent), interview with Terry O'Neill, March 1983, Tibnin, Lebanon
9   Goulding, 'The Evolution of United Nations Peacekeeping', p. 452
10 Ibid., p. 453
11 Ibid.
12 Brian Urquhart, 'UN Peacekeeping in the Middle East', *The World Today*, March 1980, p. 41
13 F.T. Liu, 'Evolution of UN Peacekeeping Operations', in Kevin Clements and Christine Wilson (eds), *UN Peacekeeping at the Crossroads*, Canberra, Australian National University, 1994, p. 64
14 United Nations, *The Blue Helmets: A Review of United Nations Peacekeeping*, 2nd edn, New York, United Nations Department of Public Information, 1990, p. 73
15 Nabil A. Elarby and Henry Wisemand (eds), 'UN Peacekeeping: The Egyptian Experience', in *Peacekeeping Appraisals and Perspectives*, New York, Pergamon Press, 1983, p. 68
16 Alan James, *Peacekeeping in International Politics*, London, Macmillan p. 217
17 Mona Ghali, 'United Nations Emergency Force I', in William J. Durch, *The Evolution of UN Peacekeeping*, London, Macmillan, 1993, p. 217
18 Alan James, *The Politics of Peacekeeping*, London, Chatto and Windus, 1969, pp. 300–1
19 Ibid., pp. 308–9
20 Ibid.
21 UN, *The Blue Helmets*, p. 25
22 Brian Urquhart, 'Beyond the Sheriff's Posse', *Survival*, Vol. 32, No. 3, 1990, p. 199
23 Bertil Stjernfelt, *The Sinai Peace Front*, London, Hurst and Co., 1992, pp. 11–12
24 Ibid., p. 61
25 Ibid., p. 68
26 Ibid., p. 67
27 Ibid., p. 99
28 Ibid., p. 100
29 Goulding, 'The Evolution of United Nations Peacekeeping', p. 453
30 F.T. Liu in Clements and Wilson, *UN Peacekeeping at the Crossroads*, pp. 66–7
31 Alan James, *The UN on Golan – Peacekeeping Paradox*, Oslo, Norsk Utenrikspolitisk Institutt, August 1986, pp. 14–15
32 Ibid., pp. 20–1
33 Ibid., pp. 30–2
34 Goulding in John Roper, Masashi Nishihara, Olara Otunnu, Enid C.B. Schoegttle (eds), *Keeping the Peace in the Post Cold War Era*, New York, Trilateral Commission, 1993, p. 95
35 Kendall W. Stiles and Mary Ellen MacDonald, 'After Consensus What? Performance Criteria for UN in the Post Cold War Era', *Journal of Peace Research*, Vol. 29, No. 3, 1992, p. 309

36 Made up of Canada, France, Great Britain, US, and West Germany. This phenomenon, an informal ad hoc cabal as opposed to the UN Security Council, would later have a significant role in Bosnia. Fortna, 'United Nations Transition Assistance Group', in Durch *The Evolution of UN Peacekeeping*, p. 354

37 Thomas Frank and George Nolte, 'Secretary General's Good Office Building', in Roberts and Kingsbury, *United Nations: Divided World*, Oxford, Oxford University Press, p. 64

38 Adam Roberts, 'From San Francisco to Sarajevo: The UN and the Use of Force', *Survival*, Vol. 37, No. 4, 1995–6, p. 16

39 Johan Holst, 'Enhancing Peacekeeping Operations', *Survival*, Vol. 32, No. 3, 1990, pp. 272–3

40 Steven Ratner, *The New UN Peacekeeping*, London, Macmillan Press Ltd, 1997, p. 10

41 Adam Roberts, 'The Crisis in UN Peacekeeping', *Survival*, Vol. 36, No. 3, 1994, p. 95

42 Mats Berdal, '*UN at the Crossroads*', IFS Info., Oslo Norsk Utenrikspolitisk Institutt, No. 7, 1993, p. 45

43 UN Peace Operations: Year in Review 2002, UN Department of Public Information: http://www.un.org/Depts/dkpo/yir/english (accessed 05/03/2003)

44 Inis Claude, *Swords into Plowshares*, London, University of London Press Ltd, 1965, p. 290

45 James, *The Politics of Peacekeeping*, p. 3

46 Maurice Flory quoted in David Ruzie, 'Maintaining, Building and Enforcing Peace: A Legal Perspective', *UNIDIR Newsletter*, No. 24, December 1993, p. 13

47 Roberts, 'The Crisis in Peacekeeping', p. 94

48 Nigel White, 'The UN Charter and Peacekeeping Forces', in Michael Pugh (ed.), *The UN, Peace and Force*, p. 115

49 Roberts, 'The Crisis in UN Peacekeeping', p. 94

50 Jarat Chopra, 'Enforcement Mechanisms for Humanitarian Crises', in Age Eknes and Anthony McDermott (eds), *Sovereignty Humanitarian Intervention and the Military*, Oslo, NUPI, 1994, p. 73

51 Shashi Tharoor, 'Should UN Peacekeeping Go Back to Basics', *Survival*, Vol. 3, No. 4, 1995–6, p. 60. Ironically, UN observers were accommodated in houses owned by 'Arkan' (Zeljko Raznaltovic, a Serbian War Criminal). Commandant Dan Murphy, Irish UN Observer, interview with Terry O'Neill, May 1998, Athlone

52 Kofi Annan, 'Challenges of the New Peacekeeping', in Olara Otunnu and Michael W. Doyle (eds), *Peacemaking and Peacekeeping in the New Century*

53 *Multidisciplinary Peacekeeping: Lessons from Recent Experience*, p. 5

54 *Comprehensive Review of the Whole Question of Peacekeeping Operations in All Their Aspects*, p. ix

55 For instance, in Lebanon, the Nordic and Irish contingents were restrained in their use of force. However, the French response to any impediment was so aggressive that that contingent was eventually withdrawn. Christopher Brady and Sam Daws, 'UN Operations: The Political Military Interface', *International Peacekeeping*, Vol. 1, No. 1, Spring 1994, pp. 66–7

56 Jerzy Ciechanski, 'Enforcement Measures Under Chapter VII of the UN Charter', in Pugh (ed.) *The UN, Peace and Force*, p. 90

57 Alan James, *Peacekeeping in International Politics*, London, Macmillan, 1990, p. 2

58 Virginia Page Fortna, 'United Nations Transition Assistance Group', in Durch (ed.), *The Evolution of UN Peacekeeping*, London, Macmillan Press, 1994, p. 365

59 Peter Jakobsen, 'Overload Not Marginalization Threatens UN Peacekeeping', in *Security Dialogue*, Vol. 31, No. 2, 2000, p. 168

60 Lt Col. Sean Kilbride, Former Military Police Officer who observed CIVPOL in Cyprus and Cambodia, interview with Terry O'Neill, 1 September 2000, in Athlone

61 Tetsuo, Ito, *UN Authorised Use of Force: Recent Changes in UN Practice*, Oslo, Institutt for Forsvarsstudier, 1995, p. 8

62 *Wider Peacekeeping, Army Field Manuel*, UpAvon British Army Headquarters Doctrine and Training, (third draft), p. 25

63 John Gerrard Ruggie, 'The UN and the Collective Use of Force Whither or Whether', in Michael Pugh (ed.), *The UN Peace and Force*, London, Frank Cass, 1997, p. 5

64 Paul Diehl, *Forks in the Road: Policy Concerns for 21st Century Peacekeeping*, p. 358

65 John Sanderson, 'The Incalculable Dynamic of Using Force', in Biermann and Vedset (eds), *UN Peacekeeping in Trouble: Lessons Learned in Former Yugoslavia*, p. 202

66 James Mayall, *The New Interventionism 1991–1994*, Cambridge, Cambridge University Press, 1996, p. 25

67 Marrack Goulding, appendix in *Keeping The Peace in the Post-Cold War Era*, Trilateral Commission, p. 97

68 Goulding, 'The Evolution of UN Peacekeeping', p. 453

69 Sally Morphet, 'UN Peacekeeping and Election Monitoring', in Roberts and Kingsbury, *United Nations, Divided World*, p. 191

70 Gareth Evans, *Co-operating for Peace*, St Leonards NSW, Allen and Unwin, 1993, p. 100

71 Anthony French, Senior Legal Adviser UNTSO, 'Peacekeeping and Impartiality', paper delivered to the Israeli National Defence College, Tel Aviv, 18 May 1993, p. 1

72 Shashi Tharoor, 'Should UN Peacekeeping "Go Back to Basics"', Survival, Vol. 37, No. 4, 1995–6, p. 60

73 *Fourth Report of the Secretary General on the United Nations Mission in Sierra Leone*, pp. 13–14

74 *Eighth Report of the Secretary General on UNAMSIL*, 23 September 1999, p. 6

75 Jerzy Cieckanski, 'Enforcement Measures Under Chapter VII of the UN Charter: UN Practice after the Cold War', in Pugh, *The UN, Peace and Force*, p. 83

76 Charles Dobbie, 'A Concept for Post-Cold War Peacekeeping', *Survival*, Vol. 36, No. 3, 1994, p. 121

77 Ghali, 'An Agenda for Peace', in Roberts and Kingsbury, *United Nations, Divided World*, p. 476

78 Ibid.

79 Gareth Evans, *Co-operating for Peace*, London, Allen and Unwin, 1993, p. 10

80 Ibid., pp. 71–75

81 Ghali, 'An Agenda for Peace', in Roberts and Kingsbury, *United Nations, Divided World*, p. 479

82 Ibid.

83 Jeremy Ginifer and Espen Eide, *An Agenda for Preventive Diplomacy, Theory and Practice*, Oslo, NUPI, 1997, p. 26

84 Roberts, 'The Crisis in UN Peacekeeping', p. 96

85 Ibid., p. 97

86 Ibid., p. 96

87 Peter Jakobsen, 'The Transformation of United Nations Peace Operations in the 1990s', *Cooperation and Conflict*, Vol. 37, No. 3, 2002, pp. 267–82

88 Ibid., p. 273

89 Benjamin Miller, 'Competing Realist Perspectives on Great Power Crisis Behaviour', *Security Studies*, Vol. 5, No. 2, 1996, pp. 334–6

90 Peter Calvocoressi, *World Politics Since 1945*, London, Longman Group, 1995, p. 132

91 Charles Pentland, 'Building Global Institutions', in Gavin Boyd and Charles Pentland (eds), *Issues in Global Politics*, London, Collier and Macmillan, 1981, p. 339
92 Durch, *The Evolution of UN Peacekeeping*, p. 7
93 Mona Ghali, 'United Nations Emergency Force I', in Durch, *The Evolution of UN Peacekeeping*, p. 111
94 Mona Ghali, 'United Nations Interim Force in Lebanon', in Durch, The Evolution of UN Peacekeeping, pp. 186–7
95 Donald Puchala, 'American Interests and the United Nations', in Steven Spiegel (ed.), *At Issue*, 4th edition, New York, St Martin's Press, 1984, p. 430
96 Charles Pentland in *Building Global Institutions*, p. 339
97 Mats Berdal, 'Fateful Encounter: The U.S. and UN Peacekeeping', *Survival*, Vol. 36, Spring 1994, p. 32
98 Augustus Norton and Thomas Weiss, 'Super Powers and Peacekeepers', *Survival*, Vol. 32, May/June 1990, p. 212
99 Adam Roberts, 'The Crisis in Peacekeeping', *Survival*, Vol. 36, No. 3, 1994, p. 97
100 Jerzy Ciechanski, 'Enforcement Measures under Chapter VII', in Pugh, *The UN, Peace and Force*, p. 84
101 Ibid., p. 85
102 Ibid. p. 97
103 Ibid., p. 98

3

ONUC AND THE CONGO, 1960–1964

Introduction

The UN operation in the Congo, ONUC (Operation des Nations Unies au Congo) is an example of what may ensue when the UN embarks on a mission without a clear plan and without establishing the role and status of the international troops employed. Ambiguous UN Security Council resolutions confused the Congolese who requested the Forces' presence and the members of the Secretariat charged with conducting the operation. As the peacekeepers engaged in armed conflict with one of the local parties, the operation could be seen as failing to adhere to the tenets of 'traditional peacekeeping': yet lacking the required military might and the authority of Chapter VII of the UN Charter, it could not be deemed an exercise in 'enforcement'.

Nature of the conflict

The operation, which ran from July 1960 to June 1964, can be viewed as a two-phase operation aimed at restoring state authority. The UN force was initially tasked with helping to restore law and order and later with preventing civil war. The operation was linked to a widespread feeling of sympathy by UN member states for the Congolese whose country had, within days of independence, been plunged into turmoil. The challenge facing the UN was that of translating goodwill into action while operating within the constraints of the UN Charter. There was the problem of trying to reconcile intervention with respect for state sovereignty and the question of whether international forces should become engaged in preventing civil war. The crisis created by civil disorder presented a challenge to the liberal belief that self-determination and democracy reduce the risk of conflict. It also raised questions as to whether limits should be set to the pursuit of self-determination and demonstrated the difficulty of trying to introduce democracy (here defined as 'rule by the people') to communities who are not informed by a common policy.

In this section of the study, these issues are considered under the headings: (1) Historical background – covering the origins of the crisis, (2) phase one – from the commencement of the operation to February 1961, and (3) phase two – February 1961 onwards. The headings 'Phase one' and 'Phase two' are also employed through other sections of the case study.

Historical background

In 1957, Patrice Lumumba, subsequently to become an icon of African nationalism, observed that in working out any far-sighted political policy, it was advisable to take account of local circumstances. The enjoyment of political rights, he wrote, presupposed that the beneficiaries have an adequate understanding of public affairs and an appreciation of the general interest. To introduce the ferment of political life prematurely would, he warned, be to introduce the ferments of discord and dissension: it would not be a victory for the democratic idea, but would, rather, open the way to a return to old tribal concepts.[1] His words would acquire a particular significance in the light of subsequent events in the Congo. However, the references to 'far-sighted political policy', 'employment of political rights', the 'democratic idea', and 'return to old tribal concepts' also raise again issues such as distinction between states and nations, sovereignty, and in particular the question of responsibility for developments both within and between states.

Much of the responsibilities of the Congo crisis of 1960 would be laid at the door of the Belgians for their failure to prepare their colony for independence. But however blameworthy the Belgians, the crisis could also be seen as a direct consequence of the widespread international support for the liberal objective of 'national self-determination'. The uncritical espousal of this objective within the UN failed in the case of the Congo to take account of 'the destabilising effects of ethnic groups single mindedly pursuing their accumulated rivalries and ancient hatreds'.[2] Insofar as the Belgians thought about the future of their colony, they imagined a slow advance by Africans to a level at which a new form of association might have been allowed. However, a transfer of power did not enter these calculations, no steps were taken to educate an elite, and at independence the country had only 17 university graduates.[3]

The situation changed dramatically following riots in the capital, Leopoldville, in January 1959. The rioting was prompted largely by unemployment and discrimination, but was also linked to General de Gaulle's offer of self-government to neighbouring French Congo. Across the Congo, political activity began engaging the interest of mass politics. By November 1959, 53 political groups were officially registered and within a few months, the number had reached over 120. Almost every party sprang from tribal origins and the vast size of the country (over 1 million square miles – see Map 3.1) hampered the formation of nationally based movements. Elements of the population of 14 million spoke different languages and had virtually no communication with others outside their own region. Thus, the desire of many of the emerging political leaders was that the ending of colonial rule would mean not so much national independence as the revival of ancient African empires.[4]

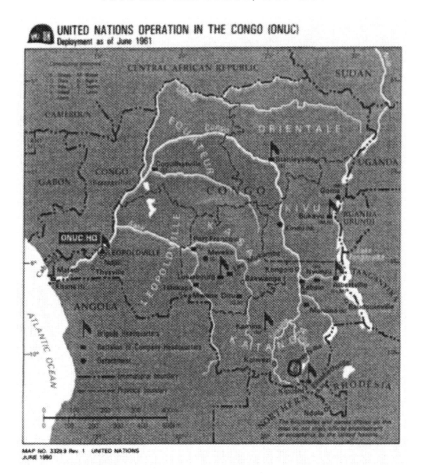

Map 3.1 Congo and ONUC: deployment as of June 1961

Source: UN Cartographic Section (Map No. 3329.9 Rev 1)

Encouraged by the anti-imperialist rhetoric from the non-aligned states, Lumumba and the other Congolese leaders were not prepared to wait for any gradual introduction to the ideas of politics and democracy and under domestic pressure the Belgian government decided to grant independence on 30 June 1960. In doing so, it hoped to be able to maintain the substance of military and commercial interest while surrendering official control to the Congolese. The Congolese nationalists found advantage in appealing to the colonisers for the application to the colony of the colonisers' own values. Democracy implied that self-government could not be refused once a convincing demonstration had been made that the nationalist party incorporated the popular will. But democratic systems required a basic consensus among most citizens about the acceptability of their state,[5] and the tribally oriented Congolese had had no opportunity to arrive at any such consensus.

What then was the nature of Congolese nationalism and popular will? Congolese nationalism represented, according to Crawford Young, 'the sublime conviction in the capacity of nationalism not only to challenge and dislodge the coloniser, but also to fulfil its own promises'. He cites the campaign platform of one party which promised complete elimination of unemployment and wage increases for all.[6] As for the 'popular will', this related largely to tribal or regional aspirations. The ABAKO party led by Joseph Kasavubu had as its ultimate dream the reunification of the Bakongo people living in Angola and the French and Belgian Congos.[7] A thousand miles away in the province of Katanga, Moise Tshombe's CONAKAT party favoured provincial autonomy. Foremost among the country's political movements was the Mouvement Nationale Congolaise (MNC) led by Lumumba: but even its support came in large measure from the leader's tribal associations.[8] In the election of May 1960 to the 137-seat parliament, the MNC gained 33 seats, the largest single total, but in crucial areas around Leopoldville and South Katanga, it got no effective support. Lumumba, nevertheless, gained sufficient support from disparate groups to force the Belgians reluctantly to appoint him premier, Kasavubu becoming non-executive president.[9]

The Congolese had elected a government, but to function effectively, it needed to enjoy general consent and legitimacy. In reality, there was little or no evidence of compatibility between the various 'peoples' whose vote determined the common government. They did not constitute a 'nation' and their allegiance as confirmed at the polls was to tribal or at best regional leaders rather than to any central authority. The situation was precisely that which Lumumba had warned against.

Five days after independence, the Force Publique, the country's 25,000-strong army mutinied and as violence spread, many of the white, mostly Belgian, population fled. In response, the Belgian government first deployed troops stationed in the Congo, then flew in reinforcements. Amid the chaos, Tshombe declared Katanga an independent state. In so doing, he had widespread support from the African population in the south of the province and from most of the 32,000-strong European community. He had control of the provincial government and access to the tax revenue of the copper industry.[10] His actions and the collapse of state authority created the need for some form of immediate action. But what action and by whom?

Uncertainty as to objectives and priorities characterised the appeals for assistance which came from the Congolese. In the first made by Lumumba on 10 July, the premier merely asked for UN assistance in training the Arme Nationale Congolaise (ANC), the former Force Publique.[11] The second came on 11 July from three Congolese government ministers who asked the US for American troops to help restore order. A third request from Kasavubu and Lumumba on 12 July asked the UN for military assistance against what they described as 'external aggression', namely Belgian intervention. Significantly, they emphasised that the assistance they requested was not for the purpose of restoring internal order. The confusion was compounded by their further request of 13 July for assistance from the Soviet Union. By this time, however, the Security Council (in Resolution 143 of 14 July

1960) had authorised Secretary-General Dag Hammarskjöld to provide the Congolese Government 'with such military assistance as may be needed, until through the efforts of the Congolese government with the technical assistance of the United Nations, the national security forces may be able in the opinion of the government to meet fully their tasks'.[12]

The wording of this resolution was certain to create misunderstanding. The Congolese authorities were entitled to believe that UN military forces were being placed at their disposal – but was this really the UN's intention? Also the term 'military assistance' was open to a variety of interpretations – was ONUC a military or police force? If the former, was it to be an actual or potential army? If the latter, how could it operate in this role without the approval of the Congolese? The UN Security Council had created an international force but confusion surrounded its purpose.

Phase one (July 1960–February 1961)

By 19 July 1960, some fourteen and a half thousand people were deployed, and the Force was made up of troops from thirty member states (see Map 3.1). Acceding to the Congolese request for neutral-country military personnel only, Secretary-General Hammarskjöld created a body that was predominantly African but included Swedish and Irish contingents to reassure the European communities.[13] Left to implement the establishing resolution, the Secretary-General laid down a set of principles based on strict adherence to the UN Charter. Hammarskjöld was emphatic about the need to isolate ONUC from any internal struggle for power.[14] However, the Secretary-General's stance called into question the whole purpose of the UN presence. The Congo was falling apart and a feeble government was being further undermined by secessionist movements in two of its richest provinces, Katanga and Kasai.[15] In the absence of a disciplined effective security force, there was every likelihood of protracted and bloody strife throughout the country. Such conflict had the potential not only for 'spill over' but direct intervention by one or more of the major powers. This was precisely the kind of situation 'preventive diplomacy' was supposed to address. However, by standing aloof and failing to take decisive action, the UN allowed a dangerous situation to escalate dramatically.

Disillusioned with the UN's failure to provide the military assistance it appeared to promise, Lumumba decided to end Katanga's secession himself and asked the Soviet Union for assistance. Supplied with Soviet aircraft and transport, Lumumba used the aircraft to ferry troops into Kasai en route to Katanga.[16] The result was a tribal massacre. The premier's action and his reliance upon the Soviet Union had major repercussions since it effectively pitched the internal struggle for power at the level of Cold War confrontation. In September 1960, Lumumba was ousted from office by the West-backed Kasavubu in a move in which UN troops had a pivotal role. This was quickly followed by a US-backed coup organised by the country's Chief of Staff, Joseph Mobutu, who expelled all Soviet personnel.[17] The circumstances surrounding Lumumba's downfall were such that the UN arguably had no option but to intervene. However, the action which was widely perceived as evidence of a Western takeover of UN effectively demolished any prospects of an agreed international approach to the Congo's problems.

The deteriorating situation was aggravated by the central government's decision to hand over Lumumba to his enemies in Katanga, who immediately murdered him. Though technically a Congolese matter, the murder of the premier of a state it had undertaken to assist could only be viewed as further evidence of the UN's inability to act decisively and effectively. (The UN's responsibility for Lumumba's death would be given as a reason for Mozambique's reluctance to accept UN help in the 1990s.)[18] Galvanised into a semblance of consensus, the Security Council in February 1961 passed a resolution (161A) urging prevention of civil war and the use of force if necessary to achieve this purpose. The implied intention to become more directly involved suggested that the hitherto perceived barriers to intervention in Congolese affairs were in fact surmountable, and that the UN proposed demonstrating its resolve.

Phase two (February 1961–June 1964)

However oblique the wording in the February 1961 Resolution, a clear purpose was the ending of Katanga's secession. To what extent then had that province succeeded in establishing a separate existence? A year after declaring its independence, Katanga was a prosperous and generally secure area in an otherwise disorganised Congo. It enjoyed support in government circles in Belgium, France and Britain and received support also from neighbouring Northern Rhodesia. It had many of the characteristics of a newly emergent state, but lacked international 'recognition'. Its prosperity, however, provided one of the main arguments for its speedy reintegration. Since the province's copper industry had, pre-independence, provided some 40 per cent of the country's revenue, a Congo state deprived of this income would not be viable.[19]

The issue facing the UN appeared clear cut. The future of a UN member state was at stake and a threat to international peace was perceived to exist. However, the operation remained in a state of paralysis and arguably no action would have been forthcoming but for, (1) the arrival in Katanga in April 1961 of a brigade of Indian combat troops, and, (2) the appointment of Dr Conor Cruise O'Brien (Ireland) as the Secretary-General's Representative in Katanga. These developments were significant for two reasons. First, India's Premier Nehru had responded to Hammarskjöld's request for troops on the understanding that if he provided personnel, the Secretary-General would not allow them to be insulted or pushed around.[20] Moreover, with tension high along its borders with China, India could not afford to leave its contingent in the Congo indefinitely. Second, O'Brien left New York persuaded that continued existence of an independent state of Katanga constituted a threat to the existence of the UN. Whereas up to the time of O'Brien's arrival, the February 1961 Resolution had remained just another formula of words, both O'Brien and the head of UN Civilian Operations in the Congo, Mahmoud Khiari (Tunisia), decided to translate it into action.

The attitude of Nehru and of O'Brien and Khiari was understandable. The Congolese leaders had asked the UN for assistance but had sought to impose their own rules on ONUC's employment. They had insisted that the ANC be recognised as a responsible security force and that it retain its arms. However, the people of Kasai and the various ONUC contingents which had suffered casualties, had paid dearly for this assertion of Congolese sovereignty. Meanwhile, proscribed 'military personnel and advisers' (foreign mercenaries and Belgian military) were actively engaged in consolidating Katanga's secession. The UN's authority was being challenged by assorted parties and action was required.

Operation 'Rumpunch' launched by O'Brien on 28 August 1961 was intended to break the back of Katanga's resistance through the arrest of mercenaries and advisers. In the operation, elements of ONUC seized key installations in Elizabethville, the Katanga capital, and arrested white officers and personnel. Encouraged by this success and the praise of Hammarskjöld, O'Brien and Khiari decided that with another quick 'push' it would be possible to effectively end Katanga's secession.[21] Operation 'Morthor' launched on 13 September 1961 was similar to 'Rumpunch' inasmuch as the taking of critical installations was an objective; this time however, the personnel on the 'arrest list' were not mercenaries but ministers of Katanga's government: the warrants of arrest which Khiari produced were signed by the Congolese authorities only. Such arrests were not authorised by any Security Council (SC) Resolution nor were they approved by the Secretary-General. O'Brien states that McKeown, Rikhye, and probably Hammarskjöld, were unaware of the existence of the warrants.[22] However, the purpose of the arrests was, in O'Brien's opinion, consistent with the Force's overall mandate. Lacking proper organisation and planning, the operation went terribly wrong. Most ministers on the arrest list, including Tshombe, escaped, scores were killed in the fighting and 150 Irish troops stationed in Jadotville were forced to surrender.[23] Hammaerskjold arranged to meet Tshombe for ceasefire negotiations but was killed in a plane crash en route.

In what appeared like a 'get tough' approach, the Security Council in November 1961 passed Resolution 169 which authorised ONUC to take 'vigorous action' including the use of force if necessary for the deportation of all foreign military personnel and declaring support for the central government. In this way, the Council sought to clear all doubts about the legal propriety of any action such as that taken in August. However, when hostilities were renewed in December 1961, it was Katanga which brought the fight to ONUC. This time the UN forces, better prepared and equipped with a limited number of aircraft,[24] gained the upper hand but not outright success. Tshombe agreed to respect government authority but fell short of abandoning secession.

Failure to end Katanga's secession at this time confirmed the UN's inability to agree on clear objectives and take the required action. It had undertaken to provide military assistance but had accepted that it could not engage in the internal security role. It had then indicated an intention to prevent civil war but employing the Force as some form of buffer was, given the size of the country, a physical impossibility. ONUC's only possible purpose, particularly in the light of the November Resolution, was its employment in crushing Katanga through the destruction of its gendarmerie. Arguably, many contributing states might have had little appetite for a major confrontation, but bestowing the force with an extra Indian brigade would, given the attitude of the Indians, almost certainly have resulted in the ending of the gendarmerie's resistance.

The Security Council showed no enthusiasm for the vigorous action it had authorised and the eventual resolution of the Katanga problem was not due to any agreed UN plan for enforcement action. There were no indications that such would ever materialise. Rather, it was over-confidence on the part of the Katangese, American determination to protect its interests in Africa, and ONUC concern for its supply routes, which led to the ending of secession. In late 1962, Katanga, encouraged by UN passivity began harassment of ONUC troops. The US, fearful that the West-oriented central government would fall and be replaced by a pro-Soviet regime, agreed to provide ONUC with extra logistical support. In the final show of strength which began in December 1962, ONUC forces met less resistance than on previous occasions and by 14 January 1963, Katanga's secession was finally ended. By mid-1963, the UN operation was being phased out and concluded in June 1964.[25]

The UN had prevented the break-up of the Congo but where did the country now stand in relation to the promotion of self-determination and introduction of democracy given the departure of the peacekeepers? The crushing of Katanga and the removal of the last vestige of external interference could, in broad terms, be seen as the completion of the Congolese movement towards this objective. However, self-determination for the Congolese was quickly to assume a different meaning as ethnic divisions exposed the inherent instability of the former colony. Within months of ONUC's departure, the government lost control of half the country, a situation not uncommon in other peacekeeping operations during the Cold War period. As if to underline the totally artificial nature of African nationalism, the two main rebel movements were led by former supporters of Lumumba and his MNC party (Pierre Mulele and Christopher Gbenye).[26] Whereas the breakup of the broad anti-colonial nationalist movement was predictable, the fragmentation of the erstwhile nationalist political movement revealed the aspirations of assorted elements to their own concept of self-determination. These rebellions were over-come but the potential for conflict based on ethnic divisions was to remain. When civil war broke out much later in 1996 and the UN considered another peacekeeping operation, even O'Brien accepted the inherent divisions declaring: 'This time let the Congo fall apart.'[27]

Political base, phase one (June 1960–February 1961)

Prior involvement of Great Powers

The superpowers had, at the time the Congo crisis erupted, accepted the global distribution of power and had developed their own spheres of influence. The Soviet Union controlled or exercised predominant influence in the zone occupied by the Red Army or other Communist armed forces, and did not attempt to extend its influence by military force. The US exercised control and predominance over the rest of the capitalist world and Western hemisphere. It did not intervene in the zone of accepted Soviet control.[28] However, in the zone of new colonial states, the superpowers competed for power and influence, engaging in proxy wars. What, then, was the attitude of the US, Soviet Union and the other permanent members of the Security Council to the Congo in the pre-crisis period?

China, at that time represented by Taiwan, had no direct involvement in the Congo. France's only involvement was through the proximity of the capitals of the French and Belgian Congos. The three other Great Powers, however, had particular reason for concern about developments within the troubled state. While both the US and Soviet Union had, after World War II, professed strong anti-colonial and pro-nationalist sentiments, their interest in the Congo was influenced by totally different concerns. For Soviet Premier Khruschev, the revolutionary potential of Third World countries was considerable; Africa had formerly been at the bottom of the Soviet agenda, but 'nationalists', provided they were moving in a Socialist direction, could become acceptable allies.[29] In the late 1950s, the Soviet Union had established strong links with the anti-colonialist Kwame Nkrumah of Ghana and Lumumba as a disciple of Nkrumah fitted Moscow's idea of an African socialist worthy of cultivation. The US had a major interest in the Congo long before 1960. The uranium of the bomb which launched the atomic age in New Mexico on 16 July 1945 had come from Katanga: so also the explosives which destroyed Hiroshima and Nagasaki.[30] The uranium was exclusively Belgian and although in the late 1950s this mineral was becoming increasingly available from other sources, the Katanga deposits continued to be a major factor in American concerns about developments within the former colony. Also, US troops, together with other NATO forces, had for many years used the giant Kamina Base in Katanga for flying and parachute training.[31] Located at the centre of Africa, the Congo was of great strategic importance to the US.

Britain had also availed of the former Belgian bases and was concerned for their future; however, its principal concern arose from its commercial interests in Katanga. In 1958, 10 per cent of the Congo's exports went to Britain and almost 33 per cent of Katanga's copper was carried by rail through Northern and Southern Rhodesia. The railway in question was owned by the British company, Tanganyika Concessions, which had a large holding in the giant mining company Union Miniere du Haut Katanga (UMHK).[32] The Copper Belt straddled the Congo/Northern Rhodesia border. The attitude of these three powers was also influenced by the prevailing political situation.

Initial position of Great Powers

In mid-1960, the superpowers were regarding each other with nervousness. The Soviet Union was worried by Washington's bellicose rhetoric and concerned by its own brawl with China. The US meanwhile faced a dilemma; it had supported the ending of colonialism, but nationalist struggles were unpredictable. American policy makers feared Soviet responses either to a power vacuum or to US involvement. Anxious to forestall any Soviet military initiative, the US supported UN intervention. The Soviet Union seeing support of forcible decolonisation as a means of gaining influence in the Third World, was prepared to support UN resolutions for the deployment of a peacekeeping force. It hoped the force would serve its purpose and avoid it having to contemplate a difficult and dangerous intervention. The Congo was 5,000 miles away, had no communist party, and was surrounded by countries hostile to communism. It expected ONUC to eject Belgian forces and end Katanga's secession.[33]

In British eyes, law and order was the most basic Congolese requirement and that, therefore, became the cornerstone of British policy. It was sensitive to the need for order; the Congo's problems if not resolved could easily spread to neighbouring Uganda, Tanganyika and Kenya. Britain accepted that there was no real alternative to ONUC but made a point of keeping a watchful eye upon the operation. Like the Soviet Union, Britain regarded peacekeeping as a job for the Great Powers. Unhappy with a UN operation composed of personnel from the smaller states, but fearing that the vetoing of such a force in the Security Council would draw the wrath of a large number of General Assembly states, Britain chose to abstain rather than oppose the first Security Council vote on ONUC.[34]

Given Soviet, American and British anxiety to retain the favour of Third World countries, it is necessary to consider the attitude of the latter to international developments. This was shaped largely at the Bandung Conference of April 1955 which was intended to stimulate cooperation among Asians and Africans. For the members of what became known as the non-aligned movement (NAM), the principal achievement was the establishment of the foundation for joint action at the UN; through solidarity they increased their security, their status and their diplomatic weight in the world. This forced the Great Powers to take them seriously. Their areas of concern were, however, limited and their attitude strongly realist. They learned how to play the superpowers off against each other, but fearing the Soviet Union more than the US, they tended to side with the communists.

When the General Assembly voted on a resolution affirming Hungary's right to independence and demanding the dispatch of UN observers to that country in 1956, such leaders of the non-aligned group as India and Yugoslavia abstained, as did every Arab country. India refused to condemn Soviet acts in Hungary and argued that a call for free elections supervised by the UN was a violation of Hungary's sovereignty. India's reaction was dictated by classic realism. It did not want to incur Soviet displeasure at a time when Pakistan and China stood on its borders.[35] The African states were chiefly concerned with anti-colonialism, the nationalist struggle in South Africa, and the problem of achieving some sort of African unity.[36] The attitude of the neutral or non-aligned African states at this time was particularly important. The Congo operation was essentially theirs: they supplied the troops (with a few exceptions), their nationals filled most of the key military and civilian posts and they sat on the Secretary-General's Advisory Committee.[37] The elements which would directly influence the operation in the Congo were therefore motivated by different concerns making a common approach to objectives virtually impossible.

UN mandate

ONUC's task during phase one was that of assisting the Congolese Government to restore law and order.[38] This task raises the issues of (1) the legality of the operation and (2) mandate feasibility. The legal basis for the creation of the Force is described by Michael Akehurst as 'obscure and controversial'. When asked to pay its share of the expenses, the Soviet Union which had earlier voted for the enabling resolutions, argued that the creation of the Force was illegal for a number of reasons. These included the fact that the Force was virtually under the control of the Secretary-General rather than the Council. The Soviet position was difficult to reconcile with its vote for the enabling resolution. Moreover, there was no reason why the Council should not delegate its powers to the Secretary-General under the terms of the Charter.[39]

The Secretary-General presented the two main elements from the legal point of view as being (1) the request from the Congolese of 13 July for assistance, (2) the circumstances being such as to justify action under the UN Charter (a perceived threat to international peace and security). Hammarskjöld sought to establish the basic principle of the operation: 'on its side the host government when exercising its sovereign right with regard to the presence of the force, should be judged by good faith in the interpretation of the purpose of the force, the UN on its side, should be understood to be determined by similar good faith in the interpretation of the purpose'.[40] The problem for both parties was that the enabling resolution did not set out the objectives for the operation and did not define what tasks were to be met by the indigenous security forces that would allow the UN to consider its work complete. The Congolese leaders could be forgiven for interpreting the Resolution as meaning that the UN Security Council was coming in as the government's right arm; that was what it had requested. Lumumba in particular wanted help to suppress Katanga's secession. When he did not get this, he set in motion a train of events disastrous both for the Congolese people and ultimately himself. The problem was compounded by lack of clarity as to how law and order was to be restored.

To the Commander of the UN troops in Leopoldville, the task of maintaining order and protecting life required the disarming of the ANC. However, he immediately found himself at odds with the Special Representative of the Secretary-General (SRSG), Dr Ralph Bunche, who held that to disarm the troops would infringe Congolese sovereignty and ordered that all impounded weapons be returned.[41] The folly of this decision became evident when within weeks, Lumumba employed the rearmed ANC to wage war in Kasai. The situation which followed served to highlight the dilemmas created by such a vague and ambiguous mandate. Concerned at Lumumba's erratic behaviour, Kasavubu in September 1960 announced the premier's dismissal, prompting the premier to announce in turn the dismissal of the president. Hammarskjöld rejected the president's request for assistance in Lumumba's arrest on the grounds that such arrests were not the UN's concern.

However, Bunche's successor, Andrew Cordier (US), acting on the basis that ONUC was responsible for the maintenance of law and order and fearing that the arrival in the capital of Lumumba's supporters would lead to major conflict, closed Leopoldville airport and the radio station.[42]

This action, which Hammarskjöld insisted did not constitute intervention since 'to intervene means taking an initiative in the use of force',[43] incurred the wrath of the Soviet Union and its supporters. Critics of the UN action justifiably argued that the action taken favoured the president. It not only prevented Lumumba from mustering support, but denied him the opportunity of presenting his case over the airwaves.

The incident was significant not merely because of its immediate consequences, but for the questions it raised about the role of the UN in restoring order in a sovereign state (see UNIFICYP). Since UN action was certain to disadvantage one party, how could the Force carry out its mandate while purporting to behave impartially? And who was to decide on the extent of UN action? The episode also highlighted another of ONUC's major problems – identifying a legitimate Congolese authority. This problem would arise again in Somalia. The coup raised the issue not only of 'which' authority but 'whose'. The mandate was based on resolutions approved by the Soviet Union and US, both of which had recognised Lumumba and Kasavubu as the legally elected Congolese authorities. But the UN force had helped albeit indirectly to oust Lumumba. How could the role played by the UN in the affair be seen as a genuine United Nations action when the outcome clearly favoured Western interests?

Given that the mandate's ambiguity had given rise to serious problems, both for the Force and for those who authorised it, why was no effort made to amend it? The reason, according to Alan James, is that the ambiguity suited the Secretary General. As early as August 1960, Hammarskjöld had decided to undercut Lumumba and had asked his friends, including Britain, not to press for a Security Council Resolution interpreting the previous resolutions for fear of a Soviet veto. This he said could drive both Ghana and Guinea into Soviet hands. This in turn might lead to independent use of the Ghanaian or Guinean contingents and so to the necessity of his having to order the Force's withdrawal.[44] Remarkably, he made no reference to the Council's role in such a decision. Regarding the problem of the initial mandate, it could be argued that since it was framed at a time of crisis, lack of clarity was inevitable. But did the Security Council and Secretary General learn from this experience and were subsequent resolutions any more satisfactory? This will be examined in 'phase two'. Meanwhile, how did the attitude and actions of the Great Powers impinge upon the operation?

Political manoeuvres of the Great Powers

The attitude of the superpowers during the first six months of the operation showed that the presence of the UN force was regarded by them as little more than a stop-gap measure. It would not, however, stop those powers from pursuing their own agendas. The Soviet Union, by its unqualified support for Lumumba, would continue to foster instability. The US would respond by taking what President Eisenhower called 'very straightforward actions'.[45] This US action would have major implications for the operation and for the long-term future of the Congo.

There is significant evidence that both the US and UN officials influenced Kasavubu's decision to remove Lumumba. Both the Special Representative of the Secretary-General, Cordier, and Hammarskjöld coordinated their activities with the US State Department and Cordier consulted the US Ambassador in the Congo before arranging for the UN troops to close the airport in September 1960.[46] The US Central Intelligence Agency (CIA) meanwhile made a special effort to gain influence in the ANC through its Chief of Staff, Colonel Mobutu. Amply supplied by the US, Mobutu distributed large amounts of money to soldiers under his command, thereby establishing bonds of loyalty. The US then advocated a military coup and on 14 September, Mobutu closed the parliament and established himself as dictator.[47] America's role in the overthrow of Lumumba demonstrated its ruthless determination to protect its interests and called into question the sincerity of its purported commitment to democracy. It also revealed its lack of confidence in the UN as an instrument for resolving international crises.

Like the US, Britain feared the influence of Lumumba and James quotes one Foreign Office official as stating: 'the single way of ensuring his removal is by killing him'.[48] There would however, be no evidence of Britain's involvement in Lumumba's downfall, although his murder in Katanga would lead to perceptions of guilt by association. Britain wanted the Congo's problems resolved by negotiation and was emphatic about the undesirability of the use of force. It was concerned about the behaviour of some Commonwealth contingents and Nkrumah was reminded that the UN operation was the only way to bring law and order to the Congo and so keep it free from outside intervention.[49]

Phase two (February 1961–June 1964)

Initial position of the Great Powers

Lumumba's murder caused the Soviet Union to break off all relations with Hammarskjöld and to effectively turn its back on the operation. As the Council considered what action it should now take, the Soviets vetoed some of the draft resolutions and abstained on the vote on SC Resolution 161A (1961). The Soviet Union's attention would soon turn to other and more important trouble spots: first to Cuba where the US would in April 1961 attempt to overthrow the Castro regime, later to Berlin where in August the infamous Wall would be erected. Meanwhile, US interest in ONUC would increase. Prior to Lumumba's death, the Afro-Asians had argued for a stronger mandate and the new Kennedy administration was sympathetic to such a move. The death of Lumumba had produced a bitter Afro-Asian reaction against the conduct of the operation and this development influenced the Americans in supporting the February 1961 Resolution.[50] Besides, with the Congo now being led by a staunchly pro-Western regime, the US had all the more reason to support the Secretariat and the Afro-Asians.

Britain held to the stance it had taken from the outset. Before casting a very unenthusiastic vote for SC Resolution 161A (1961), it made clear its understanding that the resolution's reference to use of force related only to clashes between hostile Congolese troops. The resolution did not, in its opinion, empower the UN to impose a political settlement by force.[51] It set about doing what it could to play down the importance of the February resolution and avert its possible implementation. France showed its feelings by abstaining from voting. The Force, therefore, lacked the unreserved collective Security Council support required to carry out its task effectively.

The mandate

ONUC's particular tasks during phase two were to secure the withdrawal of all foreign personnel and political advisers not under UN control and mercenaries, and assist the government to restore and maintain political integrity and independence and to prevent civil war.[52] SC Resolution 161A provided the basis for these activities. The resolution expressed concern at the danger of 'widespread civil war' and urged the UN to take immediate appropriate measures including, if necessary, the use of force in the last resort to prevent its occurrence.[53] Confusion of purpose within the UN was however evident in the fact that while the resolution spoke of the use of force to prevent civil war, its preamble declared that 'the solution of the problems of the Congo lies in the hands of the Congolese people themselves without any interference from outside'.[54] This was just one of many extraordinary aspects of the resolution. There was the reference to the danger of civil war. But in February 1961 the prospect of civil war seemed distinctly remote. The collusion of the Leopoldville and Elizabethville regimes in Lumumba's death indicated a considerable measure of communication between the two parties.

There was also the legal aspect – civil war was an internal Congolese matter. There is no rule in international law to prevent civil wars: neither is there any law forbidding the mother state from crushing any secessionary movement.[55] (ONUC had done nothing to prevent attacks on the population of secessionist Kasai: UN troops had instructions not to intervene in fighting between Katanga Gendarmerie and pro-Central Government Baluba in North Katanga.)[56] Reference to civil war also raised the questions: (1) What action and involving what parties, was to be regarded as civil war? (2) How and in what way was force to be used to prevent it?

In relation to the first question, Sture Linner (SRSG May 1961–January 1962) indicated that 'If the Government used military force to impose its control in the entire national territory and if resistance by local authorities led to bloodshed, the UN would not regard this as a civil war and would do nothing to prevent it.'[57] Since the only 'local authorities' in any meaningful sense were those in Katanga, this statement appeared to rule out any UN interference in the event of a clash between central government and Katanga forces. This new mandate was no more clear than the original, but the lack of clarity was much more critical because of the reference to the possible use of force.

How then was force to be used and to what extent was its use a genuine option? In regard to action in or against Katanga, it did not seem to those on the ground to be a reasonable prospect. At 13,000 men, Katanga's gendarmerie which could bank on considerable local support, greatly outnumbered ONUC's forces in the province. UN troops were extremely conscious of the superior armament and mobility of the Katangese. Military concern at ONUC's vulnerability was reflected in the fact that Force security and freedom of movement were the principal topics at all top-level military conferences held between January and July 1961.[58]

Regarding the use of force, did the UN indicate any change in ONUC's status by providing the means by which force could be used? No change was in fact evident on the ground: no extra arms were provided, nor even mentioned.[59] Subsequently questioned as to whether the Secretariat had considered the need for extra fire power to give credibility to the February resolution's implied threat, O'Brien replied that he 'presumed the Secretary General had discussed the matter with his military advisers'.[60] This statement is remarkable given that the peacekeepers had from the outset been armed with weapons for self-defence only, leaving them highly vulnerable. ONUC's vulnerability had been demonstrated through the murder of nine Irish soldiers by tribesmen employing bows and arrows, by the expulsion of the UN garrison from the port of Matadi by the ANC, and the murder of 44 Ghanaians in one afternoon at Port Francqui.[61] So from whence came the pressure for the 'use of force' and how serious were perceived supporters of such action?

O'Brien maintained that the Afro-Asian governments carried the February resolution because 'they interpreted it as providing a means in effect of using the Force to end secession'.[62] This assertion, while perhaps true in respect of views expressed in the General Assembly, is however not supported by either the actions or subsequent statements of several of the Afro-Asian states directly involved. Rather than demonstrating their support for action through their continued participation in the operation, Guinea, Morocco, and Indonesia withdrew their contingents.[63] Presented with a much depleted force, the Secretary-General, in late February wrote to several African states concerning the need for troops; the response was distinctly at odds with O'Brien's contention.

The Ethiopian government declared that 'the UN forces in the Congo must not be found third party to any dispute which might arise'. Tunisia stated that it had no intention of engaging one or other of the parties concerned. Sudan took a similar line. Hammarskjöld assured these states that the basic intention of the resolution was that resort to force would only be taken if all other efforts such as negotiation, persuasion or conciliation were to fail. He further assured them that if, following such efforts UN troops engaged in defensive action to prevent a civil war risk, such action would not in his opinion mean that they became a party to the conflict.[64] This reply, however, did not clarify the issue of what form of civil war was envisaged, how ONUC was to engage better equipped forces or the distinction between defensive and offensive action. So, despite the Security Council's authorisation of the use of force and perceived demands for the Afro-Asians for action, there was no clear indication of a widespread desire for or commitment to military action. What action did come resulted directly from O'Brien's frustration with the delay in mandate implementation and the desire of the Indian contingent to complete the task which they believed they had been sent to perform.

Any suggestion such as that made by Marrack Goulding that action taken in Katanga subsequent to the passing of SC Resolution 161A amounted to 'enforcement'[65] is not supported by the facts. ONUC was not, as Britain was careful to note, one of those enforcement measures referred to in Article 2, para. 7, of the Charter.[66] Moreover, the Soviet Union interpreted the UN Charter as conferring the powers of enforcement upon the Great Powers only. There had been no formal move to Chapter VII of the Charter, nor any attempt to set a process in motion by first trying such non-coercive measures as economic sanctions. Most importantly, a Force which was neither equipped nor mandated to fight a military campaign could not become the kind of coercive unit envisaged in the Charter simply by vague references to the 'use of force'.

The notion that ONUC engaged in enforcement action in Katanga may also be linked in the eyes of some observers to the passing of SC Resolution 169 of 24 November 1961 described by Parsons as 'tough'.[67] But how tough was it in terms of intent? The answer as indicated by subsequent developments is 'not very'. The fighting which broke out in December 1961 in Elizabethville was triggered not by any military initiative on the part of ONUC, instead it was an attempt by the Katangese to cripple ONUC by attacking its supply lines which led to conflict.[68] Again, it was harassment of ONUC forces which led to the eventual showdown between the UN and Katangese forces in December 1962 and January 1963. What therefore was the difference between military action taken in 1962–3 and that which had gone before?

According to personnel who participated in the 1962–3 operation, the taking of 'vigorous action' amounted to no more than the authorisation of the use of a battery (four) of 120 mm mortars.[69] As the ONUC troops moved against the road-blocks and positions constructed by the Katangese to impede ONUC movements, considerable use was made of these heavy weapons. In proper peacekeeping spirit and practice, the shells were directed not at, but close to, the successive Katangese positions. The occupants of these, realising that direct strikes were possible, quickly vacated them and opposition crumbled. The action was well conducted but far from large scale. The Katangese had overplayed their hand and lacking international support, were no longer capable of sustained action.

What therefore can be learned from comparison between the wording of the resolutions and the action taken? The tasks prescribed in phase two of the mandate, particularly the prevention of civil war suggested that those in the Security Council who authorised the operation were either woefully ignorant of the true situation or were engaged in a dangerous game of bluff. There had been no collective support from the Security Council, no proper planning, no assignment of specific tasks and the operation had been totally under-resourced. Whether ONUC had prevented civil war would remain open to dispute and the Force's position had been at all times precarious. The experience called into question the UN's ability to engage in a collective operation involving activities other than the simple interpositioning of troops.

Let us look therefore at the role played by the members of the Security Council during the period in question.

Political manoeuvres of the Great Powers

The behaviour of the Great Powers continued to reflect the total disarray which had, bedevilled the Security Council. China continued to make no contribution whatever. When in November 1961 the Council considered the taking of more 'vigorous action', the Soviet Union vetoed a US amendment which would have deprecated all action against the UN and the Congolese government. However, with an eye to the Afro-Asians, it gave its support to SC Resolution 169 (1961) of 24 November 1961. France's attitude to the UN continued to be one of contemptuous silence. President de Gaulle had from the outset been contemptuous of the UN and all its works.[70]

Despite its support for the resolution's contents, Britain warned that it might withdraw its support from the Secretary-General if his actions pushed Katanga to defiance. But Britain's position was at all times problematic. It was anxious not to offend Commonwealth states but its Foreign Minister warned: 'if in our desire to please some of the Afro-Asians we get every element of stability pushed out of East and Central Africa, we shall have done a great disservice to the African continent'.[71]

Having faced down the Soviets over the Cuban Missile Crisis, the US was in a stronger position to assert itself. It wanted to establish good relations with Asian and African states but most particularly wanted a strong Congolese central government. With the situation remaining unresolved, fears that their plans for the Congo would come unstuck forced the Americans to take an even more positive role. In late 1962, the US, while opposed to an unprovoked attack on Katanga, agreed to supply aircraft in support of the UN operation.[72] America's contribution to the overall operation, both financially and logistically, was enormous.[73] However, its covert activities in relation to Lumumba revealed a fine line between its support for and use of the UN. Its deliberate efforts to conceal these activities and systematic distortion of the public record also clashed with the concept of democracy which it so loudly advocated.[74]

Throughout the operation, all the Great Powers had to some degree been less than supportive. But while China and France had generally stood aloof, Britain, the US, and the Soviet Union had sought to influence developments in a way which served primarily to favour their own interests rather than those of the Congolese. Having looked at the attitude of the Great Powers to the operation, let us now look at the force which the Security Council established to carry out the tasks detailed in the resolutions and how it was commanded and controlled.

Operational base

The Secretary-General

Dag Hammarskjöld's role in the ONUC operation was of enormous significance not merely because of his direct personal involvement, but because of his efforts to further establish the 'ground rules' for peacekeeping. His ideas on the composition of a force, equipment, use of force, and the UN's non-involvement in the host state's internal affairs helped confirm the image of UN peacekeeping created with UNEF 1 (1956–67). However, these rules and restrictions which he sought to impose merely told the peacekeepers what they could not do. The most serious problems for the ONUC Force arose from the Secretary-General's inability to communicate to his subordinates precise instructions on what it was they should do. Hammarskjöld frequently complained that the Security Council had failed to give him any guidance over the Congo and that, therefore, he was compelled to make decisions in the light of his judgement.[75] However, when re-appointed in 1957, he told the members of the Security Council that he believed the Secretary General should be expected 'to act without guidance should this appear to be necessary'.[76] The UN had a Secretary-General who attracted wide respect but who had also conceived ambitious hopes about the role he might be able to secure for the organisation.

To have expected guidance on the exercise of preventive diplomacy in the Congo was unrealistic. 'Keeping the Cold War out of Africa' was, as Kissinger observed, an abstraction and one which could not possibly succeed without at least agreement on some ground rules between the US and the Soviet Union.[77] In the prevailing political climate, it was inevitable that the relevant UN SC resolutions would reflect compromise and an absence of clarity: such consequential ambiguities were, O'Brien argues, not altogether undesirable since they provided the Secretary General with a wide range of interpretations. It was through ambiguities resolved and margins skilfully explored that the office of the Secretary-General had grown in authority.[78] However, Hammarskjöld's failure to foresee the consequences of ambiguity in ONUC's mandates ensured ongoing confusion as to objectives and the means of achieving them.

Many of his problems arose from his excessive reliance upon his advisers who were almost exclusively civilians with a poor appreciation of the 'military' perspective. By insisting that overall military command was vested in the Secretary-General and through him, his special representative, he created a command structure which was civilian dominated, resulting in sustained civilian–military friction evident from the very first days of the operation. The consequences of establishing the primacy of his political agents were twofold: first, it resulted in a Force that was widely scattered with inevitable problems of communication and command, and, second, a military leadership which was rarely consulted. But there were other critical players who were neither consulted nor informed by the Secretary General.

O'Brien speaks of a sense of shock on discovering that neither the Security Council nor the General Assembly had the full material necessary for adequately informed decisions on the UN operation.[79] However, he also argued that the Secretariat was justified in playing its cards close to its chest in order that it (the Secretariat) 'should win'. Such 'cabinet' as existed was not the Security Council but the so-called 'Congo Club', a group within the Secretariat whose daily meetings were presided over by the Secretary General. The 'Club' which consisted of an inner core of Americans and an outer layer of neutrals mainly Afro-Asians, tacitly accepted the 'Afro-Asian thesis' that the secession of Katanga would have to be ended and that the UN would have to help in ending it.[80] They were, however, out of touch with the realities of the situation.

Ralph Bunche, in his earlier role as SRSG and acting Force Commander, had flung the troops in small units without any apparent appreciation of the requirements for effective command. He also displayed his lack of understanding of military problems by issuing a three-page legally worded instruction on the 'dos' and 'don'ts' of opening fire to a Force most of whose members were illiterate and who moreover would have little time for consultation of such a document in a crisis.[81] Bunche obviously never foresaw ONUC being employed as a military force. Hammarskjöld's military adviser, General Indar Rikhye, was also a poor choice, being, not only resented by many ONUC officers but also poorly informed.[82] O'Brien had no experience of the Congo before taking up his appointment in Katanga and had no knowledge whatever of military affairs.[83] This lack of knowledge made him amenable to persuasion by the bellicose Indian commander (Brig. J.A.S. Raja) that military action in Katanga presented no serious problems.

Responsibility for many of the problems which arose in Katanga could be laid at Hammarskjöld's door. Arguably, he had little option but to accept the Indians, but their deployment in Katanga where their arrival immediately provoked opposition, suggests that despite his apparent opposition to violence, he was content to accept the 'Afro-Asian agenda' and the risks this involved. He could moreover, be seriously faulted for his failure to react to the February 1961 resolution. His failure is seen as relating to a lack of clarification of the 'civil war proviso', and the associated issue of 'use of force'. The Secretary General had been willing to accept the 'use of force' proviso without making any provision for its possible military action. When he discussed with Force Commander Gen. Carl von Horn (Sweden) the possibility of war between ONUC and Katanga, von Horn had made him aware of what this might involve. He provided a list that included five to six brigades, reconnaissance aircraft and sufficient transport aircraft to maintain an adequate airlift. Hammarskjöld's response was to ask: 'Do you think I want to start an armaments race'?[84] A year later, when Von Horn's successor General Sean McKeown (Ireland) raised the relatively uncontroversial issue of providing ONUC troops with armoured personnel carriers (APCs), his proposal was dismissed with the identical reply.[85]

After operation 'Morthor', Hammarskjöld insisted that the UN troops had used force only in self-defence and technically this is true. However, to O'Brien, 'Morthor' was the 'use of force' as referred to in the February resolution, namely, action to end Katanga's secession.[86] The Morthor debacle can therefore be seen as the direct consequence of the Secretary-General's failure to provide clarification of the mandate or to make provision for contingencies. The decision of the Security Council members to 'leave it to Dag' placed an enormous burden on his shoulders, but his decision to run a virtual one-man show resulted in a situation where even his most trusted acolytes were never sure of what he had in mind.

Hammarskjöld's successor, U Thant, had little to agonise over. He did concede that 'for a peace force, even a little fighting is too much and only a few casualties is too many';[87] but the UN force he would employ in subsequent operations would at least be better prepared for action, having both aircraft and heavy mortars and knowledge of the Katanga gendarmerie's capabilities.

The Force Commander

The Commanding Officer (CO) of the first Irish contingent on arriving in his operation area discovered to his alarm that elements of his battalion had been dropped 350 miles away and two months were to pass before he would have an opportunity of meeting them.[88] This random dispersal of the UN forces across the face of the Congo by civilian officials was a consequence of demands to 'do something' and do it quickly. Putting UN flags across maps of the Congo, would help reassure delegates in New York that the organisation was acting with all haste. However, 'painting the Congo blue' with flags alone was just another manifestation of the gap in perceptions of UN operations between those directing and those required to execute them, between the civilian and military personnel concerned with putting UN resolutions into effect.

In theory, the Force Commander (FC) had the task of exercising command of the military operations in accordance with the political guidance relayed from the Secretary General. Therefore, before arriving at a decision on any proposed course of action, the Secretary-General should have consulted his expert on the ground, the military commander; Hammarskjöld chose not to do so. The FC was thus largely isolated. General von Horn, the first Force Commander, was presented with an ill-defined mandate and inadequate resources in men and military materiel; he was responsible for a military force that was organised on an improvised basis and made up of contingents which had little in common. When, several weeks into the operation, the CO of the Irish contingent asked von Horn for details of the 'mission', the FC replied that he was unable to provide any satisfactory information since he himself had been kept in the dark.[89] His Operational Directive served to highlight the ambiguity of ONUC's position and his own dilemma. It stated: 'The UN Force in the Congo serves as a security force at the request of the Government of the Congo', but then went on: 'The UN Force shall NOT, repeat, NOT be a party to or in any way intervene in or influence the outcome of any internal conflict, constitutional or otherwise.'[90]

The work of the FC was from the outset made considerably more difficult by the realisation that some contingents whose governments empathised with Lumumba, for example, the Guineans, Ghanaians and Egyptians, might become involved in the Congo's internal affairs. Another problem was the fearsome reputation of other contingents. The reputation of the Moroccans for heavy-handedness was such that the cry 'Moroc no good' was a common utterance whenever that contingent served.[91] The Ethiopians also established such a reputation that the mere threat of their arrival was calculated to bring order to areas where disturbance seemed likely to escalate.[92] A consequence of these problems was a significant reduction in the pool of reliable 'peace' keepers, troops willing to negotiate and resolve a crisis by diplomacy rather than force.

A particular problem for the FC, especially in relation to the task of foreign military advisers, was the lack of an Intelligence Service. As O'Brien notes, 'The UN, having no intelligence, could not know with certainty who all the advisers to the Katangese were'.[93] Gen. Bjorn Egge (Norway, former Military Information Officer, ONUC HQ) goes further stating that 'Rumpunch' and 'Morthor' served as 'reminders and a strong incitement to acknowledge the need for Intelligence information to support the activities of ONUC'.[94] What was euphemistically described as a Military Information Branch at ONUC Headquarters did manage to gather limited intelligence from various sources; for example, Col. Jonas Waern, (Swedish Commander in Southern Katanga), by use of photographs, newspapers and general observations built up a file on the strength and dispositions of the gendarmerie.[95] However, by the time conflict broke out in Katanga, the FC had in effect become a minor player in the whole operation.

He continued to exercise command over the entire operation area, but his authority became undermined with the arrival of O'Brien in Katanga in January 1961. O'Brien had a direct link to New York and while Force Headquarters in Leopoldville was consulted on pending developments, communication was, according to the then FC Gen. McKeown, minimal. McKeown was informed of the impending operation 'Morthor' less than twenty-four hours before the event.[96] This sidelining of the FC (and O'Brien's ignorance of military matters) had major consequences for the operation. Asked as to why prior to 'Morthor' the Irish company had been sent to Jadotville against the recommendations of Col. Waern who regarded the post as dangerously isolated, O'Brien would say only that it was a decision 'taken at the top'.[97] This extraordinary decision which effectively presented the Katanga regime with 150 hostages, revealed just how little military considerations influenced the deliberations of the Secretariat. In a situation where the FC was effectively denied any authority or influence, responsibility for actions of contingents inevitably devolved upon commanders and their officers. How contingents perceived their role and the factors which influenced their performances are therefore the basis for the next part of the case study.

Tactical capabilities

Scattered across an area equivalent to Western Europe, ONUC was in many respects not one but many peacekeeping forces. These forces were contingents whose performance and behaviour was determined by their background, training and perception of ONUC's role; their response to different crises was also greatly influenced by such factors as communications, logistics and equipment. We shall look first at some of the contingents.

Contingents

The attitude of contingents both to their work and to the Congolese was largely influenced by cultural, religious or historical factors. The Irish empathised with the Belgians because they were Catholic: the Swedes had Congolese links through the presence of Swedish missionaries. Both those European contingents identified closely with Katanga: their values and general attitude to the troublesome Baluba (who in November 1960 murdered nine Irish soldiers) are evident in a report of December 1960 emanating from the Swedish and Irish-staffed local headquarters. It noted: 'the rule of law must be imposed on these people for their own good. They respect only power and force'.[98]

The Indian contingent also believed in power and force, but in a different context. Indian officers on their arrival in Katanga made it quite clear that what they fore-saw as their effective use was a role totally at odds with what subsequently became known as 'traditional peacekeeping'. Col. Eugene O'Neill (Commanding Officer 34 Irish Btn) recalls being greeted by officers of the Indian Brigade with the questions: 'where is the enemy'? 'Where is the action'?[99] Colonel Maitra, CO of the newly arrived Gurkha Battalion, frequently declared that 'his chaps' were 'straining at the leash' and that the Indian force was in the Congo to 'finally settle the Katanga question'.[100] The Congolese in turn were united in their dislike of the Indians. The paramount Chief of the Baluba in South Katanga denounced them as 'uncivilised'. (When asked why, he replied: 'They don't believe in God, they eat with their fingers and they don't speak French'.)[101]

Having just arrived from the border confrontation with China, the Indian con-tingent, Gen. Egge observes, perceived its task in Katanga as an ordinary military fighting job. 'They had apparently not been properly briefed on the basic idea and special procedures of UN peacekeeping.'[102] But few of the other contingents had been briefed on the ideas and special procedures of UN peacekeeping. What briefing personnel received almost exclusively passed on when contingents were being replaced. Moreover, the 'special procedures' were still only being developed. What distinguished the Indians from other contingents was the fact that they arrived into the mission satisfied that their task was to fight a war against Katanga.

Equipment

ONUC's equipment reflected the total lack of organisation and planning which characterised the operation. In particular, the armament and transport with which it was forced to operate, made nonsense of any claims that it had engaged in enforcement action. Troops arriving in July 1960 were largely equipped as per instruction with rifles, low calibre machine guns and light (60 mm and 81 mm) mortars.[103] They were equipped to defend themselves, not make war. Even the Indians drafted in after the February 1961 resolution were lightly armed. These weapons were appropriate to the task of peacekeeping as undertaken in UNEF I: they were totally inadequate for a 'use of force' mandate, particularly when that task implied engaging the Katanga gendarmerie.

When UN forces confronted the gendarmerie in September 1961, their weapons and equipment were proved to be inadequate and unreliable. The gendarmerie had modern APCs, heavy machine guns, anti-tank weapons, the latest FN rifles, and three jet aircraft. In contrast, the Irish armoured cars, built in Ireland during World War II, were 'museum pieces' penetrable even by the gendarmerie rifles. The Irish and Indians were forced to rely on bolt-action rifles including World War I Lee Enfields. ONUC's obsolete/obsolescent equipment created other problems. In December 1961, mortar shells fired by the Irish at a military barracks in Elizabethville fell short, hitting a hospital, killing three patients and wounding many others. The official Irish inquiry revealed that the range tables available were long out of date.[104] The incident provided Katanga with a propaganda coup and was highly embarrassing for those troops who had come to bring peace, not wage war.

Almost from the outset, ONUC operations were seriously handicapped by a lack of mobility. Six months into the operation, the vehicles which contingents had brought with them were reduced to 40 per cent efficiency through excessive wear and tear, and the Moroccan contingent was forced to rely on 'cannibalised' trucks abandoned by the Belgians. These transportation problems assumed major importance during 'Morthor'. Troops sent in a vain attempt to relieve the beleaguered Jadotville company travelled not in military vehicles – none were available – but in commandeered civilian omnibuses. Summarising the Swedish experience in the Congo, Nils Sköld observes that casualties could have been considerably smaller if the Swedish battalion had been provided with heavier support weapons and more armoured cars.[105] His comment is particularly significant since the Swedes were recognised within the Force as being by far the best equipped of ONUC's contingents.

Failure to make provision for possible military action revealed serious failures on two levels. First, the Secretary-General had either ignored or failed to understand the consequences of the February 1961 resolution. Second, the Security Council's members had blithely authorised use of force, but had not concerned themselves about whether this threat could be implemented. That a single tiny jet could effectively paralyse UN military activity in September 1961 pointed to Hammarskjöld's naïveté and the Security Council's lack of concern for the mission it had authorised.[106] This failure in responsibility could be traced in part to the failure in communications at all levels which bedevilled the operation.

Communications

Reporting on the final 'push' against Katanga, in January 1963, Bunche refers to 'a rather disconcerting picture with regard to communications'.[107] In the incident a field commander, his troops under fire, needed clarification of instructions from New York. Conscious that because of time difference a decision would be slow in arriving, he chose to deal with the situation himself. Although his decision to advance on Jadotville effectively ended Katanga's military resistance, his perceived unauthorised advance became the subject of a UN HQ investigation. The incident illustrated the extent to which military activity was still tightly controlled by the civilian element but also the difficulties created for commanders through lack of effective communications.

The political decision to scatter small bodies of troops across the Congo placed particular emphasis on the need for effective communications between the higher and lower echelons of command. Battalion commanders discovered that not only were elements of their contingents located 100 to 150 miles from local headquarters, but that the signal equipment upon which they were forced so heavily to rely was, because of atmospheric conditions or age, highly unreliable. In some cases, equipment was just not available. A section of Irish soldiers massacred near Niemba in November 1960 had, it was later discovered, no signal equipment with which to communicate with its platoon HQ.[108]

There were also communication problems at the personal level. These involved not just the clear failure of the Secretary-General to communicate his intentions to his civilian and military subordinates, but the difficulties created by the language barrier. A major problem during the conduct of 'Morthor' arose from the failure of the Indians and Swedes, who theoretically had a good knowledge of English to fully comprehend the precise details of the operation. As a result, certain critical objectives, such as the arrest of Tshombe were not achieved.[109]

The student of UN peacekeeping might be tempted to regard the misunderstanding which arose as just another 'unfortunate incident' in the history of UN operations. However, 'Morthor' was no sudden response to a crisis but effectively a military operation planned by UN civilian and military personnel. Thus many died, arguably unnecessarily, as a result of communication failure. Many were also to die, albeit indirectly, because of logistics problems.

Logistics

Putting UN flags across the map of Africa was easy: supplying the personnel based in the locations indicated by those flags was not. From the beginning to the end of the mission, the primary concern of the UN force would be protection of its supply lines. Given the nature of the Congo's infrastructure, getting essential supplies to such a scattered force would, in normal conditions, have represented a formidable challenge: in a situation where services had broken down, providing the UN troops with rations and fuel was a task both difficult and dangerous. Supply routes were often highly vulnerable to attack and in times of tension, sub-units could effectively be cut off. In such situations, rations and fuel, were, where possible, flown in by helicopter: but even this means of re-supply involved problems. Aviation fuel for the helicopter was usually transported in bulk by train: this involved a heavy commitment of troops to train-guards.[110] While the re-supply of platoon-size outposts constituted the major problem for most contingent commanders, it was the plight and subsequent surrender of the Jadotville Company which exposed the vulnerability of ONUC's supply system.

Jadotville, located approximately 80 miles north-west of Elizabethville, was served by one of the finest roads in Africa. However, at a point 15 miles from the town, the road passed over the Lufira river. Any party holding the bridge could interdict movement in either direction. This point was not lost on the commander of the Swedish troops (Col. Waern). Realising the vulnerability of his personnel located in the heavily white, pro-Tshombe town, Waern, in the weeks preceding 'Morthor', withdrew his company. A company of Irish troops was sent as replacement. In the days preceding 'Morthor', officers from the Irish company visited the UN Headquarters in Elizabethville to warn that their situation was highly precarious. According to one of the officers involved, their pleas for the company to be withdrawn were summarily dismissed.[111]

Following the outbreak of fighting in Elizabethville, the gendarmerie occupied the Lufira bridge effectively cutting off the Irish company's only supply route. Within hours, the company came under attack and the local authorities in Jadotville cut off the company's water supply. A relief column was easily repulsed at the bridge and a helicopter carrying provisions was shot down. Deprived of essential supplies, the UN company was forced to surrender, thereby bringing 'Morthor' to an inglorious end. The message of Jadotville was clear. For the Katangese, the objective now more than ever was to cut ONUC's supply links: for ONUC, those links had to be protected at all costs. It was an attempt by the Katangese to block ONUC access to Elizabethville airport, the local forces' only lifeline, which led to the fighting in December 1961 in which 25 UN personnel died. It was an effort to carry out a similar operation in December 1962 which led to the outbreak of hostilities: this in turn led to the final and decisive effort by ONUC to remove the ongoing threat to its lifeline.

While it could not be disputed that by December 1962 many within the UN and particularly the US, were anxious for a final showdown with Katanga, that effort when it came was not the result of a deliberate decision to conduct a military offensive aimed at preventing imminent civil war. It was a simple but determined effort to ensure that the UN forces in Katanga would not suffer the humiliation of another 'Jadotville' that brought an end to Katanga's secession.

Analysis

Mandate performance

Given the constraints under which ONUC operated, its mandate(s) made little sense and their fulfilment effectively impossible. Restoring law and order and preventing civil war were tasks which required direct involvement in the Congo's affairs, but the UN Charter's provisions, the Secretary-General's instructions and the attitude of the host state appeared to preclude any considered and organised effort to engage in such action. In effect, the Force was employed to carry out tasks which were theoretically proscribed and attempts to implement the mandate were at all times tentative. Its controversial role in Lumumba's overthrow aside, the Force had no direct involvement in matters of law and order within the state. Its mere presence undoubtedly had a stabilising effect in the early weeks but it could never, as many hoped it could, create the basis for lasting peace. Whether, through its action in Katanga, it prevented civil war is uncertain. Given the resources available to the perceived possible protagonists, it is highly unlikely that the central government would ever have confronted Katanga in large-scale warfare. Had such a confrontation taken place, ONUC would have been incapable of preventing it. As subsequent events showed, ONUC did not prevent war between the Congolese, it merely delayed such hostilities.

Facilitating conflict resolution

The outbreak of civil war in the wake of ONUC's departure confirmed the message that whereas peacekeepers can facilitate conflict resolution, it is the responsibility of the combatants to settle their differences. ONUC's arrival prevented the spiral into anarchy and provided a breathing space during which the many disparate elements, political and tribal, had an opportunity to consider their role in the new democratic state, assuming they were so disposed. Whereas the sources of political conflict were myriad, the most serious was that created by Katantga's attempted secession. ONUC's presence in the province helped restrain the province's move towards total independence and kept alive the possibility of reconciliation between Leopoldville and Elizabethville, and in this respect its contribution was not insignificant.

Unfortunately, the problem in the Congo was not just a dispute between central authority and one province, but the disruptive potential of ethnic dispute at many points throughout the vast country. Facilitating conflict resolution between the scores of real or potential combatants in the Congo was a task beyond the capabilities of any peacekeeping force, particularly given the absence of any effective efforts at mediation.

Conflict containment

If one accepts the proposition that in 1960 the superpowers or neighbouring states were prepared to become directly involved, then ONUC's efforts could be seen as having prevented a catastrophe. However, the Soviet Union's timid acceptance of the expulsion of its personnel following Mobutu's coup would indicate that it was content to operate through proxies. That the US alone became directly involved in 1964 also shows that any enthusiasm for involvement by the Soviet Union or African states had quickly evaporated. Nevertheless, the support given to Katanga in 1961 by elements in Rhodesia and incursions from Angola and Rwanda in the succeeding decades, indicates the potential for 'over-spill' which existed in 1960. The tribal loyalties which had shattered the fragile unity of the Congo had the potential to lead to cross-border disputes, leading eventually to a succession of inter- and intrastate conflicts. ONUC provided a means by which member states could display their desire for a restoration of order and respect for the boundaries, however artificial, that were to become sacrosanct in the new Africa that was emerging.

Assessment

The UN's performance in the Congo, characterised by a marked lack of unity and purpose, represented a major setback to hopes that the UN could provide a safer, better-organised world. In several respects, the handling of the crisis reflected the climate of the times. Cold War rivalry diluted Security Council consensus making effective action problematic. But efforts to assist the Congolese had also been heavily influenced by the presence in the General Assembly of an increasing number of states whose internal qualities differed in a significant way from those that had set the old patterns of international relations. What these new states failed to appreciate was that the end of colonialism did not mean the end of nationalism in the sense of manifestation by peoples of their perceived ethnic identities. The achievement of independence had, rather than bringing peace led to a re-awakening of communal antagonisms. In a world of independent states, nationalism had become as much a disruptive force as it had been in a world of colonial empires.

The idea that artificial units created by colonisers could automatically become stable viable states was totally unrealistic. This was particularly so in the case of a country as vast, diverse and ill-prepared for self-government as the Congo. In a situation requiring political as well as military assistance, the Security Council had addressed only the security issue and this in a half-hearted and inept manner. The absence of even the semblance of effective government required the introduction of some form of caretaker administration to enable the fledgeling state to find its feet, but the Council had excluded this course of action. (Interestingly, as part of its efforts to 'nation-build' in the 1990s, the UN would take this course in its operation in East Timor – United Nations Transitional Administration for East Timor). The Security Council was obviously influenced by the reaction such a step would produce among newly emergent states but its inaction represented a total abdication of responsibility.

Failure to follow through on the action prescribed in successive SC Resolutions damaged the UN's credibility. But equally the approved use of force within a member state, appeared to undermine the provisions of the UN Charter and run counter to the liberal concept upon which the UN was theoretically based. The threatened use of force was particularly unfortunate since it (1) created confusion as to the exact circumstances in which it might be employed, (2) helped foster the myth that lightly armed peacekeepers could be instantly transformed into an army; that peacekeeping and enforcement could be combined. Arguably, it was a total overestimation of ONUC's 'military' achievements in Katanga which led to the UN's subsequent blunders in Somalia and former Yugoslavia.

The crisis in the Congo represented an opportunity for the member states of the UN to unite in helping one of their members. But rather than demonstrating what could be achieved through international cooperation, the Congo operation exposed the extent of divisions within the UN. It also demonstrated the UN's critical weaknesses in the area of decision-making and leadership. Faced with a situation for which the UN Charter did not provide, the Security Council had adopted vague resolutions and passed the problem to the Secretary-General. He, in turn, let the Congolese dictate the pace of events. In the absence of any clear plan, individual member states and UN officials (O'Brien and Khiari) had sought to impose their own solutions. Translating perceived needs into policies required leadership and this had been noticeably lacking. It was clear from the experience of the League of Nations that the United Nations could not function effectively without the backing of the major powers, but the two powers who really mattered at this time, the US and the Soviet Union, could not agree on a definite course of action. What little purpose the operation possessed had only come when the Soviet Union had lost interest and the US, for its own ends, sought to help bring matters to a conclusion.

Solving the Congo's problems presented an enormous challenge, but the UN's response had been little more than a succession of disorganised ad hoc measures. The major lessons of the operation – the need to (1) determine clear objectives, (2) provide clear mandates, (3) ensure that the personnel are provided with resources commensurate with their task, and (4) establish from the outset whether the troops were to be employed as symbols or soldiers, were clear to see. The question was whether those responsible for authorising and conducting operations, the UN Security Council and the Secretariat, were prepared to learn them.

Notes

1 Patrice Lumumba, *Congo my Country*, London, Pall Mall Press, 1962, p. 31
2 Henry Kissinger, *Diplomacy*, New York, Simon and Schuster, 1994, p. 808
3 There were no Congolese lawyers, doctors or engineers. Anthony Parsons, *From Cold War to Hot Peace*, London, Penguin Group, 1995, p. 79
4 Martin Meredith, *The First Dance of Freedom*, London, Abacus, 1985, p. 120
5 Eric Hobsbawn, *Age of Extremes: The Short Twentieth Century 1914–1991*, London, Abacus, 1995, p. 136
6 Crawford Young, 'Decolonisation in Africa', in L.H. Gann and Peter Duignan (eds), *Colonialism in Africa 1870–1960*, London, Cambridge University Press, 1982, p. 461
7 Peter Calvoceressi, *World Politics Since 1945*, 6th edition, London, Longman, 1991, p. 521
8 Martin Meredith, *The First Dance*, p. 121
9 Ibid. p. 124
10 Ibid., p. 126
11 William Durch, 'The UN Operation in the Congo: 1960–1964' in William Durch (ed.), *The Evolution of UN Peacekeeping*, London, Macmillan Press, 1993, p. 319
12 Robert C.R. Siekmann, *Basic Documents on UN and Related Peacekeeping Forces*, Dordrecht, Martinus Nijhoff, 1984, p. 75
13 Durch, 'The UN Operation in the Congo', p. 336
14 Anthony Parsons, *From Cold War*, p. 82
15 Meredith, *From Cold War*, p. 125
16 Alan James, *The Politics of Peacekeeping*, London, Chatto and Windus, 1969, p. 358
17 Meredith, *The First Dance*, p. 131
18 Marrack Goulding, Peacemonger, London, John Murray, 2002, p. 178
19 Meredith, *The First Dance*, pp. 135–6
20 Rajeshwar Dayal, *Mission for Hammarskjöld*, London, Oxford University Press, 1976, p. 237
21 Conor Cruise O'Brien, *To Katanga and Back*, London, Hutchinson and Co., 1962, pp. 242–3
22 Donald Harman Akenson, *Conor, A Biography of Conor Cruise O'Brien*, Vol. II, Montreal, McGill, Queens University Press, 1994, p. 58
23 O'Brien, *To Katanga*, pp. 257–62
24 Sweden and Ethiopia each provided four jet fighters; India provided six Canberra light bombers. Durch, 'The UN Operation in the Congo' (n. 11 above), p. 336
25 Martin Meredith, *The First Dance*, p. 139
26 Ibid., p. 140
27 Conor Cruise O'Brien, *The Times* (London), 19 November 1996, p. 16
28 Hobsbawn, *Age of Extreme*, p. 226
29 Ibid., pp. 435–6
30 Richie Calder, *Agony of the Congo*, London, Gollancz, 1961, p. 129
31 James, *Britain and the Congo Crisis 1960–63*, New York, St Martin's Press, 1996, p. 47
32 Andrew Boyd, *United Nations Piety, Myth and Truth*, Middlesex, p. 129
33 Durch, *The Evolution*, p. 323
34 James, *Britain and the Congo*, p. 35
35 Kissinger, *Diplomacy*, pp. 563–4
36 Calvocoressi, *World Politics*, pp. 145–6
37 Boyd, *United Nations*, p. 43
38 Rosalyn Higgins, *United Nations Peacekeeping 1946–1976, Documents and Commentary, Vol. III, Africa*, Oxford, Oxford University Press, 1980, p. 41

39 Michael Akehurst, *A Modern Introduction to International Law*, 3rd edition, London, Allen and Unwin, 1970, pp. 209–10
40 Siekmann, *Basic Documents*, p. 76
41 Carl von Horn, *Soldiering for Peace*, London, Cassell and Co., 1966, pp. 140–6. This decision is particularly interesting in the light of the UN's subsequent operation in Somalia (see Chapter 5)
42 Dayal, *Mission*, p. 37
43 Ibid.
44 James, *Britain and the Congo*, pp. 66–7
45 David Gibbs, 'Secrecy and International Relations', *Journal of Peace Research*, Vol. 32, No. 2, 1995, p. 220
46 Stephen Weissman, *American Foreign Policy Towards the Congo 1960–1964*, Ithaca, NY, Cornell University Press, 1974, p. 90
47 Gibbs, (n. 45 above), pp. 220–1. See also Madeleine Kalb, *The Congo Cables: The Cold War in Africa from Eisenhower to Kennedy*, New York, Macmillan, 1982, p. 96
48 James, *Britain and the Congo*, p. 53
49 Ibid., p. 60
50 James, *The Politics*, p. 414
51 James, *Britain and the Congo*, pp. 88–9
52 Siekmann, *Basic Documents*, p. 81. Note: When accused of using 'mercenaries', Tshombe on one occasion pointed towards some sunbathing Swedish troops who were being paid 120 dollars a month allowance and declared: 'There are your true mercenaries.' Recollection of Terry O'Neill
53 Ibid.
54 Higgins, *United Nations Peacekeeping*, p. 41
55 Akehurst, *International Law*, p. 57
56 History of 33 Irish Battalion, Irish Military Archives, Dublin, p. 6
57 Ernest Lefever, *Crisis in the Congo: A UN Force in Action*, Washington, Brookings Institute, (1956), p. 56
58 Gen. Noel Bergin, Irish Contingent, Military Information Officer, 34 Bn, January–July 1961, interviewed by Terry O'Neill, 25 May 1995, Kildare
59 ONUC troops in Katanga were alarmed that they might be required to engage in action for which they were not equipped. Recollection of Terry O'Neill
60 Dr O'Brien, at a symposium on Peacekeeping, held at Irish UN Training School in June 1995, attended by Terry O'Neill
61 UN, *The Blue Helmets*, 2nd edition, UN Publications, pp. 230–3
62 Conor Cruise O'Brien, *To Katanga*, p. 270
63 Alan James, 'The Congo Controversies', in *International Peacekeeping*, Vol. 1, No. 1, 1999, p. 53
64 Siekmann, *Basic Documents*, pp. 109–10
65 James, *Britain and the Congo*, p. 82
66 Marrack Goulding, 'The Evolution of UN Peacekeeping', *International Affairs*, Vol. 3, No. 69, 1993, p. 453
67 Parsons, *From Cold War*, p. 89
68 Col. Patrick Rohan (Irish Contingent) maintains that no plans existed for ONUC to go on the offensive. Col. Rohan interviewed by Terry O'Neill, 10 September 1996, Athlone
69 Col. Patrick Rohan and Lt Col. Patrick Molloy (Irish Contingent) interviewed by Terry O'Neill, Athlone, 20 January, 1995
70 James, *Britain and the Congo*, p. 34. Note: France refused to allow Irish troops travelling to the Congo access to its airspace
71 Ibid., p. 163
72 Ibid., p. 186

73 The US contributed 48 per cent of the cost of the military operation. Durch, (n. 11 above), p. 33
74 Gibbs, 'Secrecy', p. 224
75 Dayal, *Mission*, p. 83
76 James, *Britain and the Congo*, p. 20
77 Henry Kissinger, *The Necessity for Choice*, New York, Harper and Brothers, 1961, p. 337
78 O'Brien, *To Katanga*, p. 47
79 Ibid., p. 50
80 Ibid., p. 58
81 Von Horn, *Soldiering*, p. 159
82 In his book, *The Theory and Practice of Peacekeeping*, London, C. Hurst & Company, 1984, p. 88, he states: 'In Bakwanga, the diamond state, Munongo declared himself king.' Bakwanga was the capital of Kasai province largely controlled by 'King' Kalonji. Munongo (Godefroid) was Interior Minister in the Katanga regime and was widely accepted as the real power behind Tshombe
83 O'Brien, *To Katanga*, p. 258
84 Von Horn, *Soldiering*, p. 176
85 General McKeown interviewed by Terry O'Neill, 30 March 1995, Athlone
86 O'Brien, *To Katanga*, p. 276
87 Lefever, *Crisis*, p. 60
88 Col. Mortimer Buckley, CO, 32 Irish Btn, interviewed by Terry O'Neill, 12 March 1995, Athlone
89 Ibid.
90 *Directive FC*, September 1960, Irish Military Archives, 2
91 Moroccan troops mounted machine guns on flat-cars when acting as train guards. At the slightest sign of hostility, they opened fire indiscriminately. Belgian personnel in interview with Terry O'Neill, March 1961, Katanga
92 Gen. Gerald O'Sullivan (Irish) Senior Staff Officer ONUC HQ 1960–1, interviewed by Terry O'Neill, 10 May 1995, Dublin
93 O'Brien, *To Katanga*, p. 127
94 Lt General Bjorn Egge, interview, 21 August 1997, Oslo, and subsequent correspondence with Terry O'Neill
95 Jonas Waern, *Experiences of a Brigade Commander in Katanga*: K. Krigsvet, Akad, Tidskript, 1962, pp. 497–8
96 General McKeown, interviewed by Terry O'Neill, 30 March 1995, Athlone
97 Dr O'Brien at UN Peacekeeping Seminar in Irish UN Training School, June 1995
98 *Report on the Situation in Katanga*, 15 December 1960, UN Records, Irish Military Archives, 12
99 Col. Eugene O'Neill, interviewed by Terry O'Neill, 14 May 1995, Dublin
100 In May 1961, Terry O' Neill worked in close proximity with the Indian Brigade
101 Col. Eugene O'Neill, interviewed by Terry O'Neill, 14 May 1995, Dublin
102 General Egge in correspondence with the Terry O'Neill
103 The Guinean contingent which arrived with heavy mortars, anti-tank and anti-aircraft guns was quickly dispatched to the crocodile infested swamps of Equateur province. Von Horn, *Soldiering*, p. 155
104 Col. Joseph Leech, Irish Contingent, interviewed by Terry O'Neill, 2 February 1996, Athlone
105 Nils Skjold, *Med FN I Kongo*, Stockholm, Probus, 1994, p. 241
106 A Fouga Magister training plane adapted by the Katangese to carry bombs was used against ONUC troops in Elizabethville, Kamina Base and Jadotville. Col. J. Leech, interviewed by Terry O'Neill, 2 February 1996, Athlone

107 Bunche quoted in Higgins, *United Nations Peacekeeping*, p. 138
108 Personnel of 33rd Irish Battalion interviewed by Terry O'Neill, January 1961, Katanga
109 O'Brien, *To Katanga*, p. 255
110 Personnel of 34th Irish Battalion interviewed by Terry O'Neill, March 1961, Katanga
111 Captain Liam Donnelly (Irish Contingent), interviewed by Terry O'Neill, 16 November 1994, Mullingar

4

UNFICYP AND CYPRUS, 1964–

Introduction

UNFICYP is an example of how the UN by attempting to interpose between the parties in conflict – one of the most common of peacekeeping activities – may itself become part of the overall problem. The operation can be seen as having played a not insignificant role in containing ethnic conflict on the island of Cyprus and preventing possible confrontation between Greece and Turkey: yet it can also be viewed as having merely kept the warring sides apart while failing to resolve the root causes of the conflict. The ongoing presence of the UN force raises the questions: is peace the absence of armed conflict or a state where the parties are agreed on a territorial or political solution; and what is the UN to do in the face of continuing intransigence on the part of both elements to the dispute?

Nature of the conflict

The conflict in Cyprus is the result of a process of political disintegration, whereby a society which for decades shared a culture and history, evolved into separate nationalities. The saga of Cyprus (March 1964–) demonstrates once again the disruptive influence of ethnic difference and how this can lead to conflict at both local and international levels. It is particularly noteworthy for its legal dimension – the questions it raises about the legitimacy and ramifications of international treaties – and how it demonstrates the importance of the legal base to disputes. It also raises questions about (1) the adequacy of the division of the world into sovereign states, (2) perceptions of sovereignty, and (3) the extent to which UN operations reflect a common approach to the problem of conflict.

In examining these issues, it is noted that while the mandate of UNFICYP (UN Force in Cyprus) has remained substantially unchanged, the environment in which the peacekeepers have operated has, since 1974, altered dramatically. The case study therefore considers the operation in two distinct phases. Phase one covers the period from March 1964 to the Turkish invasion of Cyprus in June 1974. Phase two looks at the period from that event onward. In examining this multidimensional problem, let us look first at the origins of the conflict which led to the UN's involvement.

Historical background

Many discussions of the Cyprus conflict start with the truism that the conflict is deeply rooted in historical enmities; however, inter-ethnic conflict did not occur until 1957.[1] It was the establishment by the British in the early twentieth century of a dual secular school system which led to the Muslims and Orthodox learning different histories and different ideologies. Thus British rule redefined the communities.[2] By the 1950s, the Greek Cypriots who formed 80 per cent of the population, alienated by a system of British rule in which they had no say, found the dream of Greek nationalism beckoning. Once it became clear that self-determination via an appeal to the UN was not forthcoming, the pro-'enosis' (union with Greece) EOKA movement led by George Grivas (an officer of the Greek Army, Cypriot by birth) launched a campaign of violence.[3] The bloody and bitter 'liberation' struggle had a profound effect on relations between Cypriots.

In the absence of their own national identity, the Muslims might have been absorbed into the Greek 'nationalist' movement.[4] However, British policy of employing Turkish Cypriots exclusively in the police force made the Turks the target of EOKA terrorism and dependent upon the British for protection. In this way the Turkish community acquired a Turkish identity, a development reinforced by Britain's decision to bring Turkey into negotiations for independence. Divisions and tensions were increased through (1) the establishment by the Turkish Cypriots of their own resistance movement (TMT – Turkish Defence Organisation) which sought partition of the island and (2) Turkey's unwillingness to countenance the despised Greeks taking possession of what they saw as 'a Cypriot dagger pointing at Turkey's heart'.[5]

Faced with a threat by Britain to implement partition, Archbishop Makarios, the Greek Cypriot leader, instead of pursuing enosis, indicated a willingness to 'accept' independence. The 1960 settlement imposed by Britain, Turkey and Greece temporarily solved their problems but not those of the Cypriots. Independence for the Greek Cypriots was a sorry compromise on the road to enosis: for the Turkish Cypriots it was a Greek plot with enosis as the objective.[6] Although theoretically sovereign, Cyprus remained in a semi-colonial status, her authority in both domestic and foreign affairs curtailed by constitutional and treaty rights given to three foreign countries. The 1959 London and Zurich Agreements provided for Cypriot independence based on the premise that while Cyprus was one state, it comprised two nations, necessitating constitutional structures to protect one regime against the other.[7] The inherent instability of the newly created state was recognised in the Zurich Agreement which included a Treaty of Guarantee, Treaty of Alliance, and Treaty of Establishment.[8]

Nothing so underlined the myth of Cypriot sovereignty as the Treaty of Guarantee. Under its terms, Britain, Turkey and Greece assured the independence, territorial integrity and security of Cyprus and guaranteed the basic articles of the Constitution. The three states agreed in the event of a breach of the treaties to consult together with a view to arriving at agreement or a concerted course of action. If agreement or concerted action were to prove impossible, each party could take action to restore the state of affairs existing at independence.[9]

There were two obvious flaws in this arrangement: first, unless the unilateral action involved Greece or Turkey taking action against 'their own', such action, in whatever form, was certain to be regarded by the other guarantors as provocative. The second flaw was the term 'action'. Greek commentators took the view that the word was not intended to include armed action; if it were, the guarantors would have spelled it out. They argued that if the Treaty did permit armed action, it would violate Articles 2(4) and 103 of the UN Charter. Britain took an opposing view holding that the Treaty contemplated the use of armed force in certain circumstances and that such force did not violate the Charter.[10] The Turks would subsequently argue that since intercommunal strife could undermine peaceful relations between Turkey and Greece, a side-effect of the accords was the maintenance of peace, a UN Charter objective.[11] Within the UN also there was uncertainty. The Security Council in 1964 abstained from expressing an opinion as to the Treaty of Guarantee's validity. The General Assembly in Resolution 2077, 18 December 1965, implied treaty invalidity; Cyprus, it declared, was entitled to enjoy full sovereignty without any foreign intervention or interference.[12] The Treaty's status in relation to the UN Charter, was and would remain uncertain. Since it was directed towards the maintenance of regional peace and security, it might appear to constitute a 'regional arrangement'.[13] However, its language revealed an intention to protect Cyprus rather than the guarantor powers. This uncertainty could only lead to problems centring on the legitimacy of intervention by the guarantors.

The UN's acceptance of the Treaty also called into question the organisation's declared commitment to self-determination for emergent states. Fundamental to the notion of decolonialisation was the idea that peoples could best govern themselves free from the influence of foreigners. The Cypriots, however, had no part in the preparation of the Treaty, were not free to opt for enosis or partition and, though the Republic of Cyprus, had the theoretical right to wage war, its army was restricted to 2,000 men.[14] The constraints on Cypriot sovereignty were quite remarkable even given the circumstances and would undoubtedly have evoked massive protest were they applied to an African or Asian emergent state. The marked absence of such protest could only be seen as evidence of the perceived distinctions within the UN between European problems and those elsewhere in the world.

From its inception, therefore, the status of Cyprus as a state was confused and confusing. It needed a political identity if it were to achieve real independence, but the very lack of independence was a major obstacle preventing Cypriots from developing a specific identity which could link the two communities closer together. The imposed accommodation remained fragile, and within three years it proved unworkable. Archbishop Makarios, in December 1963, proposed amendments to the Constitution including abrogation of the Treaties of Guarantee and Alliance. Not surprisingly, these proposals were regarded by the minority community as an attack on their safeguards. Their rejection of the amendments was followed almost immediately by large-scale intercommunal violence in which up to 500 people were killed. The majority of the casualties were Turkish Cypriots. Also, 103 Turkish Cypriot villages were attacked and 30,000 Turkish Cypriots made refugees.[15] The Turkish fleet prepared to sail and Turkish military aircraft overflew the island. Makarios called on Britain to intervene and the three guarantor forces formed a peacekeeping force under British command.[16] A truce was arranged and a 'green line' of ceasefire (so called simply because a green pencil was used to mark the map) was drawn through Nicosia. However, there was now no hope of restoring the Constitution.

The crisis created alarm within NATO. Because of the perceived threat to NATO stability, Britain proposed that the existing peacekeeping force be strengthened with other forces from that body. The proposed force of approximately 10,000 would include 8,000 British and 1,000 US soldiers; Germany, it was hoped, would provide a sizeable number. But Makarios, by now a prominent figure in the non-aligned movement, rejected the idea.[17] While this might seem unsurprising, James Stenenga argues that Makarios may have had a 'hidden agenda', one linked to small emergent states' perception of the UN and its purpose. Makarios, he claims, may have purposely provoked violence in the hope of securing UN involvement for changes which could not be made in a peaceful legal way. Violence had worked against the British and might now secure a UN umbrella under which to complete the struggle for Cyprus.[18] James Boyd maintains that Makarios did not really want any international force but wanted a free hand from the UN to subjugate the Turkish Cypriots. It was with this purpose in mind that he established the National Guard.[19]

On 26 December 1963, Cyprus, Turkey, Britain and Greece requested the Secretary General to appoint a peacemaker on the island (General G.S. Gyani of India was appointed). Cyprus however remained unhappy with the existing guarantor force and on 4 March 1964, the Security Council in Resolution 186 recommended the creation of a UN peacekeeping force. The Force's task was that of restoring peace: significantly, the task of promoting a peaceful solution and an agreed settlement was assigned to a mediator.[20]

The creation of the UN force raised a number of questions. What was UNFICYP expected to do that the guarantor force or a NATO force could not? Was it expected to assist the Cypriot government impose its brand of law and order? What was the status of the Force vis-à-vis the guarantors and their obligations? The UN gave no indication of providing clarity as to the situation it now faced: the treaties remained valid and the question of how peace was to be restored and in what form was to remain unclear.[21] There was, however, no clear path forward. In a situation where the communities distrusted each other, there could be no political solution without the military security issues being first addressed. But action in this regard faced the UN with a classic peacekeeping dilemma. It would, the Secretary General observed, be incongruous for the Force to set about killing Cypriots whether Greek or Turkish to prevent them killing each other.[22] Moreover, to foster stability and constructive ethnic relations, it would be necessary to secure the rights and position of the minority. But who now were the minority? The notion of majority and minority had dissolved once Turkey became involved in Cyprus.

Phase one (1964–1974)

The Force (6,400) was deployed throughout the island (see Map 4.1) but despite its best efforts sporadic violence continued, punctuated by outbursts of heavy fighting in which peacekeepers were fired upon by both sides. On 9 May, the Security Council adopted Resolution 193 (1964) which called for a ceasefire and this was agreed to by both the Greek and Turkish governments.[23] Although it was the Cypriot government which had appealed for UN assistance, UNFICYP's efforts were from the outset severely impeded by lack of that government's cooperation. Freedom of movement was an essential prerequisite for the prevention of renewed fighting, but it was only in November 1964 that the Force Commander got an agreement from the National Guard declaring the whole island open to UN forces. Even then, certain areas covering approximately 1.65 per cent of the country were accessible only to UNFICYP senior officers.[24] This in effect provided the Cypriot government with the opportunity for large scale importation of arms. It also allowed Greek military personnel to come ashore unobserved. The UN's authority was dealt a further blow with the rejection in 1965 of the mediator's efforts.[25] Meanwhile, the problem had gradually acquired an international dimension.

For both Greece and Turkey, a major concern was the increasingly independent course pursued by Makarios. Faced with the prospect of a non-aligned Cyprus, both mainland parties sought to strengthen their own security.[26] In clear defiance of its treaty undertakings, Greece moved against Makarios by sending Grivas to command the Cypriot National Guard. The threat to Cypriot independence was further increased by the overthrow of the Greek government in April 1967 by a group of right-wing colonels. Emboldened by this development, Grivas on 14 November sent armed patrols into the 'Turkish' village of Ayios Theodoros where they murdered 17 villagers.[27] Again a Turkish invasion appeared imminent. But the Secretary General's representative and President Johnson's 'trouble-shooter' Cyrus Vance, induced Turkey, Greece and Cyprus to reach an agreement whereby Greece undertook to withdraw all its military personnel in excess of the 950 it was entitled to maintain on Cyprus under the Treaty of Alliance.[28] Turkey had sent only a few officers and volunteers.[29] When the negotiation process began, it was discovered that Greece had concealed over 6,500 troops and 60 armoured vehicles including tanks.[30]

The November attacks and their aftermath were noteworthy for several reasons: (1) they demonstrated Greece's disregard for the treaties it had signed; (2) they revealed the bad faith of Makarios who had to be aware of the illicit troops' presence; (3) they further undermined relations between the communities; and (4) they provided Turkey with an excuse for greater involvement in Cypriot affairs. They also highlighted UNFICYP's limitations in regard to maintaining the peace.

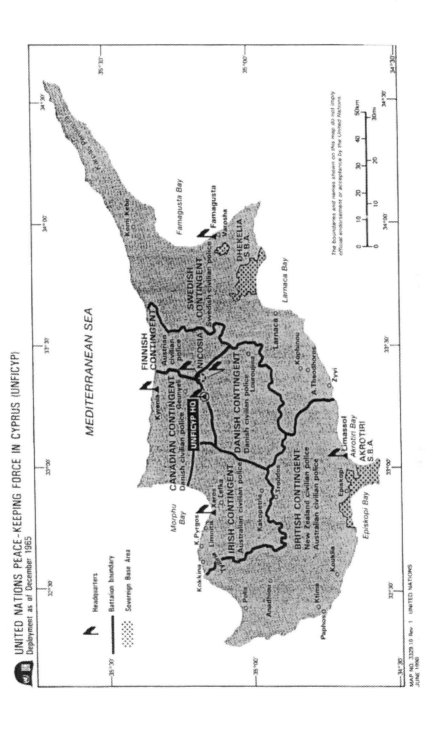

Map 4.1 Cyprus and UNFICYP: deployment as of December 1965

Source: UN Cartographic Section (Map No. 3329.10 Rev 1)

The events of late 1967 also forced Makarios to accept that independence was now the only option. This decision led to three developments. The first was UN-sponsored talks between the Turkish Cypriot representative (Rauf Denktash) and the Greek Cypriot representative (Gleckos Clerides). These talks quickly foundered. The second and third developments were linked. Hard-line enosis supporters recommenced organising opposition to Makarios and Grivas returned to the island to set up EOKA 'B';[31] gradually the Greek troops repatriated in 1967 filtered back. Meanwhile, the plot to remove Makarios acquired a Cold War dimension. The insecure Greek junta, in attempting to gain respect and acceptance, decided to play 'the NATO card'. The Arab–Israeli war of 1967 and its effects on the Middle East lent urgency to Western efforts to incorporate Cyprus into NATO. Grivas therefore worked on the basis of a common understanding with the Americans[32] and even his death in January 1974[33] did not halt the movement towards Makarios's overthrow.

On 15 July 1974, the National Guard (effectively a Greek force), overthrew the Cypriot government and declared Makarios dead. (In fact, he escaped to the British base at Akrotiri). Nicos Sampson, a virulent anti-Turk was installed as President. Turkey responded by calling in Britain as a co-guarantor of Cypriot independence to halt the Greek intervention, but the British turned to the Americans to defuse the situation. The US, ostensibly preoccupied with the resignation of its president in the wake of the Watergate scandal, declined to become involved. On 18 July, Turkey sent an ultimatum to Greece demanding Sampson's resignation, withdrawal of all Greek soldiers and pledges to uphold the independence of Cyprus. Greece, mistakenly believing that it could rely on US support, refused to comply, and on 20 July Turkey began landing troops and equipment near Kyrenia. The Turkish assault resulted in the occupation of the Turkish Cypriot enclave of Nicosia and areas to the north and west.[34] The Security Council in its resolution called for a ceasefire and demanded an immediate end to foreign military intervention. It also called on Turkey, Greece and Cyprus to enter immediately into negotiations for the restoration of peace and constitutional government on Cyprus.[35] By asking all parties to cooperate with UNFICYP, the Council indicated that the Force was expected to continue to function; however, UNFICYP's task was complicated by the uncertainty surrounding the purpose and duration of the Turkish presence (see Map 4.2).

Phase two (1974–)

Before considering the consequences of the invasion, let us look at Turkey's justification of its action, namely that it was exercising its rights and obligations under the Treaty of Guarantee and had intervened to protect the independence of Cyprus and to some extent, the Turkish Cypriot people.[36] There can be no doubt that the coup on Cyprus by what were essentially Greek military personnel was a clear case of illegal intervention which called for action under the Treaty of Guarantee. Greece had sought to impose its will upon the internal affairs of Cyprus for the purpose of altering conditions there. Thus, according to A.J. Thomas, the Greek

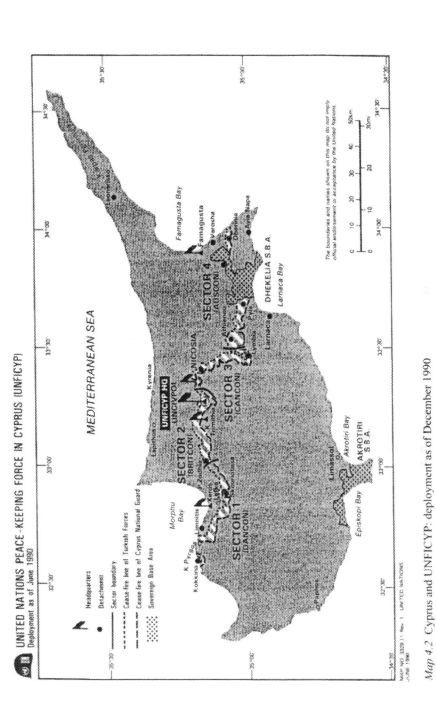

UNITED NATIONS PEACE-KEEPING FORCE IN CYPRUS (UNFICYP)
Deployment as of June 1990

▲ Headquarters
● Detachment
—— Sector boundary
∙∙∙∙∙∙ Cease fire line of Turkish Forces
–∙–∙– Cease fire line of Cyprus National Guard
⠿ Sovereign Base Area

MEDITERRANEAN SEA

Morphu Bay

Kyrenia

NICOSIA

UNFICYP HQ
UNFICYPOL

Famagusta Bay
Famagusta
Varosha

SECTOR 4
(AUSCON)

SECTOR 2
(BRITCON)

SECTOR 3
(CANCON)

SECTOR 1
(DANCON)

Larnaca
Larnaca Bay

DHEKELIA S.B.A.

Limassol

Akrotiri Bay
AKROTIRI
S.B.A.

Episkopi Bay

The boundaries and names shown on this map do not imply
official endorsement or acceptance by the United Nations

MAP NO. 3329 11 Rev 3   UNITED NATIONS
JUNE 1990

Map 4.2 Cyprus and UNFICYP: deployment as of December 1990

Source: UN Cartographic Section (Map No. 3329 11 Rev 1)

action fell within the rubric of aggression.[37] The Turkish action was apparently justified, but was it legal?

As required under the Treaty of Guarantee, Turkey did consult Britain regarding what representations or measures were necessary to ensure observance of the Treaty's provisions. Britain's response exposed the emptiness of that guarantor's original undertaking. It resisted Turkey's appeals to allow its troops to land at the sovereign bases but in so doing, found itself faced with the task of overthrowing Sampson; this it was unwilling to attempt. Britain had a further problem; it recognised that it would not be sufficient merely to restore the status quo because that would be to ratify the wrongs of 1963–4. Greece, the other co-guarantor, was not present for the Britain–Turkey discussions since its government was in the process of being overthrown. Thus, Turkey's action which enjoyed the support or at least understanding of a large section of world opinion,[38] might have appeared perfectly legal. However, the issue was far from clear-cut. Uncertainty arose from the question of whether the Treaties had created a regional organisation. If the Turkish action was an enforcement measure, according to Ann Thomas it would 'apparently require Security Council authorisation for legal regional action'.[39] This it did not have. Moreover, the Turkish objective, to be perceived as legal, would have to have been the restoration of the status quo.[40] Turkey's subsequent action reflected that this was not its intention.

The Turkish action and the doubts surrounding its legality, emphasised by Ann Thomas's use of the word 'apparently', raise major questions not only about the legitimacy of the Treaty of Guarantee, but highlight the limitations of international law in relation to acts of international aggression. Had Turkey not intervened, Greek aggression would have succeeded and Sampson would have been illegally installed as ruler of Cyprus. Britain had dithered, the US had failed to intervene. UNFICYP did make a major contribution towards limiting Turkish designs by preventing the seizure of Nicosia airport. However, this operation which prevented the spread of conflict was not a considered UN collective security response but a local measure of questionable legitimacy. Its success was a bonus for the operation but the UN's only official response to the crisis – a request to all states to exercise the utmost restraint – underlined the organisation's uncertainty as to what it could and should do.

Security Council Resolution 353 (1974) created the basis for talks between Turkey, Greece and Britain: but those talks (which began in Geneva on 25 July 1974) quickly collapsed. Turkey launched a second phase invasion which consolidated its hold on territory already occupied. In Resolution 360, the Security Council expressed formal disapproval of 'the military action taken against the Republic of Cyprus' and on 16 August 1974, a ceasefire came into effect. However, by this time the invasion had resulted in Turkish seizure of 40 per cent of Cyprus together with the displacement of approximately 200,000 Greek Cypriots who sought refuge in the south.[41] In December 1974, Makarios returned to power but the declaration in February 1975 of a Federated Turkish Cypriot state meant in effect that the Republic of Cyprus as originally established had ceased to exist.[42]

The ongoing Turkish occupation of northern Cyprus in defiance of over fifty unanimous Security Council Resolutions raises two issues: (1) Turkey's justification of its continuing presence, and (2) the UN's ability to impose its 'rules'. The return of an internationally recognised Cypriot government would suggest that the Turkish occupation was neither morally nor legally justified. However, Turkey sought to justify its action in 1974 by arguing that it had exercised its rights under the Treaty of Guarantee, not only to return the island to constitutional rule but to protect the Turkish community's rights.[43] Opponents of Turkey's position might well argue that the Turkish community were Cypriots not Turkish citizens; but the Treaty of Guarantee and the provisions of the Constitution were about nothing if not the protection of the island's communities. The Ayios Thedoros incident and the 1974 coup showed that the Turkish community needed protection from some quarter. Whereas this might seem a task for the UN, its record in the role of protector had been in the Cypriot case as elsewhere, dismal. This task would therefore seem to devolve on the Turks. They quite fairly argued that 'it did not require a prophet to anticipate what could and would happen if the Turkish forces were to be withdrawn'.[44]

The ongoing Turkish presence appears to constitute defiance of SC Resolution 353 (1974) which called for an immediate end to foreign military personnel other than those there under international agreement. But how authoritative is that resolution? Much confusion arises from its wording and from the Council's failure to state the article of the UN Charter on which it was based. A mere 'request' can hardly be considered as creating a legal obligation: a 'demand' would imply a threat of action in the event of non-compliance. Resolution 353 carried no explicit threat: it was not an enforcement measure as defined by Articles 41 and 42.[45] The resolution appeared, in the opinion of Ann Thomas, to fall under Article 40 which would be no more than a 'call' upon the parties concerned to comply with such provisional measures as the Council deemed necessary or desirable. There is, she goes on, disagreement as to whether 'calls' are binding; nevertheless, there is general agreement that 'calls' can be considered obligatory when it is clear that the resolution is founded on Article 40. But even under Article 40, the language of the resolution must be couched in legally binding terms; it must be mandatory against those to whom it is directed. Resolution 353 included no such terms.[46]

The resolution did 'demand' an end to foreign military intervention which amounted to a command to be obeyed. Turkey, by failing to end its intervention, defied the resolution and in effect violated the UN Charter. However, the Turks apparently interpreted the provisions of the resolution as non-obligatory unless certain conditions including progress towards a settlement be met.[47] Given the position of the parties, such progress was always unlikely. The declaration of a Turkish Republic of Northern Cyprus (TRNC) in 1985 confirmed Turkish defiance of the UN. Why then have UN resolutions gone unheeded? The answer relates both to Cold War realities and the UN's inability to honour its undertakings.

From 1974 onwards, the attitude of the superpowers was inclined towards acceptance of the status quo as the preferable option. For the US to have applied pressure on a very unstable Greece would not have been in the interests of NATO. Equally, Turkey was one of Washington's favourite protégés. Even the Soviet Union was not likely to go too far in criticising Turkey – always first among non-communist recipients of aid.[48] Besides, given the peaceful situation since 1974, 'rocking the boat' would be difficult to justify. Viewed from the wider international perspective, the Cyprus problem presented no clear villains and victims. Resolution of the problem would obviously lie ultimately with the Greek and Turkish Cypriots but these parties have at all times concentrated on antagonistic positions. What is a guarantee of security from one side – the presence or absence of Turkish troops – is perceived as the main source of threat and insecurity for the other.

The UN's failure to solve the Cyprus problem has brought calls for the withdrawal of UNFICYP, an option which it is argued would force the parties to solve the dispute between them.[49] This 'solution' takes little account of the military realities.[50] The departure of UNFICYP would likely be followed by friction between the two armed forces. Conflict, even on a small scale, could lead to the replacement of shaky democracies in Greece and Turkey, and eventually to military confrontation in the region and possibly beyond. Faced with such a scenario, the UN has chosen to continue with its peacekeeping operation.

Political base

Phase one: prior involvement of Great Powers

The UNFYCP mandate was broadly defined in terms reflecting a wish to buy time in a search for a solution to a problem in which it was clear neither sides' argument was without merit or justification. Significantly, the Security Council which set up the operation avoided the use of the word 'shall' in any of its early resolutions. Arguably, it was this cautious approach, further emphasised by the limiting of the duration of the mandate to three months, which induced permanent members of the Council to give the operation their assent. China and France were largely unconcerned about the crisis.[51] China had no involvement in the region. France considered the problem Britain's affair.[52] But Britain, the US and the Soviet Union all had a particular interest in developments. Quite apart from its concern for NATO integrity, Britain had good reasons for wanting stability in Cyprus. Having encouraged lurking antagonism between Greece and Turkey, it was now required to act as stabiliser. The moral case for intervention remained but there was nothing Britain wanted less than a return in force to the island. Its resources were already stretched and the Suez experience had killed any inclination to meddle in other states' politics unless the Americans were involved.[53]

The island's geo-strategic significance ensured US concern at political developments. Even without any indication from Moscow, Soviet interests had to be assumed. America favoured a reactive policy, responding to the inter-communal violence through a high level diplomatic mission to Athens, Ankara and Nicosia. In February 1964, Under-Secretary of State, George Ball, conferred with Makarios but neither side was impressed with the other. Ball meanwhile summed up the US perception of Cyprus by describing it as 'a strategically important piece of real-estate'.[54] Alarmed by Makarios's non-aligned stance and maverick behaviour, American policy reflected a concern with international law insofar as it related to the establishing treaties and NATO's strategic interests. When Cyprus sought to argue that the principle of sovereignty proclaimed in Article 2(1) of the UN Charter invalidated the treaties imposed on Cyprus at independence, the Americans insisted that all treaties had to be honoured.[55] Since military intervention would have represented a departure from reactive policies, President Johnson accepted the UNFICYP option. Perceived as an 'unsinkable' aircraft carrier and used as both a staging post for Britain and as a surveillance post for US intelligence, the island was of more than passing interest to the superpowers.[56] The Soviets expected to benefit from the intra-alliance cleavages which the US feared. In supporting Makarios, it could hope for a veto on additional bases in Cyprus and the Archbishop's standing in the Third World made him a potentially useful ally.[57]

Initial position of the Great Powers

Security Council members were less than wholehearted in their support for a UN force. After the controversies of ONUC, Britain, the US, and the Soviet Union had to adjust to a new and very different mission. Britain had been highly critical of UNEF I and ONUC. It was unhappy with the idea that through the US the Soviets and Afro-Asians would have an opportunity of meddling in an area of such strategic importance.[58] However, it could only regard with relief the deployment of UNFICYP. British forces on the island (7,000) were barely adequate for its peacekeeping and NATO tasks.[59] Its earlier peacekeeping effort having failed, it could persuade itself that its treaty obligations to Cyprus were being kept through its direct contribution to UNFICYP. However, Britain faced the dilemma that whereas the presence of a UN force would tend to freeze the situation, Britain was still bound by the Treaty of Guarantee to restoration of the state of affairs established by the Basic Articles of the 1960 Constitution. France, like the Soviet Union, was unhappy about delegation of power to the Secretary-General.

For the Americans, power plus legitimacy remained the key to leadership. It was imperative to be seen to support UN efforts while at the same time engaging in diplomatic activity. That diplomatic activity nevertheless involved taking a strong line with both Greece and Turkey. President Johnson reminded Turkey that a direct intervention in Cyprus could lead to Soviet involvement. He warned that if there were a consequential clash between those powers, NATO might not be bound to come to Turkey's assistance. At the same time, in an extraordinary outburst, he warned Greece's UN ambassador: 'if your Prime Minister gives me any talk about democracy, parliament and constitution, he, his parliament and his constitution may not last very long'.[60] Washington's realpolitik in relation to Cyprus was clear: Greece and Turkey were accorded quasi-proprietary rights: NATO had the overarching authority and the Cypriots did not exist or were a mere nuisance.[61]

The Soviets, having lost face in the Congo, had good reason to be less confrontational. Cyprus was not a Third World country but a relatively prosperous European state which, if the majority community had its way, would become part of a NATO member state. For the Soviets, the presence of UNFICYP had the particular merit that it ruled out the possibility of a NATO solution being imposed on a non-aligned state. Makarios's enthusiasm for a UN operation, agreement that costs be borne on a voluntary basis, and the limited (three-month) mandate were further reasons why the Soviet Union (like France) should unite with the other Council members in approving the mission.[62] Ninety per cent of funds provided for the first five years of the operation would come from NATO states.[63]

The mandate

The mandate for the force in March 1964 was even more vague than that provided for UNEF I and ONUC. In September 1964, the Secretary General told the Security Council that there was need for clarification: however, he received no such clarification, only tacit approval for his actions and initiatives.[64] Resolution 186 (1964), in referring to Article 2, paragraph 4, of the Charter and through reminding member states of the Charter's obligations, indicated that though the Cypriot communities were the principal parties in the dispute, each of the supporting actions had a major role in the drama. On 29 April 1964, Secretary General U Thant presented UNFICYP's mandate as being: (1) to prevent the recurrence of fighting; (2) to contribute to the maintenance of law and order; and (3) to contribute to a return to normal conditions.[65] Let us look at the legal basis for the operation, the difficulties created by the Treaty of Guarantee, and the feasibility of the mandate.

While the enabling resolution did not refer to any specific paragraph of the Charter,[66] the apparently sound legal basis is indicated by the consent of Cyprus, the guarantor powers and the contingent-supplying states. Of particular note was Makarios's attempt to have the mandate's terms of reference refer specifically to the protection of Cypriot territorial integrity: such a reference would have been consistent with the Charter's provisions and would later appear in SC Resolution 353 (1974). His hope, according to James Boyd, was that such a statement would provide an argument against the legality of the Treaty of Guarantee and that it could be used to support claims that any armed intervention by Turkey was an act of aggression under the Charter.[67] This issue underlined the complexity of the Cyprus problem. If the UN accepted Turkey's right to intervene, then to what extent was the organisation prepared to dictate the conditions of intervention? For how long was this extraordinary arrangement to be allowed continue?

UNFICYP's mandate was highly problematic; the Force had neither the resources nor authority to prevent fighting or restore law and order – the Secretary-General insisted that UNFICYP could take no action that would affect the outcome of the final settlement.[68] This stricture bore directly on the task of 'restoring normal conditions', but that term provided its own problems. 'Normal conditions' depended upon one's point of reference.[69] Just as the Greeks believed the mandate required UNFICYP to help quell Turkish Cypriots' rebellion against the legitimate government, the Turkish community believed the Security Council through Resolution 186 intended a complete restoration of the 1960 constitutional position.[70] Nor was confusion as to the UN's intentions limited to the parties alone. Ireland hesitated before supplying a contingent, fearful of finding itself involved in a partitioning exercise, and other states, mindful of the ONUC experience, were also reluctant to commit themselves.[71]

As events were to show, these uncertainties had a significant impact on the mission. Marios Evivriades and Dimitris Bourantonis maintain that the 1964 fighting could have been checked had UNFICYP been fully operational in the sense of possessing freedom of movement, the right of 'self-defence'[72] and interposition, the right to dismantle fortifications and create buffer zones.[73] The limitations of the mandate might arguably have been offset by the presence of a much larger force: but in June 1964, at 6,400,[74] the Force was, given the task and terrain, far from imposing. The glaring weaknesses, quickly exposed, could only raise doubts about the seriousness of UN intent. A key issue in all interventions in cases of ethnic conflict is the credibility of the international commitment.[75] UNFICYP's mandate did nothing to reassure the Turkish Cypriots that they would not be liable to further attack: neither did it suggest to the Greek Cypriots that a Turkish invasion would be opposed. In effect, the UN failed dismally to create the atmosphere in which trust could develop and mediation become effective.

Political manoeuvres of the Great Powers

Developments in 1974 presented Britain with exactly the situation it had hoped to avoid. Secure in its sovereign bases and contributing to UNFICYP, it had between 1964 and 1974 kept a low profile and accepted the 1967 Greek coup as a fait accompli. It was content to let the Americans handle the Greeks and Turks. US policy continued to be dictated by the need to keep Cyprus under NATO control. For that reason, it remained concerned about Makarios.[76] The Greek junta enjoyed benign tolerance – American military leaders praised 'the colonels', military assistance continued and grew, despite the fact that Greece had been expelled from the Council of Europe and blocked from joining the EEC.[77] Washington pressurised NATO allies to stop calling for the expulsion of Greece from the Alliance.[78] US–Cyprus relations became markedly influenced by Henry Kissinger's appointment as National Security Advisor. Kissinger distrusted Makarios and feared that Cyprus and its problems might upset the Soviet–American détente he had worked so hard to create. Equally motivated by Cold War realities, the Soviet Union had not hesitated to exploit successive crises on Cyprus. When Turkey threatened invasion in 1964, Moscow supplied Makarios with arms and a year later, provided 70 million dollars worth of military aid,[79] while in 1965 shifting over to the Turkish side. Predictably it denounced the 1974 coup as an American plot and demanded restoration of Makarios.

The behaviour of these three Great Powers was in the circumstances unsurprising. The US was the only power capable of exerting pressure on the parties but such developments as there had been served NATO and American interests. However, pressure alone, even if exerted by a totally united Security Council, would merely have contained the conflict since the parties had become steadily more entrenched and their positions irreconcilable.

Phase two (1974–): position of the Great Powers

The Turkish invasion of 20 July 1974 faced Britain with choices, all problematic. It could attempt as the 'neutral' guarantor to overthrow Sampson, but such international action could prove extremely difficult; it could take joint action with Turkey, but that option involved the risk of completely alienating the Greek Cypriots: in opting to do neither, it could be seen as handing the initiative to Turkey. The Geneva Talks offered a glimmer of hope for a peaceful resolution but Britain's obvious reluctance to engage in positive action was tantamount to a green light for further Turkish action. Britain's only positive response therefore would be its support for UNIFYCP in the Nicosia Airport incident in which it had little choice since British and Canadian lives were at stake.

It is clear that the US had no intention of preventing the second Turkish invasion. On 13 August, the State Department referred to the position of the Turkish community as requiring considerable improvement and protection, and indicated its support for greater autonomy for them. An appeal by the US Ambassador in Greece to have the US Sixth Fleet prevent the invasion was described by Kissinger as 'hysterical'. He also told the US envoy in Nicosia to receive the Foreign Minister of the Sampson regime, in effect making the US the only government to accord that regime de facto recognition. Most significantly, it emerged that the Turkish plan for the partition of Cyprus presented to the failed Geneva Talks was written in consultation with Kissinger.[80] The Soviet response was limited to expressions of condemnation of Turkey's action. Superpower reaction to the Turkish invasion carried one clear message. Whatever the perceived rules and principles of international behaviour outlined in the UN Charter, it was Cold War considerations which ultimately dictated great power behaviour.

The mandate post-1974

The events of July and August 1974 faced UNFICYP with a situation unforeseen in its original mandate. The functions laid down in SC Resolution 186 (1964) did not relate to large-scale hostilities arising from the actions of armed forces. A redefining of the mandate emphasising the interstate level of conflict might therefore have appeared both desirable and likely. However, on seeking a redefinition, the Secretary General found that there was by no means full agreement among the parties as to how, and with what objectives.[81] Moreover, the Nicosia Airport incident had shown what could be achieved through availing of mandate flexibility.

Adjusting to the new situation, the Force's functions became (1) maintenance of the military status quo and prevention of a recurrence of fighting, and (2) humanitarian and economic activities to promote a return to normal conditions.[82] Secretary General Kurt Waldheim's response turned UNFICYP from a dispersed force into one which interposed itself along and watched over the demarcation line drawn across the island (See Map 4.2). The effective creation of a state for each community greatly reduced the 'peacekeeping' problem and placed responsibility for a return to normal conditions firmly in the bailiwick of the diplomats.

It is argued by Cooper and Berdal that UNFICYP in contributing to a return to normal conditions had by stabilising the situation done the opposite. Just as 'peace' in 1964–5 had meant freezing the situation in favour of the Greek Cypriots, UN efforts post-1974 had frozen the situation created by Turkey's purported attempt to return the island to constitutional rule.[83] But this is to credit UNFICYP with having had the power and authority to keep the parties in check. Developments from 1964 onwards showed that it was the parties, with the acquiescence if not the connivance of the West, which had frozen or unfrozen the situation with general disregard for UNFICYP. The Turks, the dominant power having taken what they wanted, had no reason to go further. It was this combination of superior strength and political satisfaction which, in the opinion of Alan James, gave the status quo such stability from 1974 onwards.[84] Given UNFICYP's powerlessness, it is necessary to consider the attitude of the Great Powers to the new situation.

Political manoeuvres of the Great Powers post-1974

In the period 1975 – 1998, the Great Powers appeared to lose interest in Cyprus and its problems. Apart from supporting SC Resolutions, neither Britain, the US nor the Soviet Union made any significant move to change the 1974 status quo. Britain's attitude reflected resignation, the Soviets only contribution would be to call for an international conference (in 1986).[85] American policy, particularly during the presidency of Jimmy Carter (1976–80), was to make gestures aimed at placating the domestic 'Greek vote', while at the same time keeping the Turks satisfied by supplying arms via NATO. A plan for constitutional revision put forward by Carter in 1978 was rejected by Greece[86] allowing the US to claim that whatever it did or did not do, it was certain to be criticised. So what of the ongoing response of the Council to the situation? Successive SC resolutions from 353 (1974) onwards and in particular SC Resolution 541 (1983) have implied that the status quo be redressed because it contravenes the norms of international law. But is this really so?

The establishment in 1983 of TRNC, condemned in SC Resolution 541 (1983), raises the seeming inconsistency between the ongoing resolutions and UN acceptance of the rights of peoples to self-determination and independence, particularly where there is evidence of human rights abuse. The constitution of the Republic of Cyprus in 1960 represented the right of self-determination by the peoples constituting the state and government of Cyprus. Arguably, developments post-1974 represented a new stage in the exercise of self-determination by one of the two communities. That Turkey's intervention was crucial to this development is indisputable but without that intervention, the minority would almost certainly have been liable to indefinite subjugation.

It is, moreover, questionable whether it is correct to talk of the illegitimacy of separation from a unitary state of Cyprus since a unitary state of Cyprus never existed. The 1960 state organisation was one state with two peoples. Even if one were to accept that the Turkish Cypriot declaration of independence in 1983 amounted to secession, it could not be secession from a unitary state but a secession from participation in a bi-communal state. Furthermore, even if there was a secession, that secession, according to Claudio Zanghi (Committee of Human Rights Council of Europe 1972–3) was justified on the grounds of ill-treatment of one of the peoples by the other. This, he claims, gives them the right to secede and establish their own government and state.[87] Assuming that Zanghi is correct, then that right is denied by SC Resolution 541 (1983) which invites member states not to recognise the newly created state of TRNC. But even in so doing, the Council implicitly accepts the existence of that state. Moreover, whatever the circumstances of its creation, TRNC appears to adhere to the international principle which says that a state exists when it combines a state apparatus within a defined territorial area and a definite collectivity of people.[88] Meanwhile, by adherence to Resolution 541, the Council confines the Turkish people of northern Cyprus either to non-existence or to negation of their rights of self-determination. This is obviously an unsatisfactory situation which the UN seems unable to address.

Operational base

Secretary-General

The relative ease with which the Security Council deputed responsibility for the operation to the Secretary-General could be viewed as a ready 'passing of the buck', but could also be seen as indicating acceptance that solutions were not readily forthcoming and that U Thant had handled the ONUC operation with confidence and skill.[89] On this occasion, U Thant chose to be cautious and legalistic. He created a small force and was ultra-conscious of the mandate's limitations. When in 1967 Greece and Turkey agreed to withdraw troops in excess of their respective contingents, UNFICYP did not, as might have been expected, oversee the withdrawals. The Secretary General deemed it outside the mandate, and even when both sides asked the UN to check the remaining contingents, the Secretary-General hesitated.[90] His successor, Kurt Waldheim, was more assertive. He immediately addressed the issue of arms importation and established an agreement with the Cypriot government whereby a substantial delivery of arms and ammunition made in March 1972 would be inspected by the Force Commander and later stored within the UN camp. This agreement proved of enormous significance in the light of the events in 1974.[91] When fighting broke out in 1974, the UN had no mandate to intervene directly. However, Waldheim took it upon himself to tell UNFICYP to 'play it by ear'.[92]

Brigadier-General Francis Henn (former UNFICYP Chief of Staff) acknowledges the outstanding role of the Force Commander, General Chand, in the Nicosia Airport takeover: but he also accepts that the success of this venture was due in large measure to the Secretary-General's readiness to take decisions without waiting for options to be debated within the Council.[93] Waldheim's gamble involved considerable risks since many UNFICYP lives were at stake and enormous international pressure was required to prevent Turkey from attacking the UNFICYP positions. The gamble, however, produced major benefits. On the Greek side, there was a new-found confidence in UNFICYP which led to greater cooperation from the National Guard. The Turks were forced to recognise that UNFICYP could no longer be ignored. Most of all the relationship established between Secretary General and FC raised force morale and gave the troops a sense of purpose which had previously been notably lacking.[94]

Force Commander

A fundamental problem for any FC is what the Force's role should be in a war situation. The Nicosia airport incident represented just such a situation and General Chand's achievement on this occasion was due in large measure to the status and authority generally enjoyed by Commanders of UNFICYP.

U Thant's original decision to send General Gyani to Cyprus in January 1964 helped the planning of the operation but also established a relationship between the Commander and New York which was notably absent from ONUC. The FC, while not directly in charge of the civilian staff, held a first among equals position with regard to the senior political and legal adviser. Moreover, the Commander was to act not as a broker seeking to coordinate independent contingents, but to directly command all units. This represented a generally successful attempt to prevent the tenuous links of command being influenced by interference from national authorities.[95]

The image of the FC as one who added diplomacy to military skills was fostered by the appointment of General Martola of Finland in May 1966. A legendary hero in Finland, he commanded respect not just within UNIFICYP, but the island's communities. This respect was enhanced by his reaction to the Ayios Theodoros and Kophinou incidents. Whereas the British sought to play down the humiliation of the UN forces at Kophinou, Martola directed that elements from all contingents be sent to the village as a demonstration of UN resolve. The National Guard, surprised by the response, rapidly withdrew allowing the speedy return of the villagers. This display of brinkmanship exceeded the terms of the mandate, but bolstered UN authority and restored Force credibility.[96] Martola's decision may well have inspired General Chand to take a similar calculated risk in taking over Nicosia Airport in 1974. This venture was considered necessary for three reasons: (1) a battle for the airport would expose the UN camp to acute danger; (2) damage to the installation would prevent its use for resupply and reinforcement; (3) a battle for the airport would cause a breakdown islandwide of the fragile ceasefire.

Chand was conscious that UNFICYP had no authority to halt the Turkish advance, but decided to take over the airport and declare it a 'UN protected area'. The military body assembled to hold the installation which included cooks, barbers and clerks was at the Commander's insistence representative of all contingents. Its military weakness would it was hoped be outweighed by its political strengths. UNFICYP won the battle of nerves, not merely because the UN action was unusually robust (it was fortified by extra British armour and the threat of British airstrikes), but because the prospect of a confrontation between UNFICYP and the Turks generated acute international anxiety.[97] A Turkish attack at the airport would inevitably have resulted in large scale casualties, not only among NATO (British and Canadian) units, but among personnel from 'neutral' Finland, Sweden, and Ireland. Reflecting on the seriousness of the situation, former British Prime Minister, Harold Wilson, later declared that at the time of the crisis, 'Britain had been within an hour of war' with Turkey.[98]

It is certain that had the FC not taken a risk, the consequences would have been catastrophic. It is equally certain that without British military support and American diplomatic pressure, the UNFICYP effort would have been doomed.[99] UNFICYP was highly unusual among UN operations insofar as reinforcements and powerful ones at that were readily available. Had the UN force been composed of weak Third World contingents, reinforcement would have been out of the question. But then Chand would hardly have made his stand at the airport had he been reliant on such contingents. What made the incident exceptional was its spontaneity. The airport 'coup', one of UN peacekeeping's greatest successes, was not the outcome of any plan dictated from New York but resulted from the Commander's initiative. It showed what could be achieved even with limited resources once support from some of the Great Powers was forthcoming. It also raised again the role of the peacekeeper – was he a policeman or a soldier?

Tactical capabilities, contingents

UNFICYP, (initially composed of contingents from Canada, Denmark, Finland, Ireland, and Sweden), never reached its proposed strength of 7,000.[100] In contrast to earlier operations, the Secretary-General found on this occasion that governments were hesitant about providing contingents. This was due largely to uncertainty as to the consequences of commitment. Canada and Finland asked for clarification about status and duties before providing troops. Sweden expressed an unwillingness to be the only neutral country represented and so Ireland was invited to contribute. The pool of potential contributors was further reduced by Cypriot and Turkish objections to the inclusion of troops from developing countries. The resultant force was consequently unrepresentative of the UN; all the countries were from Western parliamentary democracies sharing a common north European culture. All were better trained and disciplined than many of the ONUC contingents but there was a marked difference between contingents in terms of preparation for and perception of the peacekeeping role.

Canadian troops reflected the military viewpoint that all UN forces were successful when they enforced their rights and proved worthless when they let local forces treat them with contempt. General Lewis Mackenzie describes his Commanding Officer's priority as simple and clear: 'the unit must always be ready to fight and the edge must not be lost while peacekeeping'.[101] The Canadian enthusiasm for 'professional challenge', a term used to describe penetrations of restricted zones, was however not well received by other contingents who regarded such activity as dangerously provocative.[102] British troops were, like the Canadians, highly trained fighting soldiers but not at all prepared for peacekeeping duties.[103] They operated on the belief that peacekeeping was not a role for 'real' soldiers but assumed that well-trained soldiers could readily adapt to the peacekeeping role. This view was shown to be badly mistaken – the humiliating incident at Kophinou in 1967 involved a unit which had just been transferred from active service in Aden, whose members were uncertain as to how to react in the new role.[104] They were also for historical reasons perceived as 'pro-Turkish' and therefore more liable to attack by Greek Cypriots. However, their fighting ability earned respect and having combat reinforcement 'on call' from the sovereign bases proved a major bonus, particularly during the events of 1974.[105]

In contrast to these contingents, troops from the other four contributors were oriented towards consent-based peacekeeping. Irish personnel, a majority of whom had served in ONUC, had learned how to exercise patience and diplomacy. These skills helped them gain the confidence of both communities. The civilianised nature of the Nordic contingents reflected the belief that the civilian doing his military service was more adaptable to peacekeeping than the regular soldier. These contingents also reflected the political emphasis of their governments. Finland, concerned with its own security, did not believe in 'wasting' trained troops on UN duties, and its UNFICYP personnel had just two months basic training. Denmark, preoccupied with its NATO commitments, pursued a similar policy.[106] Sweden, on the other hand, took its UN commitment very seriously. Its troops were required to undergo ten months of rigorous training.[107] Nordic troops were generally regarded as efficient in the performance of their duties and effective in cooperating with the local communities. (The Swedish, Irish, Danish and Canadian contingents would later be replaced by Austrian and Argentinian units).

The Force HQ, reflecting the quality of the contingents, was efficient and smooth running. Personnel were generally of a high calibre and general proficiency in English and familiarity with NATO staff procedures facilitated smooth operations.[108] Untroubled by the ideological and cultural differences which bedevilled ONUC, UNFICYP was a competent, well-organised body. However, it lacked a clear mission and the means of achieving it.

Communications

UNFICYP enjoyed the advantage of having available the well-established signal communication service of the British Army already in situ and the skills and services of the Canadian signal personnel who had served with UNEF I and ONUC. It also benefited from the fact that a majority of personnel either spoke English fluently or had a working knowledge of the language.[109] However, it was unable to capitalise on these assets because it lacked freedom of movement, resources in terms of numbers and equipment, and was prevented from intelligence-gathering. The sporadic violence and the omnipresent threat of attack made acquisition of information vitally important; troops seeking to interpose effectively needed information on 'hostile' elements, both for their own safety and to allow them to address the party posing the greater threat. In the absence of such information, the scale and boldness of the attacks on Ayios Theodoros and Kophinou took UNFICYP completely by surprise. It was known that there were secret camps but when in December 1967 an entire Greek army brigade emerged from its hideout in the Troodos mountains, the UN personnel were both amazed and alarmed.[110] The coup of 1974 re-emphasised the problems created through denial of an intelligence service. UNFICYP Headquarters only became aware of significant international developments when heavy firing from the nearby Turkish position disturbed the morning staff conference of 15 July. In the weeks preceding the coup, the unusual movement of prominent Greek army and National Guard personnel had been noted by individual officers but not commented upon since such comment was deemed inappropriate for peacekeepers.[111] Thus, not only UNFICYP HQ but New York were taken unawares.

As the Security Council's response to a perceived threat to international peace and security, UNFICYP should have been in a position to advise that body of any serious developments. In the absence of critical information, the Force however became effectively an independent body forced to undertake tasks for which it was not prepared. The problems created through the unavailability of intelligence re-emphasised the enormous weakness of consent-based peacekeeping. Were it UN policy that under no circumstances should UN peacekeepers engage the parties, then a prohibition on intelligence gathering might be supportable. However, the Nicosia airport incident had shown that on occasion peacekeeping personnel had to assume the role of soldiers. To perform in this role, they required both information and also equipment.

Equipment

UNFICYP was unusual insofar as the UN administrative, logistical, financial and procurement regulations and procedures which cause the military element massive frustration on most missions were not a problem. The British Army on the island provided troop transporting vehicles, food, fuel, maintenance organisation and ordnance stores.[112] In keeping with the practices established through UNEF I and ONUC, and in accordance with the Secretary-General's aide memoire, national contingents brought their own weapons and combat vehicles. Armament included the usual infantry battalion weapons up to and including medium mortars and heavy machine guns (HMGs).[113] It was the decision to bring HMGs, armoured vehicles and other forms of 'heavy' equipment which revealed the concerns of troop-contributing states and underlined their lack of confidence in the UN Secretariat.

In recognition of the non-aggressive nature of the mission, APCs were at first considered unnecessary by most contingents. However, a majority were equipped with assorted forms of armoured fighting vehicles. These small vehicles provided patrols or outposts with an element of support, but were nevertheless little other than mobile gun and mortar platforms. Very quickly the need for greater protection and extra 'muscle' was recognised, the Canadian contingent being reinforced by the arrival of an anti-tank element, APCs and reconnaissance vehicles.[114] The Irish decision to include heavy (120 mm) mortars in their arsenal was a sign that a force which had been caught unprepared in the Congo was on this occasion taking necessary precautions. That contingents saw the need for such equipment and that the UN agreed to its availability indicated both uncertainty as to what UNFICYP's role might involve and the Force's obvious vulnerability. UNFICYP's very defensive posture was obviously consistent with the traditional operating concept of peacekeeping but it also signalled the Force's inability effectively to halt armed conflict or to prevent its recurrence.

Analysis

Mandate performance

UNFICYP's mandate was of the kind referred to by Bratt: 'cooked up to satisfy the Security Council's domestic interests. Nobody in the Security Council in their wildest dreams thought (it) would be implemented'.[115] Since the status quo ante was in itself wholly unsatisfactory, a return to normal conditions was an impossible objective, since there was nothing 'normal' about Cyprus. The guarantor arrangements amounted to recognition that problems were anticipated, problems which could only be solved by goodwill. This was notably lacking, and since UNFICYP could not create good will, it could merely attempt to deal with the consequences of its absence.

The Force had been unable to prevent recurrence of fighting in late 1964, 1967 and 1974 and even its humanitarian activities had been dependent upon the cooperation of the parties. By its presence, UNFICYP had reflected international concern, but the Security Council's unwillingness to provide adequate resources at the initial stage or to change the mandate could only be read as an indication that the organisation was merely 'going through the motions'. It could be argued that peace having reigned for over twenty years, 'normal conditions' can now be perceived to prevail. However, the continuing UN presence would indicate that the mandate's objective remains unachieved.

Facilitating conflict resolution

Resolving the Cyprus conflict required an evolutionary process that would incrementally lower the fears and raise the hopes of both sides by phases which would allow flexibility, interaction and reciprocity.[116] The success of such a process, however, would depend upon opportune circumstances, the existence of institutional mechanisms for conflict resolution, and the political will for settlement by the protagonists and their allies or supporters. Such conditions did not exist on Cyprus. The situation from the period 1950s onwards was one involving lack of trust in the intentions of the other side and fears of domination by a more powerful adversary. This had been exacerbated by the actions of Greece and then Turkey which effectively nullified any efforts by the peacekeepers to lay the ground for confidence building. From the period 1968 to 1974 when military sobriety had replaced military violence, the complementary development of a peacemaking initiative was missing. It was at this time that a new trust and confidence needed to be created through a process of reconciliation, one involving the Turkish community on a more equal basis. The organisation did not react to the changing circumstances, the mandate remained unchanged, and specialised agencies aimed at conciliation were not employed.[117]

Moreover, high politics also intruded to subvert the UN-sponsored intercommunal dialogue begun in 1968. These politics involved the destabilising role of the Greek junta which the West did nothing to prevent.[118] The geographic partition which followed the Turkish invasion complicated even further any search for a political solution. In 1992 for the first time UN negotiation tackled substantive issues relating to the internal aspects of the problems such as territory, settlement and ownership of property: past negotiations had focused on constitutional positions only. But nothing came of this, largely due to the intransigence of the Turks.[119] Equally damaging to any prospect of resolution was the fact that the Security Council continued to show an unwillingness to assume direct responsibility for the issue and was unwilling to alter the political mandate of the Secretary-General or of UNFICYP.[120]

In November 2002, the UN Secretary-General put forward proposals for the reunification of Cyprus on the basis of a two-component state federation. The proposal engaged the support of the EU and US. Under the proposal, the Turkish controlled area would reduce from 36 per cent to 28.5 per cent and approximately 85,000 Greek Cypriots forced to flee their homes after the 1974 invasion, would be able to return to areas that would again come under Greek-Cypriot administration. The UN force would remain on indefinitely, bolstered by Greek and Turkish soldiers.[121] Hopes for such a solution were dashed when the proposal was rejected by the Turkish Cypriot leader, Denktash. The UN was quoted as saying that it would give up trying.[122]

Conflict containment

While outbreaks of fighting, particularly that in 1974, might suggest otherwise, UNFICYP can be said to have played a not insignificant role in limiting conflict. In such a mixed, distrustful and trigger-happy state as Cyprus, it would, as James observes, have been almost impossible to prevent the escalation of all the many incidents which occurred without the presence of UNFICYP.[123] It could not prevent conflict but the barbarity to which war gives rise was to a considerable extent stemmed by the presence of UN troops. Through negotiation and persuasion, local fighting was stopped and often prevented from occurring. When it did take place, UNFICYP assisted civilians evacuated wounded and endeavoured to resolve its underlying causes. If UNFICYP's primary purpose was to prevent Greece and Turkey going to war, then it would appear to have succeeded. Undoubtedly the primary restraining force was the US but even if peacekeepers were on their own unable to prevent direct conflict, they did at least constitute a useful and apparently effective 'trip-wire'. This very limited capability highlights the UN's reliance upon the parties to keep the peace. (Whether, and what, action might follow a 'tripping of the wire' is open to speculation).

Assessment

Events in Cyprus from 1960 onwards demonstrated the intractability of intra-state disputes, especially those having an ethnic dimension. They also revealed the UN's acute limitations when dealing with such disputes. In particular, they showed that by embarking on a mission without clear objectives or agenda, the organisation could, through its efforts, complicate rather than help resolve an issue. The problem of Cyprus was arguably beyond the UN's power to resolve right from the outset. The antagonism between the communities, fuelled by the majority community's pursuit of enosis, was certain to find greater expression in the newly created state. Efforts to safeguard the interests of the minority through the Treaty of Guarantee could only highlight the divisions and add to the complexity of the problem. Subsequent interventions by Greece and Turkey were guaranteed to complete the polarisation and make harmonious relations between the communities an impossibility. Both sides would in time agree that a solution could only be found with the framework of a bi-communal, bi-zonal Cypriot federation with one nationality and one sovereignty. But this formula repeated in numerous UN resolutions assumed that the island's constitutional territorial and economic problems could be resolved and this had proved impossible.[124]

Throughout, the UN approach to the Cyprus problem had been confused and inconsistent. The organisation, while encouraging 'self-determination' allowed the new member state's independence to be circumscribed by an international treaty which gave three outside states authority to intervene on the island. It gave its peacekeeping force the tasks of preventing a recurrence of fighting and helping to maintain law and order, but made achievement of these tasks impossible by

(1) accepting that the Force be denied freedom of movement and (2) instructing the peacekeepers to refrain from intervening in Cypriot affairs. It has, since 1964, continued to seek a return to normal conditions, but in so doing, created for itself an ongoing dilemma. By maintaining a Force along the line established in 1974, it has created what amounts to a border between the two communities. What now should be UN's reaction were the Greek Cypriots to drive north into the illegal Republic of North Cyprus in an effort to recover territory from which they were driven in 1974? Would such armed attack be treated as legitimate and if not, to what status quo would the parties be required to return?

The operation revealed the aspirational and largely symbolic character of UN peacekeeping. Denied authority and resources, UNFICYP could never of itself separate the parties or prevent hostilities. It could at no time 'keep the peace'. The UN had by sending in a peacekeeping force 'done something' but the operation had shown that there was a vast difference between responding to clamour for action and taking positive action to address conflict. The benefits of positive action had been demonstrated by the 'airport incident'. It had shown how an effective commander and efficient force, if given support and resources, could assert UN authority. This lesson would however, go unheeded.

Notes

1 Adamantia Pollis, 'Colonialism and Neo-Colonialism: Determination of Ethnic Conflict in Cyprus', in Peter Worsley and Paschalis Kitromilides (eds), *Small States in the Modern World*, Nicosia, New Cyprus Association, 1979, p. 58

2 Ibid., pp. 51–4

3 Costas Melakopides, 'Making Peace in Cyprus: Time for a Comprehensive Initiative', in *Martello Papers*, 15, Ontario, Ontario Centre for International Relations, Queens University, 1996, p. 4

4 Pollis, in Worsley and Kitromilides, *Small States*, pp. 56–8

5 Anthony Parsons, *From Cold War to Hot Peace*, London, Penguin, 1995, p. 170

6 Vangelis Vitalis, 'Cyprus, Divided People, Divided Land' *New Zealand International Review*, January/February 1992, p. 14

7 Pollis, (n.1 above), p. 60. The Turkish Cypriots insisted on interpreting the constitution as a federation, although the term did not appear in the document itself. Makarios feared that it left the door open to partition. He claimed that what had been granted was a state but not a nation. Robert McDonald, 'The Problem of Cyprus', *Adelphi Papers 234*, 1999, p. 11

8 The constitution included the powers of veto over legislation and cabinet decisions to the President (Greek Cypriot) and Vice President (Turkish Cypriot): the appointing of a civil service and a police on a 7:3 ratio, and the creation of Greek and Turkish communal chambers to handle cultural and religious affairs. Significantly, it also gave Britain sovereign rights to bases at Akrotiri and Dhekelia. Melakopides, 'Making Peace', p. 9

9 James Boyd, *United Nations Peacekeeping Operations: A Military and Political Appraisal*, New York, Praeger, 1971, p. 24

10 Ann Wynen Thomas, 'The Turkish Invasion of Cyprus: Legal Aspects of the Regional and United Nations Action', p. 205

11 Ibid., p. 204

12 A.J. Thomas Jnr., 'International Law and the Turkish Invasion of Cyprus', in Worsley and Kitromilides, *Small States*, p. 190

13 'There shall be considered as regional arrangements, organisations of a permanent nature, grouping in a given geographic area, several countries which by reason of their proximity, community of interests or cultural, linguistic, historical or spiritual affinities make themselves jointly responsible for peaceful settlement of any dispute which may arise between them and for the maintenance of peace and security in their region, as well as for the safeguarding of their interests and the development of their economic and cultural relations.' Ann Wynen Thomas, 'The Turkish Invasion of Cyprus: Legal Aspects of the Regional and United Nations Action', in Worsley and Kitromilides, *Small States*, p. 200

14 Ali Sirmen, 'The Notion of the Small State: Cyprus, Its Security and Survival', in Worsley and Kitromilides, *Small States* p. 89

15 Mumtaz Soysal, 'Turkish Position on Cyprus', in Kjell Skjelsbaek, (ed.) *The Cyprus Conflict and the Role of the United Nations*, Oslo, Norsk Utenrikspolilisk Institutt, 1988, p. 73

16 UN, *The Blue Helmets*, p. 284

17 Karl Birgisson, 'United Nations Peacekeeping Force in Cyprus', in William Durch (ed.), *The Evolution of UN Peacekeeping*, London, Macmillan Press, 1993, p. 221

18 James Stenenga, 'UN Peacekeeping: The Cyprus Venture', *Journal of Peace Research*, Vol. 7, 1970, p. 2

19 Andrew Boyd, *Fifteen Men on a Powder Keg*, London, Methuen & Co. Ltd, 1971, p. 280.

20 UN, *The Blue Helmets*, p. 285

21 While Makarios continued to hope that the presence of a UN force could be used to nullify the Treaty of Guarantee, Britain and the US secured the support of the Sec. Council for the view that that body had no power to interpret or annul the treaties and on this issue, Makarios failed to carry even the support of Greece. Rosalyn Higgins, *United Nations Peacekeeping, Documents and Commentary*, Vol. 4, Oxford, Oxford University Press, 1981, p. 92

22 U. Thant quoted in Marios Evriviades and Dimitris Bourantis, 'Peacekeeping and Peacemaking: Some Lessons From Cyprus', *International Peacekeeping*, No. 4, 1994, London, p. 398

23 UN, *The Blue Helmets*, p. 294

24 Ibid., p. 293

25 The mediator (Galo Plaza of Equador) found that any proposed settlement involving enosis was unacceptable to the Turkish Cypriots just as partition was totally unacceptable to the Greek community and this rejection of Turkish calls for a federation led Ankara to break off discussions. Vitalis, 'Cyprus', p. 15

26 Pollis, in Worsley and Kitromilides, *Small States*, p. 71

27 UNFICYP forces attempting to intervene were shelled. The National Guard also attacked the village of Kophinou, over-running UN positions and seizing arms and equipment. General M.J. Murphy (Irish Contingent), interviewed by Terry O'Neill, 24 February 1995, Athlone

28 James Wolfe, 'United States Policy and the Cyprus Conflict and the Role of the United Nations', in Skjelsbaek, *The Cyprus Conflict*, p. 48

29 Boyd, *Fifteen Men*, p. 295

30 General M.J. Murphy (Irish Contingent), interviewed by Terry O'Neill, 24 February 1995, Athlone

31 *Keesing's Contemporary Archives*, Bristol, Keesing Publications, 1969–70, 25033–25243

32 N. Kadritzke and W. Wagner, 'Limitations of Independence in the Case of Cyprus', in Worsley and Kitromilides, *Small States*, p. 104

33 Pollis, 'Colonialism and Neo-Colonialism', in Worsley and Kitromilides, *Small States*, p. 70
34 Vitalis, 'Cyprus', p. 16
35 Ibid.
36 A.J. Thomas, 'International Law and the Turkish Invasion of Cyprus', in Worsley and Kitromilides, *Small States*, p. 195
37 'Delictual conduct which violates the right of territorial integrity or political independence of a sovereign state thus placing the security of the state in danger'. A.J. Thomas, in Worsley and Kitromilides, *Small States*, p. 118
38 Keith Kyle, 'British Policy Towards Cyprus', in Skjelsbaek, *The Cyprus Conflict*, p. 64
39 Ann Wynen Thomas, in Worsley and Kitromilides, *Small States*, pp. 202–3
40 A.J. Thomas, in Worsley and Kitromilides, *Small States*, p. 202
41 Alan James, 'The UN Force in Cyprus', in *International Affairs*, Vol. 65, No. 3, 1989, p. 483
42 Over the following years, groups from both communities moved north and south. By November 1988, only 639 Greek Cypriots remained in the north. There were no more than 100 Turkish Cypriots in the State. (UN Brief for VIP Visitors, UNFICYP, UNFICYP Headquarters, Nicosia, 5)
43 Ann Wynen Thomas, in Worsley and Kitromilides, *Small States*, p. 203
44 Ibid., p. 211
45 Ibid., p. 209
46 Ibid.
47 The others being that a feeling of security be re-established and that the humanitarian problem including that of refugees be solved. Ann Wynen Thomas, (n.1 above), p. 211
48 Melakopides, 'Making Peace', p. 64
49 Ibid., p. 29
50 Turkish troops in Cyprus in 1995 were estimated at between 20,000 and 30,000. The Cypriot National Guard comprised 13,000: there were also 1,750 Greek Army troops on the island. UN Brief for VIP Visitors, UNFICYP Headquarters, Nicosia
51 Even after the Chinese seat on the Council was assumed by the Communist regime in 1971, China refused for ten years to have anything to do with the establishment or extension of peacekeeping forces. Alan James, 'The UN Force in Cyprus', *International Affairs*, Vol. 65, No. 3, 1969, p. 486
52 Ibid., p. 489
53 Kyle, in Skjelsbaek, *The Cyprus Conflict*, p. 63
54 Ball, quoted in Melakopides, 'Making Peace', p. 15
55 James H. Wolfe, in Skjelsbaek, *The Cyprus Conflict*, p. 46
56 Pollis, in Worsley and Kitromilides, *Small States*, p. 10
57 Melakopides, 'Making Peace', p. 19
58 Boyd, *Fifteen Men*, p. 279
59 Alan James, *The Politics of Peacekeeping*, London, Chatto and Windus, 1969, p. 321
60 Melakopides, 'Making Peace', p. 14
61 Ibid., p. 15
62 Birgisson, 'United Nations Peacekeeping', p. 223
63 Boyd, *Fifteen Men*, p. 283
64 Ibid., p. 285
65 Ibid., p. 224
66 Akehurst suggests it 'is based on paragraph 39 of the Charter'. Michael Akehurst, *A Modern Introduction to International Law*, p. 213
67 James Boyd, *United Nations Peacekeeping Operations, A Military And Political Appraisal*, New York, Praeger Publishers, 1971, p. 67

68 Marios Evriviades and Dimtris Bourantonis, 'Peacekeeping or Peacemaking: Some Lessons From Cyprus', in *International Peacekeeping*, Vol. 1, No. 4, 1994, p. 400
69 According to Karl Birgisson, 'normal conditions' before 1974 referred to economic and social life and governmental Terry O'Neillity as it was before the fighting of 1963. Birgisson, in Skjelsbaek, *The Cyprus Conflict*, p. 224
70 *The Blue Helmets*, p. 293
71 James, *The Politics*, p. 226
72 The UN troops did on occasion fire their weapons to protect civilians or to provide covering fire when removing dead or wounded. General J.M. Murphy, (Irish Contingent), interviewed by Terry O'Neill, 24 February 1995, Athlone
73 Evriviades and Bourantonis, 'Peacekeeping', p. 397
74 UN, *The Blue Helmets*, p. 293
75 Donald Lake and Daniel Rothchild, 'Containing Fear, The Origins and Management of Ethnic Conflict', *International Security*, Vol. 21, No. 2, 1996, p. 42
76 Ball declared: 'That son of a bitch will have to be killed before anything happens on Cyprus'. Melakopides, 'Making Peace', p. 15
77 Christopher Hitchens, *The Trial of Henry Kissinger*, London, Verso, 2002, p. 81
78 Mekalopides, 'Making Peace', p. 16
79 Ibid., pp. 19–20
80 Ibid., p. 17
81 James, 'The UN Force', p. 485. When the possibility of a change was raised at UNFICYP HQ in August 1974, General Chand had insisted that the mandate was adequate. General James Flynn, (Irish Contingent), interviewed by Terry O'Neill, 3 June 1995, Dublin
82 UNFICYP, 'Briefing for VIP Visitors', 11 March, 1995, UNFICYP HQ. This was the first time ever the Sec. Council exercised a humanitarian right to intervene in the internal affairs of a member state. Evriviades and Bourantis, 'Peacekeeping', p. 411
83 Martin Cooper and Mats Berdal, 'Outside Intervention in Ethnic Conflicts', *Survival*, Vol. 36, No. 1, 1993, p. 122
84 Alan James, 'The UN Force', p. 485
85 Costas Melakopides, 'Making Peace', pp. 20–1
86 James Wolfe, 'United States Policy and the Cyprus Conflict', in Skjelsbaek, *The Cyprus Conflict*, pp. 53–4
87 Claudio Zanghi, 'The Inter-Relationship between the Cyprus Question and Human Rights', in *New Cyprus*, Lefkosa, Turkey, Vol. 7, No. 1, January 1992, p. 24
88 Ibid.
89 James Boyd, *United Nations Peacekeeping*, p. 86
90 Rosalyn Higgins, 'United Nations Peacekeeping 1946–1967', in *Documents and Commentary*, Vol. 4, p. 139
91 These arms were still in UN custody in 1995. Paul Kavanagh, Civilian Advisor to the Force Commander, interviewed by Terry O'Neill, 16 March 1996, Nicosia
92 Francis Henn, 'The Nicosia Airport Incident of 1974', *International Peacekeeping*, Vol. 1, No. 1, 1994, p. 83
93 Ibid., p. 96
94 Gen. James Flynn, (Irish Contingent), interviewed by Terry O'Neill, 3 June 1995, Dublin
95 Michael Harbottle, 'UN Peacekeeping, Past Lessons and Future Prospects', David Davies Lecture, 25 November 1971
96 Gen. M.J. Murphy, (Irish Contingent), interviewed by Terry O'Neill, 24 February 1995, Athlone
97 Francis Henn, 'The Nicosia', pp. 92–4
98 Ibid., pps 92–3

99 Ibid.
100 Boyd, *Fifteen Men*, p. 289
101 Lewis Mackenzie, *Peacekeeping: The Road to Sarajevo*, Vancouver, Douglas and McIntyre, 1993, pp. 22–32
102 Gen. Murphy, interviewed by Terry O'Neill, 24 February 1995, Athlone
103 Ibid.
104 Ibid.
105 Henn, 'The Nicosia', p. 93
106 Prior to UNPROFOR, Danish regular officers regarded UN service as an inferior form of service and unhelpful to career prospects. Lt. Col. Bengt Sohnermann, Danish UN School, interviewed by Terry O'Neill, 10 September 1994, Karup, Denmark
107 Charles Moskos, *Peace Soldiers: The Sociology of a UN Military Force*, Chicago: Chicago University Press, 1976, p. 57
108 There were some 'odd' choices. A long-serving Danish officer, notable for his unfamiliarity with formal military procedures, was, it emerged, a highly esteemed hero of the Resistance in World War II. Gen. Gerald O'Sullivan, Former Staff Officer, UNFICYP, interviewed by Terry O'Neill, 10 May 1995, Dublin
109 General Patrick Dixon, (Irish Contingent), interviewed by Terry O'Neill, 24 May 1995, Athlone
110 General M. Murphy, interviewed by Terry O'Neill, 24 February 1995, Athlone
111 General J. Flynn, (Irish Contingent), interviewed by Terry O'Neill, 3 June 1995, Dublin
112 General Patrick Dixon (Irish Contingent), interviewed by Terry O'Neill, 24 May 1995, Athlone
113 Aide Memoire of Secretary General, 10 April 1964
114 Lt. Col. Patrick Freeman, (Irish Contingent), interviewed by Terry O'Neill, 21 November 1994, Athlone
115 Duane Bratt, 'Assessing Peacekeeping Success', Michael Pugh (ed.) *The UN, Peace and Force*, London, Frank Cass and Company Ltd, 1997, p. 67
116 Maria Trigeorgis and Lewis Trigeorgis, 'Cyprus, An Evolutionary Approach', *The Journal of Conflict Resolution*, Vol. 37, No. 2, June 1993, p. 357
117 Michael Harbottle, 'Cyprus: An Analysis of the UNs Third Party Role in a Small War', in Worsley and Kitromilides, *Small States*, p. 218
118 Evriviades and Bourantonis, 'Peacekeeping', p. 408
119 Paul Kavanagh, Civilian Advisor to the Force Commander, interviewed by Terry O'Neill, 16 March 1996, Nicosia
120 Evriviades and Bourantonis, 'Peacekeeping', p. 409
121 *The Economist*, 16–22 November, 2002, p. 32
122 *The Economist*, March 15–21, 2003, p. 6
123 James, 'The UN Force', p. 483
124 Heinz, Kramer, 'The Cyprus Problem and European Security', *Survival*, Vol. 39, No. 3, 1997, p. 21

5

UNOSOM AND SOMALIA, 1992–1995

Introduction

UNOSOM can be seen as an attempt by the UN and the Secretariat in particular to adapt to the changed post-Cold War international environment, and by availing of the greater harmony within the Security Council, engage its forces in a new, more robust form of action than that associated with earlier consent-based operations. However, as James Mayall observed: 'The major powers might have been better advised to have taken the Congo operation as their model and warning than to have allowed public opinion to lure them into the belief that the success of Desert Storm and enforcement action under Chapter VII could be repeated in quite different circumstances.'[1]

The nature of the conflict

In Somalia, as in the Congo, the UN presence was linked to the collapse of state authority and once again UN forces sent to save lives had become involved in bloody conflict with citizens of the 'host state'. Again, the UN was plagued by an inability to decide whether its purpose was the restoration of the political status quo prior to the outbreak of hostilities or the creation of a totally new situation. And as with ONUC, there was an incoherent mixture of peacekeeping and enforcement. The operation involved a move from a humanitarian operation and Cold War type peacekeeping to an experiment in 'peace-enforcement'. However, the latter proved to be an ill-defined concept which became confused with the much broader concept of enforcement under Article 42 of the UN Charter. This case study, 'UNOSOM' (United Nations Operation in Somalia), covers the sequential operations UNOSOM I (July 1992–May 1993), UNITAF (United Nations Task Force, December 1992–May 1993), and UNOSOM II (May 1993–March 1995).

Historical background

Unlike in other African states, the problems of Somalia were not 'ethnic' in origin. In the general 'Somali' area, there was perhaps the most homogeneous ethnic community in a single place in the African continent. Almost the entire population were Sunni Muslims: Somalis spoke the same language and shared common customs, traditions and cultures. Of the population estimated in 1992 to be 6.5 million, 98.9 per cent were ethnically Somali. Despite this homogeneity, Somalis did not identify with other Somalis regardless of origin but differentiated themselves according to their patrilineal genealogical origins.[2] These clans further divided into sub-clans and eventually immediate families. With such complete fragmentation, it is hardly surprising that Somalia should have descended into the perpetual and internecine violence of the kind that characterised 1991 and which led to UN intervention.

A military coup by General Siad Barre in 1969 had temporarily stabilised the regional conflict. However, it also involved Somalia more deeply in Cold War rivalries, resulting in the regime having access to plentiful and relatively sophisticated military supplies. In 1977 Djibouti's independence from France triggered a Somali–Ethiopian struggle for control of the disputed Ogaden region (See Map 5.1). The outcome was a crushing military defeat for Somalia which had two interlocking consequences: (1) it burdened the country with a seemingly permanent refugee problem, and (2) Barre was quickly faced by an insurrection of northern clans in the former British protectorate and north east. The first development helped create an economy of dependence on humanitarian aid and the second tied the country into a pattern of regional and global rivalries that would continue until the end of the Cold War.[3] Defeat at the hands of Ethiopia led to an upsurge of clan antagonisms as each group sought scapegoats to explain the failure. And when an abortive army coup in 1978 brought armed insurrection to the north east and north west, the US and its Western allies, especially Italy (which until 1960 controlled part of the country), added to the problem by providing equipment to what remained of Barre's Soviet arsenals.[4] The pressure of human rights activists on Western governments appalled at the suppression of northern dissidence, led to the virtual cessation of aid by 1990, by which time the area under Barre's control hardly extended beyond Mogadishu. When the dictator was finally dislodged by clans led by General Farah Aideed, the country had disintegrated into traditional clan segments.

Barre's defeat in June 1991 accelerated the disintegration of Somalia for several reasons. First, the opposition parties had only one objective in common, the defeat of the dictator. Second, when Barre was overthrown, power was immediately assumed by the Hawiye clan who had only entered the anti-Barre struggle shortly before his downfall. Having ousted Barre, the Hawiye leaders, Aideed and Ali Mahdi, could not agree on how to share power. The conflict which ensued split Mogadishu into two armed camps, quickly engulfing the city in a protracted blood bath. Aideed and Ali Mahdi continued to fight each other fiercely through 1991 and 1992 and this struggle in effect unravelled the last shreds of the Somali social fabric. Between November 1991 and March 1992, war accounted for approximately 30,000 deaths and 27,000 wounded. By June 1992, 5,000 were dying each day, 1.5 million were on the brink of death, and 4.5 million were nearing starvation. There

Source: Map No. 3710, United Nations, October 1992
Reprinted with permission of the Cartographic Unit, United Nations

Map 5.1 Somalia and UNOSOM: deployment as of October 1992
Source: UN Cartographic Section (Map No. 3710)

were no basic services such as electricity, communication, transportation or health facilities. Only 15 hospitals remained partially operational and these were entirely dependent on external assistance. War also devastated farming areas, and a two year old drought severely compounded this situation.[5]

The international response to this crisis was slow and fragmented.[6] This alienated Somalis and turned them against the UN even before the peacekeepers' arrival. In the successive battles into which Mogadishu descended after Barre's defeat, foreign embassies and most agencies, including the UN, abandoned southern Somalia to its fate. Alex De Waal describes the response of the UN agencies and bilateral institutions as 'straightforward – they withdrew and did nothing'.[7] In March 1992, a ceasefire between Ali Madhi and Aideed made possible the resumption of humanitarian relief. However, fighting and looting by various factions seeking to control ports and distribution routes greatly reduced the effectiveness of aid deliveries. Factions levied heavy taxes on cargoes and charged exorbitantly for providing relief agencies with armed escorts to protect food deliveries. Foreign NGOs were consequently trapped in a web of protection rackets.[8]

The power of the few NGOs that had remained after the 1991 crisis was magnified by the international media. Foreign journalists who visited Somalia stayed with the aid agencies, accepted their analyses and prognoses and in turn quoted them at length and gave them enormous publicity. The symbiotic relationship between the Western media and its favourite aid agencies became even closer and some journalists admitted that they deliberately selected their pictures so as to exaggerate the human degradation in the feeding centres. Significantly in the light of America's subsequent involvement, it was CARE-US which led the calls for military intervention. The stated rationale was not that the intervention would serve Somalia, but that it would serve the CARE-WFP relief programme.[9]

In trying to push Somalia onto the international agenda, the UN Secretary General faced an uphill struggle. The initiative was his, not that of member states, who were largely preoccupied with problems elsewhere, such as the Balkans. There was also the question of what form UN action should take. The situation in Somalia was markedly different to that experienced in earlier operations. There were no precedents for deploying UN forces on a humanitarian rather than a peacekeeping mission where there was no government with which to negotiate and where the practical decision, therefore, was always going to be whether to appease those with power on the ground or oppose them with force.[10] Meanwhile, the Security Council had in late February 1992 approved the ambitious operation in Cambodia (UNTAC): Croatia was in turmoil and Bosnia was about to dominate the international agenda.[11]

UNOSOM I

UNOSOM I was a 'traditional peacekeeping' mission. Although it was realised by the UN that the civil war was a significant cause of the famine, the organisation did not assume any direct responsibility for ending the fighting or resolving the political impasse. UNOSOM I operated within the context of a ceasefire agreement between Mahdi and Aideed and covered the Mogadishu area only.[12] Under Security Council Resolution 751 (April 1992) (See Appendix N), 50 military observers were to be deployed to monitor the ceasefire and to provide security for a humanitarian operation. The strategy was not to marginalise the Somali de facto leaders, but to take them along so that, although the need to engage international military personnel to provide security for relief operations was an objective, their deployment could not take place until August 1992 when the consent of the de facto political leaders was given.[13]

In addition to the military observers, the Secretary General envisaged a force of just 500 infantry soldiers to escort deliveries of humanitarian supplies and to provide security for personnel and supplies. Far from being a new world order type operation, this was a reversion to the practice of employing minimal resources and hoping that the problem would sort itself out. The Secretariat and the Security Council seemed not to be unduly concerned about the planning of the proposed mission. The decision to send the 500 was taken without consultation either with Aideed or Mahmoud Sahnoun, the Secretary-General's representative, and even before these troops had arrived, a further 3,000 troops were approved by the UN.[14] But without Aideed's cooperation, the deployment of the 500 was doomed to failure. The situation, Sahnoun later claimed, could have been markedly different had UN HQ acted more effectively and decisively. He claimed that whatever their earlier differences, all the Somali leaders had consented to working with the UN for a comprehensive solution. Ali Mahdi had agreed that he would resign as acting president as soon as the UN announced a date for a meeting with other Somali leaders. Also, by mid-October all faction leaders and community elders had given their assent to a conference on national reconciliation.[15]

Unfortunately, serious problems were created by UN management at Headquarters and by some agencies' representatives in the field. First, despite significant contributions from donor states, UN agencies were unable to provide relief on the scale seen in Ethiopia in the early 1980s. Second, by centralising everything in Mogadishu, the UN gave Aideed and his allies considerable leverage and undermined efforts to organise structures in the local communities. Third, there was the reluctance of most agencies to cooperate with Sahnoun. He had proposed monetisation of a reasonable percentage of food delivery to encourage cooperation of the local merchants who were prepared to use their influence to limit the activities of looters and militia leaders.[16] The agencies rejected this proposal. Fourth, Sahnoun further argued that had the 500 Pakistani peacekeepers been deployed before September, this would have made a significant difference. The delay in their arrival (they arrived in October) he attributed to bureaucratic factors.[17] Finally and arguably most significantly, there was the UN's failure to investigate the crash in July 1992 of a Russian plane with UN markings leased to the World Food Programme (WFP). This plane had apparently delivered arms and military equipment to Ali Mahdi. Such flights were in contravention of SC Resolution 733 of 23 January 1992 which imposed a general embargo on all deliveries of weapons and military equipment to Somalia. UN inaction over these flights rekindled the old perception of many Somalis that the organisation was biased in favour of Ali Mahdi. In particular, it infuriated Aideed.[18] UNOSOM I proved incapable of meeting the challenge it faced due to its small size and the limited scope of its mandate. The Pakistanis could not leave the harbour and airport of Mogadishu due to the lack of consent of the de facto political authorities.[19] The proposed extra 3,000 troops never arrived but it was unlikely that their arrival in the prevailing circumstances would have made any fundamental difference to the security of humanitarian activities. The overall flaw of UNOSOM I was the UN's failure to address the fundamental problem, namely collapse of state authority. The UN had behaved towards the factions as it would with sovereign governments. Thrust into a situation of virtual anarchy, the lightly armed UN troops thus became hostages not peacekeepers.

UNITAF (United Nations Unified Task Force)

By November 1992, the two principle problems in Somalia were perceived at the UN to be famine and weapons. A WFP cargo ship was shelled and the Pakistani troops at the airport came under heavy fire from Aideed's forces. The Security Council and Secretary-General agreed the situation had become intolerable and that resort to force under Chapter VII to deliver humanitarian assistance should be considered. On 25 November, the US Secretary of State, Lawrence Eagleburger, informed Boutros-Ghali of the readiness of the US to 'take the lead' in an enforcement operation. This decision was taken by the National Security Council because of the scale of human disaster and the realisation that the US was the only nation perceived by Somalis and by the regional states as being in a position to maintain neutrality and with the ability to launch the necessary large scale aid operations . The Pentagon was also among the bodies calling for intervention but only because it saw institutional advantages and new expanded roles at a time when budgets were being cut. Further, there was also the fact that George Bush, architect of the 'new world order' having lost the presidential election, and no longer constrained by domestic considerations, wanted to do 'a last good thing'.[20]

On 25 November 1992, the Secretary-General proposed five options to the Security Council. First, continue and intensify efforts to deploy UNOSOM I in accordance with its existing mandate and authorised strength. This he dismissed as inadequate. The second option, complete withdrawal of military assistance, was rejected. The third option, 'a show of force' in Mogadishu raised questions as to the UN's will, the kind and degree of force and the tenure of its presence. The fourth option was a countrywide enforcement action authorised by the Security Council under Chapter VII; the fifth option, an operation to be commanded and controlled by the UN.[21] While the Secretary-General would have preferred this fifth option, he conceded that the UN did not have the capability to command and control an enforcement operation of the size required.[22] However, the fourth option could be taken by member states responsible directly to the Security Council. In this regard, he mentioned the US offer to organise and lead such an operation. He emphasised that unlike the Gulf operation, enforcement by member states in this instance would have to be defined and limited in time in order to return to

112

peacekeeping and to another concept from *An Agenda for Peace*, namely 'post-conflict peace-building'. On 3 December 1992, the Security Council adopted Resolution 794 (Appendix O) which explicitly authorised the Secretary-General, the US and other troop-contributing countries to 'use all necessary means to establish a secure environment for humanitarian relief operations in Somalia'.[23] The UN was able to organise broad international support (including that of China) and so legitimise the operation, but it was to be the Americans who would impose peace on the warring factions.[24] There was however, disagreement as to the precise form and direction of the intervention.

As SC Resolution 794 was being drafted, the Secretary-General began urging that the coalition disarm the Somali factions before handing the operation back to the UN. The US however, declined to make any such commitment. Bush wrote to the Secretary-General: 'I want to emphasise that the mission of the coalition is limited and specific objectives can be met in the near term and as soon as they are, the coalition force will depart, transferring its function to the UN force.'[25] He did not define 'specific objectives'. In addition to the Pakistani forces already committed, support for the Americans was to be provided by twenty other contingents of various sizes and specialised functions. Under 'Operation Restore Hope', the US was to provide 28,000 troops and UNITAF ended up with 37,000 troops when at full strength (see Table 2.1). The deployment plan focused on the worst areas of famine and was constrained by Bush's pledge to have troops home by January 1993.[26] The first US units arrived in Mogadishu on 9 December and were joined by the French Foreign Legion and later Belgian, Canadian, Egyptian, Italian, Saudi Arabian and Turkish forces. With their arrival, Somali armed groups left Mogadishu, this move serving to spread the conflict to the regions.[27]

The operation was directed by US diplomat, Robert Oakley (Former US Ambassador to Somalia) whose task was that of coordinating the work of UNITAF with that of UNOSOM, now led by Iraqi diplomat, Ismat Kettani, Sahnoun's replacement as SRSG. One of the main tensions arose from UN pressure for UNITAF to enlarge its role to include disarmament and thus aid the process of negotiation and reconciliation among the main parties. The Americans however, conscious of the spectre of Vietnam, were anxious to stress the limited and short term character of their intervention. They feared 'mission creep'.[28]

After a few weeks UNITAF succeeded in opening up supply routes and getting food through to most of the needy areas. When Aideed and Ali Mahdi realised that American intervention was inevitable, both sides welcomed the new force and attempted to extract advantage from it for themselves. This guarded acceptance of the Americans was not surprising, both Aideed and Ali Mahdi had strong links with the US. In the weeks which followed, heavy weapons and military trucks disappeared from the streets; some were hidden locally, others moved to the interior. Many of the citizens saw the Americans as saviours who could restore normal life and rebuild their country. Outside Mogadishu, the US military pressure enabled local elders previously threatened by rival militias to regain some of their traditional authority.[29]

Despite the operation's achievements, it was to encounter major criticism from some NGOs; the London-based African Rights claimed that there was no real need for the military intervention in the first place, arguing that the obstacles to food delivery were not as bad as commonly assumed. The claim by SRSG Kettani that 70–80 per cent of the food was failing to reach the hungry was rejected not only by African Rights, but also by WFP and Medecines Sans Frontieres (MSF). More important, however, was the criticism that UNITAF had missed the opportunity which was perceived to exist for the disarming of warring factions and gangs.[30] While some of the population expected UNITAF to disarm the gunmen, as time went by, Somalis placed less hope in the UN and the gunmen became more confident.[31]

The issue of disarmament which became the subject of major dispute between the Secretary-General and the Americans arose from the differing interpretations of what constituted a 'secure environment for humanitarian aid'. Did it mean protecting corridors for delivery of food supplies or the wider task of creating secure conditions in which the UN could freely operate? Achievement of the latter would require a willingness on the part of the Americans to address the root cause of anarchy. They did not see this as their task and called upon the UN to deploy a strong enough force to protect humanitarian activities under the existing security conditions. But the Secretary-General was quick to point out that this was to misunderstand the capacity of the UN to manage or finance such a force.[32]

The attitude of Aideed to both parties at this time was particularly significant. He perceived Boutros-Ghali as having a hidden agenda, that of seeking to make Somalia a UN trusteeship and of wishing to restore Barre. He claimed to have accepted UNITAF because of the humanitarian needs and because he believed the US had no colonial interests in Somalia.[33] The Somali attitude was reflected in the positive reception accorded to Bush on a visit on New Year's Eve and the hostile reception accorded Boutros-Ghali on a visit to Mogadishu some days later.[34] The Secretary-General did succeed in arranging a peace conference in Addis Ababa in January 1993 at which agreement in principle on a ceasefire was reached.[35] However, a marked hardening of Somali feeling towards international intervention followed the arrival of the new US administration. Whereas Bush feared involvement in a civil war, the Clinton Administration seemed more receptive to calls from the Secretary-General for more resolute action by UNITAF. The confidence of Aideed was lost when he perceived that the US was at least cooperating with the UN. This turned him against the US and the opportunity for disarmament by agreement was lost.

Failure to do more to disarm the warlords could be viewed as tragic because a concentrated effort to remove and destroy heavy weapons would have sent a message that the US/UN meant business. Instead, in attempting to avoid possible confrontation with the militias and in seeking to appear impartial, the US/UN force ended up enhancing the roles and status of the warlords. The third UN coordination meeting in Addis Ababa in March 1993 was attended by a wide range of Somali peace groups who stressed the urgent need for improved security. The agreement, signed on 27 March by the leading warlords and representatives of assorted clan movements, committed their organisations to complete disarmament and urged that UNITAF/UNOSOM apply 'strong and effective sanctions against those responsible for any violation of a ceasefire agreement of January 1993'.[36]

Arising from an understandable desire to cobble together a Somali government as soon as possible, the agreement also provided for the establishment over two years of a transitional system of governance. This included a Transitional National Council (TNC) with representatives from the 18 regions where regional and district councils would be established. However, it was characteristic of UN policy at the time that the aspirations of some of the regional leaders were allowed to go unrecognised.[37] Also, the momentum towards an effective settlement was lost with the departure of the large American force. The Americans, in trying to get in and out of Somalia as quickly as possible, had simply postponed the problems that logically followed from intervention.

UNOSOM II

Security Council Resolution 814 of 26 March 1993, made Somalia in effect a testing ground for new peacekeeping ideas. The resolution mandated the peacekeeping force to protect humanitarian supplies and personnel. But unlike UNITAF whose participation in the disarmament process was subsidiary, UNOSOM II was mandated to disarm Somali militias under Chapter VII of the Charter. It also contained a 'nation-building' element as well as ensuring security throughout the country (UNITAF covered only 40 per cent).[38] UNOSOM II was the first peace-keeping operation in UN history to be given a mandate to use force, not merely in self-defence but in pursuit of its mission. Contingents were to operate in a traditional peacekeeping fashion when use of force was not required. They were authorised however to act as 'peace enforcement units' in situations where the use of force was required for them to carry out their mission.[39]

The mandate of UNOSOM II was not enforcement in the manner of reversing acts of international aggression. It was seen as 'peace-enforcement' which was something less, but exactly what, was not clear. The term 'peace-enforcement' which was referred to in Paragraph 44 of Boutros-Ghali's *An Agenda for Peace* was a proposal, not so much for a concept but rather a mechanism, namely 'peace-enforcement units'. This was intended to distinguish them from the forces envisioned in Article 43 of the Charter. The units were to be available on call, undergo advance training, and be deployed under the authority of the Security Council and commanded by the Secretary-General.[40] However, no such units were established and when UNOSOM II commenced operation, the force was just a collection of assorted national contingents, some well equipped, some not so.

Months before the commencement of the mission, the US administration and the Secretary-General indicated that they had widely differing perceptions of the objective of the proposed force. At meetings between the US Secretary of State, Lawrence Eagleburger and Boutros-Ghali in December 1992, the US indicated that on the handover of UNITAF to UNOSOM II it was prepared to entertain specific requests for logistical support but no more. No discussion of nation-building or anything remotely like it took place. There was however, considerable discussion of what UNOSOM II would look like.[41] The Secretariat, according to Bolton, 'foresaw something very like a traditional small-scale UN peacekeeping operation'. However, US Department of Defence officials believed that such an approach would not work and wanted a much more muscular operation.[42] This presentation of the Secretariat's position is difficult to accept since this was a Chapter VII operation. But the failure of the Americans to appreciate the difficulties of the undertaking was unsurprising given the American Administration's unfamiliarity with the nature of UN operations (see below). What is clear however, is that both parties had widely divergent views on the purpose and nature of the operation and on who would provide the 'muscle'.

From its peak in mid-January of 25,800, the US contingent dropped by the end of February to 16,000, while non-US troops increased from 10,000 to 15,000.[43] The US did not want to maintain its forces. The UN on the other hand, needed American participation in UNOSOM II for continuing logistical support and military muscle, should this be required.[44] With the passing of SC Resolution 814, the US appeared to change its attitude to involvement. The new administration's Permanent Representative to the UN, Madeline Albright, declared: 'With this resolution, we will embark on an unprecedented enterprise aimed at nothing less than the restoration of an entire country.'[45] This smacked of President Bush's 'new world order' and American prestige was now invested in the operation. In these circumstances, both the transition to a UN command and its organisation and leadership were of importance to the Americans.[46]

The Secretary-General calculated that if the operation was headed by an American, this would guarantee strong US support. Such an appointment would also be necessary if, as planned, a US force was to serve for the first time under UN command. The arrangement reached gave military command to Turkish General Cevik Bir but Kettani was replaced as SRSG by US Admiral Jonathan Howe who had served as a security adviser to President Bush. Resolution 814 provided for a multinational force of 20,000 peacekeeping troops, 5,000 logistical support staff and 3,000 civilian personnel.[47] To indicate its support, the US undertook to provide as required a tactical Quick Reaction Force (QRF). Numerically the American presence had been greatly reduced but this arrangement gave UNOSOM II a strongly American orientation which when the UN forces became embroiled in fighting, made it difficult to decide whether the Pentagon or the Secretary-General was making the vital decisions.

In March 1993, the Secretary-General noted that the effort undertaken by UNITAF to establish a secure environment in Somalia was far from complete and that the threat to international peace and security still existed. In these circumstances, UNOSOM II had little option but to move beyond humanitarian concerns and address the issues of institution-building and reconstruction.[48] Since any such moves represented a threat to the authority of the warlords, it was inevitable that a confrontation between UNOSOM II and the Somali factions, whether over ceasefire violations or disarmament matters, would occur.[49]

The growing tension between UNOSOM II and Aideed's Somali National Alliance (SNA) was reflected in the increasingly anti-UN broadcasts of Radio Mogadishu, controlled by Aideed. (Radio Mogadishu was a particularly important propaganda tool since 70 per cent of Somalis were illiterate.) Concerned at the propaganda campaign which accused UNOSOM II and the US of being aggressive and trying to colonise Somalia, Force HQ in mid-May instructed the Pakistani brigade to shut down or effectively silence Radio Mogadishu. The Pakistanis argued that they did not have the expertise to handle such a task. The suggestion that the US supply the experts was not acted upon.[50] On 5 June 1993, UNOSOM II decided to inspect five authorised weapon storage sites (AWSS) in Mogadishu. This they were entitled to do under their mandate, and the Pakistani brigade deployed a large enough force to indicate that they would use force if necessary. Since Radio Mogadishu was located in one of the AWSS, it was decided that during the weapons inspection, US Special forces would make a survey of the radio equipment. The Somalis were notified twelve hours in advance and replied that any such inspection would lead to war.[51] In the course of carrying out their 'inspections', the Pakistani forces came under attack and in the ensuing battle, 24 Pakistani soldiers were killed and 35 Somalis, including women and children, also died in the confrontation.[52] Instead of holding an independent legal inquiry and seeking to marginalise Aideed politically, the Security Council effectively declared war on him by passing SC Resolution 837 on 6 June. The Resolution blamed the SNA for inciting the attacks on the Pakistanis and authorised the force to take all necessary measures against all those responsible for the armed attacks.[53]

With this very explicit Resolution, obviously intended to step up the UN's authority, UNOSOM II ceased to be a 'peacekeeping' force. Passage of the Resolution also turned the spotlight on the role of the US forces. The mission to 'go after' Aideed was clearly beyond the capabilities of other UNOSOM II forces and the QRF (1,150 men) augmented with more helicopters and gunships (converted transport planes armed with cannons), spearheaded the hunt. The QRF was joined in late August by a 400 strong Ranger task force[54] and Resolution 837 led to a virtual war situation between UNOSOM II and the SNA as the two sides attacked each other over a period of four months. In June, UNOSOM II conducted aerial attacks and ground searches of SNA leaders' residences. In early July, the SNA retaliated with increased attacks on UN forces using a variety of weapons including rocket propelled grenades.[55] The denouement came on 3 October when Aideed's forces succeeded in shooting down two helicopters, capturing an American airman and inflicting serious casualties on US and UN personnel (18 US and 1 Malaysian soldier were killed; 78 US, 9 Malaysian and 3 Pakistanis were wounded; 300–500 Somalis were killed).[56] The CNN factor which had led to US involvement in Somalia also ended it when the images were broadcast of an American soldier's body being dragged through the streets of Mogadishu. The single question posed by US Senators Dole and Byrd was 'why are we there'?[57]

The public outcry forced President Clinton to announce on 7 October that all US forces would leave Somalia by 31 March, 1994; the Belgians, French and Italians announced their intention to withdraw in early 1994.[58] Withdrawing with honour, the Americans believed would require in the short run military reinforcements and a change in political direction. To meet the first requirement, Clinton announced the sending of additional troops and naval forces and re-appointed Oakley in order to secure the release of US prisoners. Oakley's return was welcomed by Aideed who, Resolution 837 notwithstanding, was reintroduced as a participant in unfolding political discussions.

The proposed US withdrawal was roughly 'in sync' with the UN timetable for establishing the TNC proposed at Addis Ababa. By the end of March 1994, an agreement was signed by Aideed and Al Mahdi forswearing violence and urging general disarmament as a precondition for reconstruction and set the date (15 May 1994) when an interim government was to be formed.[59] However, no real progress was made towards disarmament or division of power in an interim administration. SC Resolution 897 revised UNOSOM II's mandate from peace-enforcement to peacekeeping and envisaged a reduced military establishment (22,000) to be drawn exclusively from the Third World. But, following a succession of confusing messages from 'the field', the Security Council, weary with the deteriorating situation and the clear inability of the faction leaders to reach any effective agreement, announced in September 1994 that the operation would be wound down as soon as possible.[60]

Just as the Pakistani troops of UNOSOM I had been virtual prisoners in the hostile environment into which they arrived in 1992, the last UN troops to leave were kept in a corner by aggressive Somalis. An international operation involving US marines, dubbed 'Operation Abandon Hope' by the *Financial Times*, was required to secure the withdrawal.[61] The warlords' authority remained intact and while mass starvation had ended with the arrival of US troops in December 1992, the prospect of ongoing anarchical conflict raised the spectre of further famine.

Political base

Prior involvement of the great powers

During the Cold War, the Horn of Africa was of considerable strategic importance. It provided a bridge from Africa to Asia and faced directly into the Indian Ocean. The US and Soviet Union, therefore, had a considerable interest in the region. However, it was the actions and decisions of the Somalis themselves which led to superpower involvement in their affairs. Britain's withdrawal from Kenya and British Swaziland in the early 1960s revived a long-standing dispute over border territories including the Ogaden. Conscious of Ethiopia's military strength, Somalia turned for help first to the US, but Washington declined to provide equipment that might be used against Ethiopia, at that time ruled by Haile Selassie. The Soviet Union was then approached and the Soviets, concerned about possible

American or Chinese influence in the Horn, sought to mediate. After talks in Khartoum, hostilities were suspended but the underlying problem remained unresolved.[62]

While Somalia had initially got little help or encouragement from Moscow, a relationship was established which in time provided Somalia with a powerful air force and armoured strike force. By 1977 some 2,400 Somali military personnel had been sent to the Soviet Union for training, more than from any other African state.[63] France and Britain, as former colonial powers in the region, were concerned at increasing Soviet influence in the Indian Ocean, but were relatively powerless to prevent it. The US meanwhile had established influence and bases in Ethiopia.[64] A remarkable realignment followed the overthrow of Haile Selassie in 1973 by Colonel Haile Mengistu. Mengistu sought military help from the Soviets and Cuba, and in 1977 thrashed the Somalis in the Ogaden. By mid-1977, Somali overtures for a military relationship with the West had begun.[65] Somalia was switched by these events from Russia to American protectorship, but continued to be a sharply divided country. Meanwhile, Mengistu's government was being drained by conflicts in Eritrea and Tigre. The peoples of the region were enduring not only the horrors of seemingly endless wars but famines so deadly as to create news headlines around the world. As the Cold War receded, the superpowers found themselves at one in wishing to end the wars.[66]

Initial position of the Great Powers

In the period 1990 to 1992, Somalia was well down the list in terms of international priorities. Britain and France were preoccupied with the Maastricht Treaty and the Gulf War. Events in the Gulf and the aftermath were America's major concern. There was a general consciousness of the ongoing decline of the Soviet Union and the possible consequences of this development. In early 1992, the taking of firm action in Somalia was not an issue. The US was so reluctant to face Congress on the issue of a UN presence that it had to be persuaded by the other members of the Council to allow the observer mission to be paid for out of assessed rather than voluntary contributions.[67] The State Department's argument that Congress would not consider another peacekeeping mission at this time was only overcome by Senator Nancy Kassebaum's visit to the region in mid-1992 and subsequent public advocacy of armed protection for UN workers and urgently needed food shipments.[68]

US reasons for eventual involvement largely related to President Bush's perception of America's role after the Gulf War. In proposing action, Bush was responding to American television viewers who saw starving Somali children and Somali gunmen stealing food before it reached its appointed destination. Having just beaten Saddam Hussein, the Americans thought they knew how to deal with those whom they saw as bullies. In a speech to the General Assembly in September 1992, Bush outlined a US commitment to UN operations and US intentions had been indicated by US involvement in the precedent-setting UN operation in

Northern Iraq in early 1991 to protect the rebellious Kurds from Saddam Hussein. The frustration of the US with its inability to prevent ethnic cleansing in Bosnia, much of it directed against Muslims, added to the incentives for helping the Muslims in Somalia. Boutros-Ghali had also told Bush that there was a growing perception in the Third World that the US was using the UN to legitimise military action only when it served American interests. Gradually, opinion in Congress and among the public swung in favour of US intervention.[69]

It is indicative of the general mood of the period that SC Resolution 794 empowering UNITAF should have gained the total support of the Council including China and a number of African members who in the aftermath of the Gulf operation had expressed their suspicions that the West might use humanitarian arguments to mask their interference in the domestic affairs of other states. China explained its apparent change of heart by describing UNITAF as 'an exceptional action under the unique situation'.[70] The Security Council asserted its authority through monitoring and reporting procedures. It also emphasised the limited nature of the mandate for UNOSOM and UNITAF's withdrawal. The unanimity of the Council and the pledge of troops from over twenty countries established the overwhelming support for the operation. However, the actions and utterances of both the Bush and the Clinton administrations revealed extraordinary uncertainty as to UNITAF's function.

Although the mission was, in Bush's term, 'humanitarian', he employed numbers (28,000) which far exceeded what many on the ground believed was required to guard the relief convoys. The American numbers were in accordance with the 'Powell Doctrine' which dictated that any force deployed by the US ought to be sufficiently large to be able to overwhelm any potential opponents.[71] Since UN members had failed to come up with the additional 3,000 promised to UNOSOM I, the US contribution was to be welcomed. But deployment of such a large and well-equipped military force could only encourage speculation as to its ultimate purpose. Confusion was increased by the foreign policy declarations of the incoming administration.

Clinton, committed to reversing the Bush administration's foreign policy, had promised a policy of 'assertive multilateralism'. This, Secretary of State Madeleine Albright defined as a 'broader strategy on multilateral forums that projects our leadership where it counts'.[72] The UN, which she described as 'one of the collective bodies that increasingly steer the course of world politics'[73] was to be the chief vehicle for the conduct of assertive multiaterism. But despite these encouraging words, the US began to press for a rapid handover to UNOSOM II. American anxiety to pass the problem back to the UN appeared to support the belief that the Americans wished to use the organisation rather than be committed members of the UN. However, the Clinton administration's policy statements at this time also betrayed what Mats Berdal calls 'a simplistic set of beliefs about the nature of conflict in the post-Cold War international system'.[74] Albright in particular was to reveal an extraordinary lack of knowledge of UN operations. In June 1993, she declared her surprise at finding that when a peacekeeping operation was launched,

120

it started from scratch. She also noted a number of problems unique to peacekeeping including the absence of contingency planning, prior knowledge of available forces, lack of centralised command and control capabilities, improvised lift arrangements and complex procurement systems.[75] She clearly failed to realise that it was the presence of American forces and the attendant reduction in the operational problems listed above which had led states unwilling to join UNOSOM I to participate in UNITAF.

It is worth noting that American policy in Somalia at this time was similar to that in Bosnia. When the US administration's Bosnian policy was unveiled in February 1993, it also represented a retreat from earlier promises. At no time was there enthusiasm for direct involvement on the ground.[76] American policy was an attempt to reconcile two contradictory aspirations; demonstrating resolve while seeking to avoid measures that would place American lives at risk. What then were the tasks presented in the assorted mandates?

The mandate

Somalia was a multidimensional problem requiring a clear mission strategy and plan of action which integrated all the relevant dimensions: humanitarian, political and security. However, at the time the Somali operation commenced, the Secretariat had scant military expertise to help in making a proper assessment upon which proposed actions could be based. The technical team sent to Somalia to determine the needs of UNOSOM I was composed of officers drawn from other peacekeeping operations. On completion of their report, they returned to their normal duties and were not available for consultations.[77] This inadequate assessment of the security situation led to a total underestimation of the task facing all elements of the UN effort.

UNOSOM I

UNOSOM I was accepted by the UN Commission of Inquiry of February 1994 as having been incapable of meeting the challenge it faced, due to its small size and the limited scope of its mandate.[78] That mandate, namely protecting UN personnel and supplies and escorting humanitarian supplies, implicitly accepted not just the possibility of armed attack by Somalis, but the possibility that the Force might have to be deployed between factions. By sending in peacekeepers, the organisation was in accordance with Security Council Resolution 751 (1992), facilitating 'an immediate and effective cessation of hostilities and the maintenance of a cease-fire throughout the country'. Even assuming agreement by the Somali parties to cessation of hostilities, maintenance of a countrywide ceasefire would have required the presence of considerably more than the proposed 3,500 troops. Moreover, any attempt to keep the elements apart would have merely cemented the divisions.

Even for the 'protection' tasks, the resources provided were grossly inadequate. The force of 500 envisioned by the Secretary General was entirely unrealistic given the very conditions he described to justify the security force. (The German contingent of UNOSOM II which numbered 1,700, although this was a logistical unit, took some 83 per cent of its force to maintain its own livelihood in Somalia, leaving only 17 per cent of the contingent to do its establishment job.)[79] SC Resolution 775 of 28 August 1992 had stipulated that the UN would have to work with the Somali factions and 'authorities'. However, while this sounded good diplomatically, in practice its fulfilment was difficult since it gave the warring parties a veto over the operation. It was largely because of frustration with the parties that Boutros-Ghali decided to seek a larger military intervention with or without the consent of the parties.[80]

UNITAF

In contrast to UNOSOM I, UNITAF appeared to possess sufficient resources in terms of men and equipment to discharge its mandate. But discharging that mandate depended upon interpretation and UNITAF did not interpret its mandate as requiring it to enforce disarmament of the Somali militias.[81] Under the terms of the Addis Ababa agreements of 8 and 15 January, 1993 the political movements implemented the ceasefire and disarmament arrangements on a voluntary and cooperative basis. UNITAF did conduct occasional weapons searches and confiscations independently of the agreements but these did not form any part of a comprehensive disarmament plan.[82] The Secretary-General argued that the coalition should not withdraw before controlling weapons and disarming lawless groups: 'Without this action, I do not believe it will be possible to establish the secure environment called for in the Security Council or to create conditions in which the UN's existing efforts to promote national reconciliation can be carried forward.'[83] However, US participation depended on the potential for results in a limited period.

But was disarmament ever really within UNITAF capabilities? This is difficult to determine. Chopra, Eknes, and Nordboe argue that if Boutros-Ghali's demands made any sense, 'it was with regard to their timing, since at that time there was a unique window of opportunity'.[84] Aideed had been intransigent prior to the arrival of UNITAF; his acceptance of its presence meant that this was the best chance to convince his forces or the majority of Somalis to disarm. US strength evoked a mixture of fear and confidence.[85] But to have availed of the 'window of opportunity', US forces would have had to be prepared to commence disarming the Somalis as soon as they landed. This would have required a decision taken in November; arguing about it in December was pointless. In this, as in previous peacekeeping operations, there had been a marked lack of planning.

A complete disarmament operation would have required enormous effort and resources since for it to be effective, there would have been a need to seal off all borders by air, sea and land in cooperation with other states. There was also the problem that to have disarmed any one part of the state would have made it susceptible to attack by neighbouring states. The UN might even have had to provide protection for Somalia for a period of years. As it was, some weapons had to be returned to individuals who needed them for protection in a hostile environment.[86] It could be argued that successful disarmament did not require the removal of every weapon in the country. In theory, a measure of disarmament would have weakened the warlords, forcing them to resort to politics rather than relying on the gun. However, an overall strategy was not explicit in the UNITAF mandate. The idea that a UN Secretary-General should propose disarming militias within a sovereign state represented a dramatic turnabout in principle since the Congo. Arguably, there was a general perception that Somalia was 'a special case'. But who was to decide and where was this erosion of sovereignty to end? The proposal was just a further manifestation of how the UN had wandered into a conceptual void.

UNOSOM II

UNOSOM II's mandate did suggest an overall strategy. However, attempting to combine 'broad based consultations' with demands that the Somali people comply fully with the commitments to disarmament, merely created confusion as to the UN's intent. Farrell notes: 'If the Security Council was serious about disarming the Somali warlords, then all attempts at maintaining consent for and the impartiality of UNOSOM II ought to have been dropped at this stage and the force should have been planned and equipped for a military campaign.'[87] In the event, it was not.

The UN Commission of Inquiry in February 1994 accepted that disarmament of the militias be abandoned: it also recommended that the UN should not insist on a particular formula for the resolution of the Somali conflict but should, within the framework of the Charter, assist all Somali political movements to reach consensus on political institutions of government.[88] This seemed to accord with Aideed's ideal of autonomous democracy. He wrote (in 1993): 'After the fair elections . . . a truly national government should be formed by inviting members from all the national parties and not just by the members of the majority party . . . the idea of inviting members from all the national parties should satisfy all voters no matter which party one has voted for.'[89] Given the problems of a 'winner takes all' form of democracy, the proposal had a certain plausibility. However, it would ensure that regardless of who won an election, Aideed would be part of the government. Would this have been acceptable to other Somali leaders? There were other problems.

Most Somalis under 25 years of age had never experienced democracy; Makinda observes 'people who have known dictatorial rule and war all their lives, might well negotiate peace in good faith but could easily be tempted to resort to force to realise their goals'.[90] There was, therefore, the need to create a favourable environment for change. The Somali people might have been willing to disarm if there were a working police force. But only some member states provided the equipment and training which they had promised to help establish the proposed force. The Somalis themselves did not, as had been hoped, provide young, enthusiastic recruits, but chose instead safe, accepted locals who were not likely to enforce the law or create controversy.[91] Ultimately, the problem of the linked nation-building and the disarmament mandate was that many who might have been willing to disarm perceived UNOSOM II as too weak to be an effective guarantor.

The decision to move the operation to nation-building revealed a failure on the part of those proposing the move to grasp the political and military ramifications of such an undertaking. Establishment of representative democratic institutions in Somalia was certain to be a long process requiring the cooperation and support of all concerned Somalis and UN member states. If there were to be a transition from anarchy and conflict to order and peace, the operation would first have to secure the reins of power. The Somalis however, had shown no enthusiasm for interference in their affairs and were unlikely to meekly accept imposition of UN authority. Equally, it was highly unlikely that China and other states would support UN assumption of control of the country, even for a limited period. In the event, the UN sought neither to assume fully the reins of power nor to propose what form any new Somali authority should take. UNOSOM II's mandate highlighted yet again the disjunction between the proposals in Security Council resolutions and the ability or willingness of member states to provide the means of implementation.

Political manoeuvres of the Great Powers

The high profile of the US in the Somalia operation underlined that power's status and perceived role in the international system and the UN. No longer was there a rival superpower and the era of the five Great Powers was, apart from their retention of veto power within the Security Council, effectively over. The US role in initiating and leading the Gulf operation had established its dominant military position in the world. Its recourse to the UN for legitimisation of that venture, the statements of Bush and Albright and the UNITAF mission all appeared to indicate that the US was presenting itself as the strong right arm of the UN. Unanimous Security Council support for UNITAF indicated general acceptance that the single remaining superpower should assume that role. Equally, it was convenient for the other former Great Powers to pass the difficult problem of Somalia to the Americans, particularly since the US had been the most recent ally of Somalia's dominant clan leaders. (Both Aideed and Mahdi had been educated in the US and each had a son in the US armed forces, Aideed's son even serving as an interpreter with UNITAF.)[92] This 'passing of the buck' was confirmed in SC Resolution 837 of 6 June 1993, which in effect required the Americans, as the only troops capable of the task, to 'go after' Aideed.

Some members of the US Congress argued that the mission had become militarised on the UN's authority and that the US was responding inappropriately to UN demands. It was the UN, they claimed, that insisted that Aideed be captured. But there is little evidence to support this contention. As Kalowatie Deonanden noted, UN military actions or major policy decisions are virtually never implemented without US consent.[93] All the major SC Resolutions were written, according to William Clarke and Jeffrey Herbst, by US officials mainly in the Pentagon and handed to the UN as faits accompli.[94] The American soldiers in Somalia had done a minimum job with maximum fire power: the bulk of the force had left prematurely without having done enough to uphold even a narrow interpretation of its mandate to create a secure environment.

Operational base

Secretary-General

The Commission of Inquiry set up by the Security Council in October 1993 after the Mogadishu battle in which eighteen American servicemen were killed, concluded that the US and UN had to share the blame with General Aideed for the descent of the humanitarian mission in Somalia into the vicious confrontation in the capital. Aideed was blamed for launching the attack, the US was criticised for operating under a separate military command and for launching raids that were inconsistent with the basic tenets of peacekeeping. The report also questioned the strategy of aggressive peacekeeping adopted by the UN under Boutros-Ghali.[95] But just how fair was it to apportion blame to the Secretary-General for the debacles of Mogadishu and for the general failure of the UN to sort out the mess in Somalia? Certainly, many of his problems resulted from his pursuit of a more 'active' UN.

Boutros-Ghali's activism surprised the Americans. In the aftermath of Operation Desert Storm and amid talk of a New World Order, the US favoured a more vigorous Secretary-General. One senior US official greeted Boutros-Ghali's election with the comment 'our fear is that he will prove to be a warmed-up version of Pérez de Cuéllar'.[96] Boutros-Ghali however, sought a more assertive UN, arguing that the organisation should have at its disposal a full range of military forces of various types. The hypothesis, according to Maurice Bertrand, was the same as those of 1919 and 1945 that a definite consensus existed among the Great Powers enabling them to constitute a military alliance.[97] However, he then proceeded to alienate rather than woo these powers. In July 1992, he had criticised members of the Security Council for giving what he maintained was undue priority to the situation in Yugoslavia. The Americans were angered at his apparently random choice of 3,500 troops for UNOSOM I. They believed 30,000 to be the required figure, but nevertheless were reluctant to see Somalia used as a test case in the reinterpretation of Chapter VII of the UN Charter.[98] His relationship with Aideed had been poor, even before the mission. This dated from the period of Barre's dictatorship. In an effort to reduce opposition, Barre had appointed opponents to diplomatic posts abroad. Aideed had thus spent a period as Ambassador to India during which he perceived that there were particularly close relations between Barre and the then Egyptian Minister of Foreign Affairs, Boutros-Ghali. He was convinced that Boutros-Ghali was a supporter of Barre.[99] But Boutros-Ghali also clashed with his own appointee and former student colleague, Sahnoun, because he felt the latter as SRSG was hindering his attempts to demonstrate the new interventionist doctrine.[100]

The Secretary-General could be faulted most of all for having failed to learn the built-in limitations of UN peacekeeping. In *An Agenda for Peace*, Boutros-Ghali implied that future peacekeeping operations could be organised without the consent of parties. However, his concept of new style peacekeeping was flawed in that it failed to pay heed to the very real differences of interests and perspectives among states in the international arena, or the very real constraints upon UN action by the many conflicts demanding world attention. Boutros-Ghali was, to a great extent, unfortunate. The failure of the Security Council and General Assembly to function effectively during the Cold War had placed a disproportionate burden on the shoulders of the Secretary-General. The chief executive had come to symbolise as well as represent the UN. He was expected to provide intellectual leadership, managerial ability, negotiating skills and in an age of mass communications, establish a rapport with an international audience. *An Agenda for Peace* was much acclaimed, but member states, Thakur noted, wanted 'excellence within the parameters of political reality'.[101] Boutros-Ghali, reflecting the widespread belief that with a more harmonious Security Council the UN would be enabled to act with greater authority, had sought to capitalise on a perceived goodwill, and assert that authority through enforcement. Unfortunately, mention of enforcement raised fundamental questions. What was to be the ultimate objective of any proposed military action? Would member states be willing to cooperate? Critical to any use of force by the UN was the relationship between the Secretary-General and the US. Poor relations between Boutros-Ghali and the Americans ensured that the task which the Secretary-General set for the mission was an impossible one.

Force Commander

US refusal to accept UN command of its forces undermined the authority of the Force Commander of UNOSOM II and proved disastrous for the operation. US planners felt that UNOSOM II Force Commander General Cevik Bik did not understand how to command such a disparate multinational operation. They claimed that he was not forceful enough in ensuring compliance with the UN mandate. However, when the Commander of the US Force, General Thomas Montgomery, tried to ensure compliance, contingent commanders complained to Bik of US dominance.[102] The question of command had become greatly confused however, not only because of the US attitude, but because of the Secretariat's failure to establish and recognise the nature of UNOSOM II: was it a 'conventional' UN force or a 'coalition'? Before considering the impact of this question on the military command, let us look at these two kinds of force.

Distinguishing between a 'UN operation' and a 'coalition', Chopra, Eknes and Nordboe point out that a 'UN operation' is collectively mandated and controlled. It is an instrument authorised by and in the service of the international community as a whole. It represents something more than the sum of the nations participating in the operation in the field or in the decision-making process. 'Coalition' in contrast refers merely to cooperation and a venture in which more than one nation is participating. It refers most specifically to the US strategy of spreading responsibility in a military venture as used in the Gulf War and then in UNITAF.[103] It is possible for a coalition operation to be a legitimate collective action but only if it is a genuine agent of the UN and mandated by the Security Council or General Assembly. If acting as such, it would fly the UN flag. However, the coalition in Somalia did not 'since the gap between a collective position in law and the operational imperatives of coalition warfare had not been bridged'.[104]

Another distinction between a UN operation and a coalition has to do with the relations between contingents and Force Commander. A critical mistake of the Secretariat in relation to UNOSOM II was to perceive command relations to be the same as in a coalition. This mistake, made through the introduction of OPLAN I, led directly to the fragmentation of the force. In the early stages of the overall operation, the question of command posed no problems. UN Commander General Shaheen worked closely with US Force Commander General Roger Johnston.[105] Good relations with UNITAF were possible because of the 'coalition' format. Since UN states had failed to come up with the additional troops for UNOSOM I, the Security Council accepted and authorised employment of a US force to deputise on its behalf. Contingents operated independently but had the binding influence of the US.[106] It was the transfer of command from the US to the UN which led to problems.

UNOSOM II was not a sub-contract like UNITAF, neither was it an exclusively military operation in design. It represented a move from a sub-contract to an integrated UN operation. The compromise solution separated political control above and military command below to one establishing UN and US command side by side, and while the UN Force Commander remained responsible to the SRSG, each contingent was separately linked to its capital.[107] The problems created by this arrangement were exacerbated by UNOSOM II, OPLAN I which read: 'The relationship between UNOSOM II command and assigned coalition forces will be the same relationship between UNITAF command and these coalition forces' (Figure 5.1).[108] Of enormous significance was the use of the term 'coalition'. Rather than returning UNOSOM II to the UN ideal of an integrated and collective command structure, OPLAN I effectively widened the gap between commander and contingents. However, at the heart of the command problems was the role and attitude of the Americans. The Commander of US forces in Somalia was also Deputy Force Commander, while the US Commander in Chief of Central Command in the United States retained command of all US forces assigned to UNOSOM II. In addition, when directed, the Commander of US forces in Somalia would assume control of the Quick Reaction Force.[109] Thus, while US personnel participated as part of a UN structure, this was always something of a fiction since a US Commander was always in control and ultimate command.

The tribalism resulting from this arrangement was detrimental to operational efficiency. There were always different responses to the Force Commander's orders;

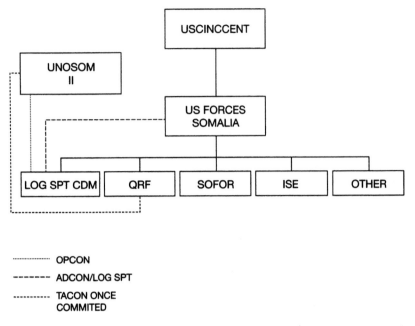

Figure 5.1 UN and US command and control relationships, UNOSOM

some followed his command, others refused to comply, and some contingents complied only after getting approval from their governments. While this insubordination might not be critical in a less complex operation, it proved disastrous in one where unity of command was essential for effective response to quickly evolving situations. The weakness of the command structure and the internal tensions thus created were demonstrated by the incidents of 5 June (Radio Mogadishu incident) and 3 October 1993 (shooting down of US helicopters). The report of the UN Commission gives as reasons for the extent of UN casualties, UNOSOM II's unpreparedness and the special status of the Quick Reaction Force.[110] Answering criticism that Italian tanks were slow in arriving on the scene, the Italian Brigade Commander stated that the order from UNOSOM II Force Headquarters arrived too late but that in any event, responsibility for assisting the Pakistanis rested primarily with the Quick Reaction Force.[111] Whatever the merits of this particular dispute, it was clear according to the UN Commission, that the Force Commander was not in effective control of several national contingents.[112]

American determination to act independently created the second major incident (3 October). While the UN was making every effort to protect its personnel and at the same time searching for Aideed, a force of US Rangers was dispatched to Mogadishu with the special task of capturing Aideed.[113] When some Rangers became trapped, an integrated rescue force had to be organised. In the clash, 18 American soldiers were killed and 78 wounded.[114] The decision to launch the operation was made in Florida (Special Operations Command). The SRSG was not informed and the Force Commander was notified just before its commencement.[115] For as long as they remained members of UNOSOM II Force Headquarters, American officers continued to operate on a dual allegiance basis. They attended conferences with officers from other contributing states but operated from separate offices to which all other contingent officers were denied access.[116] To the problems created by command structure were added those resulting from the presence of many diverse contingents.

Tactical capabilities, contingents

Before looking at some of the contingents, it is worth recalling that Pakistan alone volunteered troops for UNOSOM I.[117] Many governments were cautious and only came to the field when promised protection through the US 'umbrella'. Disagreement about the use of force caused contingents to label themselves 'Chapter VI' or 'Chapter VII' nations: this shorthand was used to differentiate those forces that had come prepared to use force proactively from those that were not prepared to use force, except in self-defence.[118] However, in the circumstances, distinctions were never clear and besides in such an operation where did 'use of force' begin and end?

An African Rights report claimed that troops from all countries used unnecessary strong-arm tactics and that up to 200 Somalis were probably killed by UNITAF. French Legionnaires, Belgian paratroopers, Canadian airborne and Pakistani troops were particularly aggressive. The Belgians managed to create a weapon-free zone in their area but this was achieved through beatings and the shooting of violators. Some were charged with 'colonial barbarism' on their return to Belgium.[119]

In contrast to these contingents, the Italians, one of the former colonial powers, behaved with great sensitivity, mingling with the local population and establishing good relations. So well were they regarded, that Somalis who attacked the Nigerian contingent in September 1993 gave as the reason for the attack, Nigerian failure to act like the Italians. The Italians in turn felt that the Americans were too quick to use force and complained that they (the Italians) were left to bear the consequences of QRF action in their sector. Their relationship with the Somalis also provided a means of obtaining the best intelligence information.[120]

The Germans were positively regarded because of the logistics resources they brought with them. However, their perceived Chapter VI role in a Chapter VII operation placed them in an invidious position on the use of force in self-defence. The German Rules of Engagement (ROE) were specific. The use of firearms was authorised only if milder means such as pushing back, hitting with a stick, fist, or rifle butts did not promise to be successful.[121] Operating under such restrictive ROE, German troops had on occasion to be escorted by Italian or Indian (Chapter VII) forces causing the Germans embarrassment and frustration.[122] Logistical limitations and concerns for their safety resulted in some contingents being unwilling to re-deploy. The Indians and Koreans refused to go to Mogadishu. Other contingents would not go elsewhere. For some, security was linked to distance from the airport: others felt the further they were from Mogadishu the safer their position.[123] Pakistani and Indian contingents conscious of how their performance might be viewed at home, were careful to ensure that reports of incidents involving their troops were channelled through their own communications system.[124] Participation had its rewards for the poorer states. The peacekeepers earned for their governments 1,000 US dollars per month per soldier.[125] There was also the prospect of picking up abandoned US equipment.

The behaviour and attitude of the American troops changed dramatically with the changeover from UNITAF to UNOSOM II. During the former, they operated with restraint.[126] However, during UNOSOM II, they demonstrated heavy-handedness in their behaviour towards the Somalis.[127] This was hardly surprising given their perceived role and the fact that they, like other contingents, were groping in the fog between peacekeeping and enforcement.

Communications

As in the Congo, the Somalia operation was dogged by an assortment of communications-related problems. From the outset, there was a breakdown in communications between New York and the field. This was due in part to the personality clash between Boutros-Ghali and Sahnoun. However, the New York–field communications system also suffered from serious organisational weaknesses. At New York HQ, responsibility for different aspects of the operation was splintered across different departments. Since it took time for coordination to develop, there was uncertainty as to what each department was doing.[128] Communication between humanitarian providers and peacekeepers was also unsatisfactory. While the head of the humanitarian section, who reported to the SRSG, participated in the daily meetings at UNOSOM HQ, the senior personnel of many of the agencies remained based in Nairobi.[129]

The gap between traditional methods of communication within Somalia and the UN's reliance on American high technology put most of the UN staff at a great disadvantage in their dealings with the local community. For example, American helicopters dropped leaflets on a population with a primarily oral tradition and known for its reliance on radio broadcasting. A proposal that UNOSOM have its own radio station was rejected by the General Assembly's Budgetary Committee. As a result, the operation did not have the right machinery to explain why it was in Somalia, why the mandates were being changed and what these changes were, what was expected of the Somali people themselves, and what they could expect from the UN.[130] Ironically, it was the UN's attempt to close down Somalia's principal communication system (Radio Mogadishu) on 5 June 1993 which proved to be the turning point in the overall operation. The incident also highlighted the UN's operational and general communications problems. In accordance with its efforts to establish good relations, UNOSOM II Headquarters was careful to notify the SNA of the UNOSOM II Headquarter's intended inspection. The SNA warned that such action could lead to war, but amazingly, the Pakistani Commander was not informed of the SNA's reaction. There was also a failure to communicate plans to the Head of UNOSOM II's Political Division who later claimed that he would not have approved the operation.[131] Reserves were not alerted from other contingents to assist the Pakistanis and in the absence of common communications facilities, the Pakistanis could not make direct contact with the Italians who were nearby. The operation in October 1993 was equally chaotic. The American plan was not communicated to other contingents, hence no contingency planning to support the operation was possible. The QRF took seven hours to plan the rescue operation.[132] In contrast, Aideed enjoyed all the advantages. He was informed of the UN's intentions on almost all occasions and was therefore able to organise demonstrations, create road blocks and deploy military forces at very short notice.[133]

Equipment

In keeping with UN peacekeeping tradition, UNOSOM I suffered from a shortage of vehicles and communication and engineering equipment.[134] In the subsequent phases of the mission, the situation remained equally unsatisfactory. Western contingents in general were well equipped and self-sufficient; contingents from developing states tended to rely on UN logistics.[135] However, the mission's outstanding equipment problem related to the inability of the Force as a whole to defend itself. The folly of sending lightly armed peacekeepers into a country awash with arms was exposed by the UNOSOM I experience. The UN then compounded the problem by undertaking 'peace enforcement' against elements armed with and experienced in the use of, a wide variety of weapons.

The Somali armed personnel were not a rag-tag militia but reasonably well-organised and trained elements operating under a good command structure. To engage such forces either aggressively or defensively, the UN Forces required a plentiful supply of powerful weapons and fighting vehicles. The events of 5 June 1993 revealed the UN Force's inadequacies. The greater part of the Pakistani casualties arose from the fact that the troops travelled, traditional peacekeeping style, in soft-skinned vehicles.[136] As in all such situations, it was all too easy to fault 'the UN' and to forget that ultimately it was member states who were responsible for the safety of their troops. The losses suffered by UNOSOM II suggested that far too many contributing states had not fully considered the consequences of involvement in enforcement action or were indifferent to the plight of their troops.

The most formidable vehicle available to the Pakistani contingent was the M42 A2 tank. This tank was a 1957 model and was totally unreliable. It was only in October, after the contingent had sustained considerable casualties, that they were provided from home with M48 A5 models with diesel engines and 105 mm guns.[137] Demands for more or better equipment did not always get a sympathetic hearing, even in the US. The American force's request for tanks, armoured fighting vehicles and artillery were turned down in early and late September 1993 by the US

Defense Secretary and Joint Chiefs of Staff. By that time, US policy makers had grown weary of UNOSOM II.[138] The Somalis, on the other hand, had abundant equipment which they used to maximum effect. They used mines to destroy the much-vaunted US HMMV (Humvees) employed in the Gulf War against Saddam Hussein; their heavy machine guns proved capable of destroying Pakistani APCs.[139] They also had 60 mm, 82 mm and 120 mm mortars (although they did not use the latter, probably because of the risk of killing Somalis). They were believed to have Stinger anti-aircraft missiles but did not need them since their RPGs proved capable of bringing down US helicopter gunships as shown in the 3 October incident.[140] Some contingents scavenged or borrowed any available American equipment. The Pakistanis, who with good reason complained of lack of air cover during operations, were towards the end of the mission given the use of several US aircraft. The Indians complained that rather than using a limited panel of pilots, the Pakistanis were flying-in new crews at 5 to 6 week intervals. The Indians feared that the Pakistanis were training personnel on US equipment for possible employment in the border dispute on the Indian sub-continent.[141]

By dropping its traditional impartiality, the UN had embarked on an operation which required the employment of troops that were not only highly trained, but equipped for all contingencies. UNOSOM II was composed of contingents from states all too many of which either had not the equipment required or were unwilling to provide it.

Analysis

Mandate performance

UNOSOM I, UNITAF and UNOSOM II all failed to fulfil their mandate, demonstrating again that to be successful, an operation requires not only a clear mandate, but the means to implement it. It was UNOSOM I's initial failure through lack of numbers which led to the subsequent reactive and poorly planned ventures. UNITAF might be seen to have achieved a measure of success in the creation of safe passage for some humanitarian relief, but while the arrival of such a powerful force caused something of a retreat by the local factions, confusion over the mandate and restrictive exercise of its powers led to the renewal of the factional offensive. Equally, the mandate given to UNOSOM II at least as it was interpreted, was too ambitious in relation to the instruments and the will to implement it.

Facilitating conflict resolution

Civil conflict in Somalia was not the UN's original concern and subsequent efforts to deal with it in tandem with the humanitarian effort were doomed to failure. A solution to Somalia's problems required the cooperation and trust of the Somalis: ending internal strife was never likely to be achieved simply by the threat implied in resort to Chapter VII of the Charter. The Secretariat's inept handling of UNOSOM I, particularly its failure to support Sahnoun's efforts and to investigate the 'Russian plane' incident, widened divisions between the major clan leaders. Reference to involuntary disarmament could only increase fears that one or other would be disadvantaged and the attempt to disarm one clan (Aideed's) but not all, was a recipe for continuous civil war. But even if the UN had succeeded by whatever means in controlling all firearms, this would not in itself have guaranteed an end to conflict. The age-old rivalries would have continued and as events in Rwanda would show, sophisticated weapons were not required for the perpetuation of bloody conflict. Conflict resolution required consultation not enforcement tactics.

Conflict containment

The Cold War over, the possibility that conflict in Somalia could spread was, to judge by international reaction to the crisis, perceived to be minimal. The abysmal reaction to appeals for troops for UNOSOM I contrasted sharply with the experience during the Cold War when contingents were, generally speaking, readily available. The reluctance of states to become involved until assured of the American umbrella, suggested that whatever the hopes for a new dawn in international relations, states' behaviour continued to be dictated by self-interest.

Assessment

UNOSOM called into question the UN's ability to implement the complex agenda of so-called 'second generation peacekeeping' namely conflict prevention, humanitarian relief, and nation building. More importantly, it highlighted the need for serious examination of what precisely this new form of UN activity involved in terms of employing military force. This vague new 'wider' peacekeeping stimulated by media images of conflict and associated human suffering might be seen as enjoying considerable support from the world community, but how to move from preventive diplomacy employed during the Cold War to a more muscular form of intervention posed problems for the doctrine makers. To attempt to ratchet-up peacekeeping simply by invoking Chapter VII and employing greater numbers was to ignore the long-established principle that peacekeeping was a consent-based activity, while enforcement, albeit in this case called 'peace enforcement', was war by another name. The world – or parts of it – might seek more positive UN action involving an undefined 'acceptable' degree of force, but use of force, as John Sanderson cautioned, should not occur as a result of decisions made in the glare of television screens.[142] Use of force in a UN operation, however well intended, required a clear objective (purpose) understood by all engaged in its use, the resources and planning critical to any successful military operation, and a readiness to inflict and sustain casualties. If one or more of the parties to the dispute being addressed was to be confronted, then the reasons for embarking on such a course of action had to be clear to all and fully justified.

133

UNOSOM demonstrated that any operation in a perceived failed state could be neither purely humanitarian nor purely military. UNOSOM I, a purely humanitarian operation, had failed through manifest lack of military resources: UNITAF in contrast had shown that if an operation arrives forcibly, its appearance can avoid the use of force. However, if any progress were to be made in resolving the underlying problem, in this case collapse of state authority, then the parties in conflict had to be persuaded that the UN's intention was to assist rather than coerce. However, instead of trying to win the confidence and gain the cooperation of the Somali factions, the UN in the person of the Secretary-General, had shown scant regard for their views, ignored the importance of their cooperation, and tried to impose a simplistic solution. In this ill-conceived endeavour, the strength of the armed opposition had been totally underestimated and the 20,000 international force had been frustrated, demoralised, and ultimately vanquished by 800 urban guerrillas.[143]

Chapter VII indicated that armed resistance was considered likely and with good reason. The old Somali principle – 'me and Somalia against the world'[144] – left little reason to doubt that, although the local factions might be engaged in civil conflict, they would resent and oppose any intrusion in their country's affairs. Moreover, in a country awash with weapons and a population long accustomed to fighting, the scale of resistance was certain to be significant. Further, little thought seemed to have been given to the reaction and attitude of the UN troops to the 'enforcement' role. Authorising troops engaged in a humanitarian operation to employ 'all necessary measures to establish a secure environment' implied that they had the necessary resources to impose the UN's will and that what constituted a 'secure environment' was perfectly clear: this of course was not so. Moreover, the taking of 'necessary measures' implied that the peacekeepers were mere trained killers now given licence to take extreme measures against the people of a state with whom neither they nor their governments had any quarrel, in pursuit of objectives about which neither the members of the Security Council nor the Secretary-General were absolutely clear. The experience of ONUC had gone unheeded and again, the peacekeepers and local population had paid a heavy price for the poorly considered approval of use of force.

Uncertainty had surrounded not only what was to be done and how, but who should do it. The US, while supporting Chapter VII measures in the Council, obviously had no intention of committing its troops to any long-term military engagement. Equally, it was evident from the presence of many Chapter VI contingents, that the other participating states expected the Americans to provide whatever military force was required. The operation was an object lesson in UN inadequacies and in particular the UN's dependence upon the major powers. The US presence had been essential to the passage of humanitarian supplies in the UNITAF phase, but equally the problem arising from the US presence had been amply demonstrated by the highly unsatisfactory command structure and the clash of military cultures. The move from a poorly planned attempt to bring humanitarian relief to the 'ground-breaking' nation-building venture was always destined to fail. Nation-building might be an admirable objective, but the creation of a stable state, especially in a country as chaotic as Somalia, required serious peace-building efforts to first establish a 'foundation', and a willingness on the part of states to give a long-term commitment to maintenance of a presence. Given the hostility of the Somalis, such a commitment was never likely. Overall, the operation provided both a reason and an excuse for states to baulk at involvement in places such as Rwanda.

Notes

1 James Mayall, *The New Interventionism 1991–1994*, Cambridge, Cambridge University Press, 1996, p. 12
2 Jarat Chopra, Aage Eknes, Torvald Nordboe, *Fighting for Hope in Somalia*, Oslo, Norsk Utenrikspolitisk Institutt, 1995, p. 20
3 Mayall, *The New Interventionism*, p. 100
4 Ibid., pp. 102–4
5 Chopra, Eknes and Nordboe, *Fighting for Hope*, p. 28
6 Ibid., p. 30
7 Alex De Waal, 'African Encounters', *Index on Censorship*, London, Writers and Scholars International Ltd, November/December 1994, p. 18
8 Mayall, *The New Interventionism*, p. 108
9 DeWaal, 'African Encounters', p. 18
10 Mayall, *The New Interventionism*, p. 109
11 Chopra, Eknes and Nordboe, *Fighting for Hope*, pp. 312
12 *Report of the Commission of Inquiry established pursuant to SC Resolution 885 (1993) to investigate armed attacks on UNOSOM II personnel which led to casualties among them*, UN HQ, New York, 24 February 1994, p. 10
13 Ibid., p. 11
14 Chopra, Eknes and Nordboe, *Fighting for Hope*, p. 36
15 Mahmoud Sahnoun, 'Prevention in Conflict Resolution: The Case of Somalia', in *Irish Studies in International Affairs*, Vol. 5, 1994, p. 10
16 Ibid., p. 11
17 Ibid.
18 Chopra, Eknes and Nordboe, *Fighting for Hope*, p. 33
19 Theo Farrell, 'Sliding into War: The Somalia Imbroglio and US Army Peace Operations Doctrine', *International Peacekeeping*, Vol. 2, No. 2, 1995, p. 195
20 Chopra, Eknes and Nordboe, *Fighting for Hope*, p. 38
21 Ibid., pp. 39–40
22 Ibid., p. 40
23 Mayall, *The New Interventionism*, p. 112
24 Ibid., p. 40
25 John Bolton, 'Wrong Turn in Somalia', *Foreign Affairs*, January/February 1994, p. 60
26 Chopra, Eknes and Nordboe, *Fighting for Hope*, p. 4
27 Ibid., p. 42
28 Mission creep occurs when there is an incremental increase in the tasks assigned UN forces to the point that the tasks far exceed initial expectations of what forces had planned for and were equipped to achieve. Michael Pugh, *From Mission Cringe to Mission Creep*, Oslo, Institutt for Forsvarsstudier, 1997, p. 9
29 Mayall, *The New Interventionism*, p. 113
30 Farrell, 'Sliding into War', pp. 196–7
31 Ibid., p. 197

32 Chopra, Eknes and Nordboe, *Fighting for Hope*, p. 43
33 Ibid., p. 38
34 Ibid., p. 46
35 Ibid.
36 Mayall, *The New Interventionism*, p. 115
37 Ibid.
38 Samuel M. Makinda, *Seeking Peace From Chaos: Humanitarian Intervention in Somalia*, Boulder, Lynne Rienner Publishers, 1993, p. 76
39 Ibid., p. 77
40 Chopra, Eknes and Nordboe, *Fighting for Hope*, p. 14
41 Bolton, 'Wrong Turn', p. 61
42 Ibid.
43 Chopra, Eknes and Nordbroe, *Fighting for Hope*, p. 47
44 Makinda, *Seeking Peace*, p. 77
45 Bolton, 'Wrong Turn', p. 62
46 Mayall, *The New Interventionism*, pp. 115–16
47 Ibid., p. 116
48 Makinda, *Seeking Peace*, pp. 79–80
49 Ibid.
50 *Report of the Commission*, 1994, p. 32
51 Ibid.
52 Ibid., p. 35
53 Mayall, *The New Interventionism*, pp. 116–117
54 Farrell, 'Sliding into War', p. 202
55 Ibid., p. 203
56 *Report of the Commission*, p. 32
57 Chopra, Eknes and Nordboe, *Fighting for Hope*, p. 99
58 Mayall, *The New Interventionism*, p. 119
59 Ibid.
60 Ibid., p. 120
61 Chopra, Eknes and Nordboe, *Fighting for Hope*, p. 7
62 Peter Calvocoressi, *World Politics Since 1945*, 6th edition, London, Longman, 1991, pp. 540–1
63 Crawford Young, *Ideology and Development in Africa*, London, Yale University Press, 1982, p. 63
64 William Foltz and Henry Bienon, *Arms and the African*, London, New Haven, Yale University Press, 1985, p. 32
65 Young, *Ideology*, p. 67
66 Calvocoressi, *World Politics*, p. 543
67 Mayall, *The New Interventionism*, p. 108
68 Durch, 'Peacekeeping in Uncharted Territory', in Durch, *The Evolution of UN Peacekeeping, Case Studies and Comparative Analysis*, London, Macmillan, 1993, p. 472
69 Farrell, (n. 19 above), pp. 196–7
70 Mats Berdal, 'Whither UN Peacekeeping', *Adelphi Paper 281*, spring 1993, p. 75
71 Farrell, 'Sliding into War', p. 199
72 Mats Berdal, 'Fateful Encounter: The United States and UN Peacekeeping', *Survival*, spring 1994, p. 32
73 Ibid.
74 Ibid., p. 30
75 Ibid., p. 33
76 Ibid., p. 36

77 Christopher Coleman and Jeremy Ginifer, *An Assessment of UNOSOM 1992–1995*, Oslo, Norsk Utenrikspolitisk Institutt, 1995, p. 4
78 *Report of the Commission*, 1994, p. 12
79 Chopra, Eknes and Nordboe, *Fighting for Hope*, p. 59
80 Makinda, *Seeking Peace*, p. 64
81 *Report of the Commission*, 1994, p. 13
82 Ibid.
83 Chopra, Eknes and Nordboe, *Fighting for Hope*, p. 43
84 Ibid., p. 44
85 Ibid., p. 45
86 Ibid., p. 44
87 Farrell, 'Sliding into War', p. 207
88 *Report of the Commission*, 1994, p. 48
89 Chopra, Eknes and Nordboe, *Fighting for Hope*, p. 55
90 Makinda, *Seeking Peace*, p. 86
91 Comdt. Richard O'Leary, Irish Contingent, UNOSOM II, interviewed by Terry O'Neill, November 1996, Athlone
92 Chopra, Eknes and Nordboe, *Fighting for Hope*, p. 43
93 Kalowatie Deonanden, 'Learning From Somalia', *Peace Review*, April 1994, p. 456
94 William Clarke and Jeffrey Herbst, 'Somalia and the Future of Humanitarian Peacekeeping', *Foreign Affairs*, March/April 1996, p. 50
95 Ramesh Thakur, 'A Second Term for Boutros-Ghali'?, *Pacific Research*, August 1996, p. 36
96 Ibid., p. 35
97 Maurice Bertrand, 'Developments of Efforts to Reform the UN', in Roberts and Kingsbury, *United Nations, Divided World*, p. 432
98 Mayall, *The New Interventionism*, p. 110
99 Chopra, Eknes and Nordboe, *Fighting for Hope*, p. 30
100 Makinda, *Seeking Peace*, p. 69
101 Thakur, 'A Second Term', p. 35
102 Chopra, Eknes and Nordboe, *Fighting for Hope*, p. 49
103 Ibid., p. 84
104 Ibid.
105 Makinda, *Seeking Peace*, p. 75
106 Chopra, Eknes and Nordboe, *Fighting for Hope*, p. 85
107 Ibid., pp. 82–3
108 Ibid.
109 Ibid., p. 86
110 *Report of the Commission*, 1994, p. 45
111 Ibid., p. 25
112 Ibid., p. 45
113 Ibid., p. 32
114 Ibid., p. 88
115 Berdal, (n. 72 above), pp. 40–1
116 Comdt. Maurice O'Donoghue, (Irish Contingent), interviewed by Terry O'Neill, December 1994, Cork
117 Durch, 'Peacekeeping', p. 472
118 Chopra, Eknes and Nordboe, *Fighting for Hope*, p. 88
119 Farrell, 'Sliding into War', p. 98. See also Chopra, Eknes and Nordboe, *Fighting for Hope*, p. 44
120 Comdt, Richard O'Leary, (Irish Contingent), interviewed by Terry O'Neill, 25 October 1995

121 Chopra, Eknes and Nordboe, *Fighting for Hope*, p. 90
122 Comdt. Richard O'Leary, (Irish Contingent), interviewed by Terry O'Neill, 3 November, 1996, Athlone
123 Chopra, Eknes and Nordboe, *Fighting for Hope*, p. 72
124 Comdt. Richard O'Leary, (Irish Contingent), interviewed by Terry O'Neill, 3 November 1996, Athlone
125 Mayall, *The New Interventionism*, p. 123
126 Farrell, 'Sliding into War', p. 198
127 Comdt. Richard O'Leary, (Irish Contingent), interviewed by Terry O'Neill, 3 November 1996, Athlone
128 Coleman, *An Assessment*, pp. 8–9
129 Ibid.
130 Ibid., p. 13
131 *Report of the Commission*, 1994, pp. 41–3
132 Ibid., pp. 86–8
133 Ibid., p. 22
134 Coleman, *An Assessment*, p. 11
135 Chopra, Eknes and Nordboe, *Fighting for Hope*, p. 71
136 *Report of the Commission*, 1994, p. 41
137 Ibid., p. 83
138 Farrell, 'Sliding into War', pp. 207–8
139 *Report of the Commission*, 1994, p. 69
140 Chopra, *Fighting for Hope*, p.82
141 Comdt. Richard O'Leary, (Irish Contingent), interviewed by Terry O'Neill, 3 November 1996, Athlone
142 John Sanderson, 'The Incalculable Dynamics of Using Force', in Wolfgang Biermann and Martin Vadset (eds) *UN Peacekeeping in Trouble: Lessons Learned from the Former Yugoslavia*, Aldershot, Ashgate 1998, p. 205
143 Lt. Col. Dermot Conway (Irish Contingent), interviewed by Terry O'Neill, 6 June 1996, Dublin
144 Chopra, Eknes and Nordboe, *Fighting for Hope*, p. 20

6

UNAVEM AND ANGOLA, 1988–1997

Introduction

UNAVEM[1] demonstrated the critical importance of cooperation by the parties in dispute to the UN's efforts. UNAVEM I, the first stage in the operation, enjoyed a considerable measure of cooperation and achieved its declared objectives. UNAVEM II and III aimed at furthering the process of reconciliation, became dismal failures once cooperation was withdrawn. Conducted at a time when the UN was attempting to deal with a variety of problems, the operation represented a test of the UN's ability and will to restore and maintain peace, not just in strategic or sensitive areas, but wherever and whenever conflict occurred. It was a test of the theory that the UN was the friend of small states and could help the promotion of the instruments and institutions of peaceful change. Rather than trying as in Somalia to impose a solution, the UN would, on this occasion, act as facilitator in efforts by the parties to end conflict and promote reconciliation.

The nature of the conflict

Election monitoring, one of the many new peacekeeping roles proposed in *An Agenda for Peace*, became one of UNAVEM's main tasks. The operation would, therefore, be expected to demonstrate the organisation's ability to (1) assist states in organising their affairs while not impinging on their sovereignty and, (2) provide help in situations where the democratic will was rejected.

Historical background

In the years prior to its gaining independence (1975), Angola, a country of 1.2 million square kilometres with a population of 10 million, lacked a cultural, economic and administrative unity on which the aspirations of the local politicians could be focused. Three nationalist movements had emerged in the fight for independence from Portuguese colonial rule in the 1950s and 1960s. The Zaire-backed FNLA (Frente Nacional de Libertacao de Angola) had its origins among the Bakongo in Northern Angola and the Western Belgian Congo. While possessing a small guerrilla force it remained relatively inactive in military terms, despite receiving military training and arms from Zaire and the US via the CIA. The MPLA (Movimento Popular de Libertacao de Angola) drew considerable support from the Mbundu tribe and from leftist and nationalist movements in the capital Luanda, and the neighbouring provinces. Its base among the more ethnically varied peoples of the capital and the coast distinguished it from the FNLA, and its 'nationalism' gave it a broad appeal. It received external support from the Soviet Union, Cuba, Yugoslavia and for a period, China. The third movement, UNITA (Uniao Nacional para a Independencia Total de Angola) was essentially built around one man. Its founder, Jonas Savimbi, had originally been a member of FNLA and later of MPLA. Disenchanted with both of these movements, he returned to his home area of Central Angola and set up the new nationalist organisation, which had at its core the Ovimbundu tribe.[2] But while the movement had a tribal core, observers on the ground dismissed the ethnic factor as the basis for the subsequent conflict, pointing to Savimbi's callous treatment of his 'own' people in Huambo which he shelled for eight weeks in 1993.[3]

Hostility between the three movements during the struggle for independence turned to armed conflict as independence approached. The Portuguese set 11 November 1975 as the date of independence, and in the meantime tried briefly to reconcile the warring groups by mediating the Alvor Accord[4] in January 1975 which set up a transitional government.[5] Renewed fighting broke out, however, and the transitional government collapsed by August of the same year. With Cuban support, (an estimated 10,000–12,000 combat troops)[6] the MPLA took control of most of the country, including Luanda, before independence day.

During the rest of the 1970s and much of the 1980s, civil war between the MPLA and UNITA, complicated by Cold War interests and the regional powers, spread and intensified throughout the country. Even before official independence, the civil war had become part of the Cold War. The Soviet Union and Cuba backed the MPLA, while the US backed UNITA. Long after the MPLA became the de facto government of Angola in 1975,[7] South Africa conducted raids into the country ostensibly pursuing guerrillas of the South West African People's Organisation (SWAPO) who were fighting South African rule in Namibia and had been given haven by the MPLA government. By 1978, the FNLA had largely ceased to be 'a player', following a rapprochement between Zaire and Angola.

In the early 1980s, the war escalated as South Africa increased its raids into Angola. Fortified by fresh military supplies and more Cuban troops, the MPLA in 1985 took the offensive against UNITA and South Africa rallied to Savimbi's support. Both sides failed. A joint UNITA–South African air onslaught at Cuito Cuanavale in 1987–8 was thwarted in the encounter and South Africa suffered heavy losses in men and equipment.[8] But UNITA, although battered in the south, was re-established in Zaire by the US, and Savimbi effectively 'recognised' as an equal with the government. By the beginning of 1987, estimated military forces included: government army 50,000, paramilitary forces 50,000, Cubans 30,000. UNITA forces were 26,000, and 34,000 support militia.[9]

In response to South Africa's increasingly aggressive actions in South Angola, the Security Council in November 1987 passed Resolution 602 condemning South Africa and demanding its immediate withdrawal from Angolan territory. By this time, the military stalemate had become painful for all parties. Greater superpower cooperation, changing domestic political conditions in South Africa, and the ever-mounting human and financial cost of the war all led the parties to the conclusion that a political settlement was desirable. The two Angolan sides were urged to meet the US and Soviet Union who were keen to test their new found cooperative spirit. Following talks lasting from May to September 1988 (which did not involve UNITA), agreement was reached on a planned withdrawal by the Cubans from Angola, to be completed by July 1991. South African forces were to be withdrawn from both Angola and Namibia. Angola and South Africa requested the UN Secretary General to verify compliance with the agreement and the UN decided to establish UNAVEM I for a period of 31 months – until one month after the completion of the Cuban withdrawal.[10] Both 'foreign' parties were relieved to be withdrawing. The Cuban force had stayed much longer than the 6 months Castro had intended, and the adventure had imposed strenuous demands and sacrifices on thousands of Cubans.[11] South Africa was under pressure from the US to seize the opportunity for a comprehensive multinational deal that would entail the departure of the Cubans, and like the Cubans, they were in a no-win situation. But the agreement did nothing to reduce the hostility between MPLA and UNITA. The war went on as before with the Angolan army unable to destroy UNITA, now well-equipped with weapons, ammunition and other war material left by the South Africans, or stamp out its widespread guerrilla attacks, and UNITA unable to pose a conventional military threat to the government.

By the early 1990s, Angola's economy was in ruins despite rich oil reserves: its infrastructure had suffered considerable damage, especially roads, while the Benguela railway, the country's east–west artery, had been especially targeted by UNITA.[12] The local currency was so worthless that foreign companies paid their employees with consumer goods. Drought added to the horrors of war. The UN addressed this problem in October 1990 by launching the Special Relief Programme for Angola, coordinated by UNDP.[13] But rather than contemplating direct involvement in Angola's political affairs, the UN was, through its UNAVEM I operation, proposing to tidy up the loose details of the departure of foreign forces.

UNAVEM I

UNAVEM I comprised unarmed observers from Algeria, Argentina, Brazil, Congo, Czechoslovakia, India, Jordan, Norway, Spain and Yugoslavia. From an initial strength of 18, it grew to 70.[14] The function of this force was 'to verify the redeployment northwards and the phased and total withdrawal of Cuban troops from the territory of Angola in accordance with the timetable agreed between Angola and Cuba.[15] The timetable for the withdrawal was set out in detail (see Map 6.1), and UNAVEM was mandated to make ad hoc inspections. (South Africa had

141

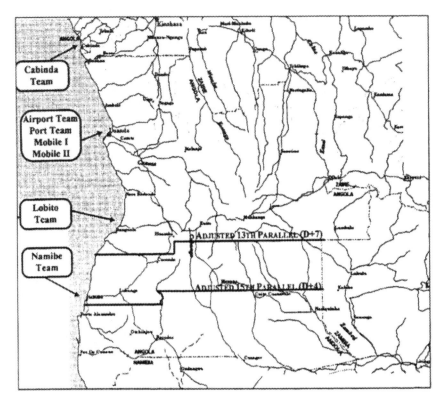

Map 6.1 Angola and UNAVEM II: deployment in 1991
Source: Krska (1997: 77)

withdrawn all its troops by August 1990.)[16] The complete withdrawal was achieved on 26 May 1991. Because of the straightforward nature of UNAVEM I's mandate, planning and implementation were relatively simple affairs. In general, the provisions of the Angolan–Cuban agreement were adhered to; the withdrawal was suspended only once (between 24 January and 25 February 1990) following two attacks by UNITA against Cuban forces during which ten Cuban soldiers were killed.[17] Although the ease with which UNAVEM I had carried out its task held out the promise of an end to conflict, there were signs that this peace would be fragile. A peace process brokered by African states[18] in 1989 between President dos Santos and Savimbi had led to a ceasefire, but within a week of its being signed each party had accused the other of violations. Nevertheless, between 1990 and May 1991, peace negotiations between the MPLA and UNITA, in which Portugal had acted as mediator and the Americans and Soviets had acted as observers, led to the Bicesse Accords. The principles of the peace package were: (1) a ceasefire to be monitored by a joint monitoring commission, (2) elections to be held under international supervision, and (3) the integration of two armies into a single national army.[19] The Bicesse Accords also provided for the planning of military assistance to the MPLA and UNITA, the confinement of all troops from both sides in assembly areas, the restoration of government administration in rebel-controlled areas, and the release of prisoners of war and political prisoners.[20] In May 1991, the Angolan government requested the Secretary General to ensure the participation of the UN in verifying the implementation of the accords. The withdrawal of the Cubans, it was clear, was only the first step in a peaceful settlement of the civil war.

UNAVEM II

Implementation of the Bicesse Accords represented a major challenge to the parties to the conflict and to the UN. The creation of trust between the Government and UNITA required the positive and ongoing involvement of a third party. By agreeing to become involved, the UN appeared to have assumed that role. However, its approach was to be uncertain and timid. Arguably it was complacency arising from the success of UNAVEM I which led it to overestimate the degree of reconciliation between the parties and, therefore, to underestimate the resources required for the new mission and the need for a clear practicable mandate. In brief, UNAVEM II's task was to verify that the joint monitoring groups established under the Bicesse Accords carried out their responsibilities. At this stage, it was clear that UNAVEM II's role was limited to observing the monitors, not organising or regulating, let alone enforcing, observance. However, UNAVEM II's mandate was expanded after the Secretary-General received two letters from the Angolan government in December 1991. One asked the UN for technical assistance during preparation for and conduct of the forthcoming elections. The other requested UN observers to follow the electoral process until its completion. On 24 March 1992, the Security Council passed Resolution 747 (1992) enlarging UNAVEM II's mandate to include election observation. This represented a change in the Force's status since the UN was not nominated in the Accords to supervise the elections. UNAVEM II's initial strength was 350 unarmed military observers and 89 police observers provided by 24 countries. These numbers were supplemented by 14 military medical personnel, 54 international civilian staff, and 41 local civilian staff. Military observers were deployed around the country at 46 assembly points as well as critical points at ports, airports and border posts. Police observers were also deployed in all provinces (see Map 6.2).[21] Based on the assumption that the factions would cooperate, the mission, although demanding, seemed relatively straightforward. However, it would emerge that there were major differences between the Angolan parties over the nature and purpose of the UN presence.

For most of 1991 and the beginning of 1992, the security situation was deteriorating. Demobilised government soldiers were not being paid or fed and many took their weapons and deserted. UNITA refused to allow government administrators access to its territory and the UN had difficulty monitoring UNITA areas. UNITA obstructed efforts to organise an electoral commission and refused to

143

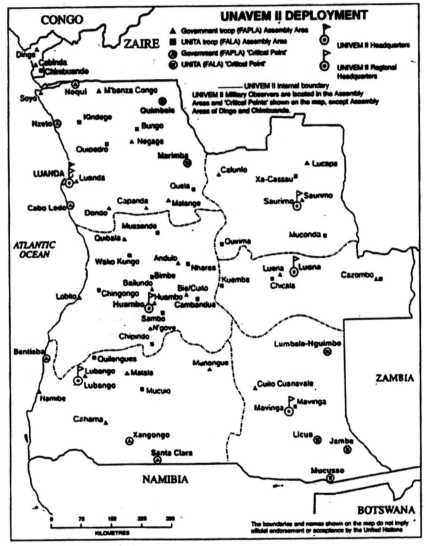

Source: UN Document 23191.

Map 6.2 Angola and UNAVEM II: 1991

Source: UN Cartographic Section (Map No. 23191)

involve itself in a multiparty conference on the preparations for the election. During this time, Savimbi sent out different signals. In April 1991, he told an audience in London that he wanted to ensure that under a future constitution no single party would have a monopoly on power. This appeared to support the belief of many commentators that the election results would produce a coalition. However, when subsequently addressing political meetings in Angola, he accused the MPLA of massacring the Ovimbundu, of violations of the peace accord, of selling Angola to foreign interests, and of plotting to kill him.[22] The major problems were, however, the pace of demobilisation and the formation of the new army. By September 1992, only 1,500 of the projected new army had been sworn in and only 8,000 more were being trained. Of particular concern was the fact that only 45 per cent of the government troops and 24 per cent of UNITA troops had been demobilised.[23] UNITA failed to hand over Stinger surface to air missiles (which would later be turned on UN planes) or American-supplied grenade launchers. The weapons assembled from both sides were of very poor quality and UNAVEM observers felt that the good equipment was being withheld for use at a later date. Presidential and legislative elections were held on 29 and 30 September 1992, and more than 91 per cent of those registered voted.[24]

Predictably, when preliminary results indicated that the MPLA had obtained a majority of seats in the new national assembly, Savimbi accused the government of electoral fraud. These accusations were investigated and the SRSG, Margaret Anstee, reported that she considered the elections to have been 'generally free and fair'.[25] As neither presidential candidate received more than 50 per cent, a second vote would be required for the presidency.[26] However, rather than face the likely outcome of a second presidential election and ignoring the legitimacy of the vote, UNITA reverted to military means in an attempt to take power. Taking advantage of the fact that its personnel had not fully disarmed or demobilised before the election, UNITA troops surrounded and occupied key towns and ports. Fighting broke out in Huambo on 17–18 December and quickly spread to Luanda. Casualties in the capital were more than 1,000, the majority of whom were perceived supports of UNITA. The government sought to deal a mortal blow to UNITA by seizing Huambo. However, by the start of 1993, the rebels were estimated to control 75 per cent of the country.[27]

From January 1993, Savimbi's forces battled to capture Huambo by shelling, despite the fact that the city, home base of the Ovimbundu, had voted for UNITA. Casualties were estimated by the UN at 15,000. Even before Huambo's fall to the rebels, the Secretary-General reported that to all intents and purposes, Angola had returned to civil war and 'was probably in an even worse situation than that which prevailed before the Peace Accords were signed in 1991'.[28] The outbreak of violence and the collapse of the joint monitoring mechanism caused the original UNAVEM II mandate to have less and less relevance. Because of the dangerous situation, 45 of UNAVEM II's 67 locations had to be evacuated. As a result, the Secretary-General decided to reduce temporarily the strength of the mission to 50 military and 18 police observers. While UNAVEM II was now effectively redundant, the Secretary-General stated that it would be unthinkable for the UN to abandon Angola and recommended an interim extension of UNAVEM II on a reduced basis and in a manner which would respond to the evaluation of the military and political situation. Its 'mission' would be to provide good offices and mediation with the goal of restoring the ceasefire and reinstating the peace process along the lines of the Peace Accords.[29] Its position was however extremely weak. By February 1993, hostility towards UNAVEM became more commonplace. Demonstrations took place outside the UN building in Luanda with people hurling insults at the UN for having led the country back to war.[30]

UN officials continued their efforts to mediate in Angola. A meeting was arranged for Addis Ababa in 1993 but Savimbi failed to turn up. Talks between the parties held in the Ivory Coast in April–May 1993 also failed to produce a ceasefire or any agreement. UNITA was generally winning the war and unwilling to negotiate seriously. However, the government's control of major oil deposits and its apparent willingness to negotiate gained it significant support. The US, which had remained hostile to President dos Santos up to this time eventually announced recognition of the MPLA government and became increasingly critical of Savimbi.[31] The UNITA leader's intransigence also led the Security Council to impose a fuel and arms embargo against the rebels. At the same time, the lifting of an arms embargo against the Angolan government and increasing sympathy for dos Santos enabled its forces to launch offensives against UNITA-held areas. These achieved a measure of success and eventually the recapture of the symbolic city of Huambo. Exploratory talks begun in Lusaka in October 1993 and as negotiations dragged on, the government offensive gained pace. With its back to the wall militarily, UNITA agreed (in Lusaka) in October 1994 to set a date for a ceasefire and to initiate a political accord allowing for UNITA participation in government (four ministerial portfolios) and for the appointment of political governors. The Lusaka Protocol was signed on 20 November by representatives on both sides.[32]

There was however, little optimism about the agreement. UNITA had signed under duress: there were also indications that the government had been willing to see delays in the signing to allow it to capture more territory, and that even after the ceasefire it would use every opportunity to extend its area of control. The positive point of the new agreement was that the UN committed itself to sending peacekeeping troops including a logistical support unit from Britain to assist in the lifting of the mines sown around the contested towns and the rich areas of most provinces.[33]

UNAVEM III

UNAVEM III authorised by SC Resolution 976 initially involved the deployment of 7,000 military personnel, 350 military observers and 200 police observers. Personnel were drawn from Uruguay, Portugal, Brazil, Bangladesh and India with logistical support from Britain.[34] It was hoped that South Africa might play a minor role in the UN operation but the Mandela government declined to do so after the Angolan government, not surprisingly, indicated its concern about South African forces returning to Angola under UN auspices.[35] Its mandate was based on the implementation of the Peace Accords, the Lusaka Protocol and relevant Security Council resolutions. Essentially, it was a reiteration of UNAVEM II's tasks with the additional one of mine clearance. As with UNAVEM II, the intransigence of

Savimbi continued to frustrate UN efforts, particularly in relation to the gathering of troops in assembly areas.

Delays in deployment of the peacekeepers meant that there had been only limited monitoring of repeated clashes and little could be done about accusations by the government and UNITA that their opponents had launched armed attacks upon them. But from the outset, UNAVEM III faced a complicated situation in part because of the loss of credibility and the reputation of UNAVEM II. As Krska noted: 'it is easy to lose confidence while to win it is very difficult and to recapture it is, in most cases, almost impossible'.[36] UNAVEM had long ago lost the confidence of the parties and UNAVEM III was, like UNAVEM II, destined to failure. Fighting would end only upon the death of Savimbi, killed in an ambush in July 2002.

Political base for operation

Prior involvement of the Great Powers

A striking feature of developments in Angola from the 1960s to the late 1980s was not only involvement of so many 'players', but the extent to which proxies were employed by the superpowers. During the 1960s, the Soviet Union had been a ready supplier of arms to African liberation movements and by the 1970s, was the major purveyor of heavy arms. It was concerned about increasing Chinese involvement on the continent, but its relations with African states suffered a reverse when it was accused by the Sudanese, in 1971, of involvement in an abortive Communist coup in that country.[37] It was happy, therefore, to have Cuba to represent its interests. There is no evidence of a Soviet role in deciding on the commitment of the Cubans, but once the Cubans were involved, the Soviet leadership ensured that they and the MPLA had the arms they needed to repel the invading South African columns. By the late 1980s, Angola had taken delivery of MIG-23 aircraft (numbers unknown) and the latest Soviet tanks with Soviet technicians building a sophisticated air defence system in the south.[38]

The US had, during the 1960s, been dependent upon Portugal for substantial naval and air facilities in the Azores and had avoided putting pressure on the Portuguese to grant independence to its colony. However, the sudden collapse of Portuguese rule in Africa in 1975 presented the US with problems. Having done nothing to assist the leaders of the African nationalist movements, it was poorly placed to influence their actions. The US was prevented from giving any assistance to groups in Angola unless specifically approved by Congress;[39] in order to protect its interests, it was obliged to act indirectly through the Zairean and more especially the South African regimes.[40]

Prior to 1975, South Africa had worked steadily to establish both an economic market and a security zone well away from its northern borders. Such plans were severely threatened by the coming to power of an MPLA regime in Angola. South Africa was not only opposed to the socialist ideology of such a government, but threatened by the MPLA's readiness to allow SWAPO to establish bases close to the Namibian border.[41] It concluded a secret agreement with UNITA. Ronald Reagan's election in 1980 brought to power a group of people who shared South Africa's obsession with Soviet imperialism and dislike and contempt for the UN with its Third World majority. In the course of the following years, a number of Council resolutions were unanimously adopted condemning South African attacks on Angola from Namibian bases and demanding South African withdrawal. But whenever measures under Chapter VII were either included or threatened, the US and Britain were quick to cast vetoes with France abstaining.[42]

The denouement came with the ending of the Cold War. The Soviets were confident that they could compete with the South Africans in the provision of military equipment: the question was whether, in the era of glasnost, perestroika and Soviet financial difficulties, such an effort was worth the financial and political cost. They concluded that it was not.[43]

Initial position of the Great Powers

The Bicesse Peace Accords were hailed as a triumph of US–Russian cooperation in the wake of the Gulf crisis. However, as Parsons notes, the accords were also a victory for Savimbi. Having been amply supplied with arms by the US, the UNITA leader had become accepted, not so much as a rebel making terms with the government, but as an equal of the government. This impression was enhanced by the fact that whereas UNITA had in effect been recognised by the US, the government had not. In these circumstances, Savimbi could with justification regard both himself and his movement as entitled not just to a share of government, but overall control of the country. But it seemed that neither the US nor Russia had given much thought to the situation in Angola. Parsons suggests that perhaps they felt that the civil war, having been perpetuated by their own past involvement, peace would automatically follow from their withdrawal of support for the combatants; perhaps they were no longer interested in what happened in an area no longer of strategic importance.[44]

There was also, according to Sommerville, a feeling of optimism about Angola. The Namibian Independence Process had worked smoothly in South Africa. Nelson Mandela had been released and constitutional negotiations were under way to draw up a democratic and non-racial political framework.[45] But the Security Council obviously failed to see the difficulties ahead. This failure on the part of the Security Council to take the Angolan problem seriously is indicated by: (1) the provision of just 450 unarmed observers for an area the size of Germany, France and Spain put together, and (2) the lack of contingency planning for rejection of the election results. No one within the Council appeared to have given any thought to the near-certainty that the losers would be unwilling to accept the role of a loyal opposition.

Mandates

Criticism of the UN's role in Angola centred almost entirely on the UNAVEM II mission. That mission's failure to prevent or contain the outbreak of hostilities in the wake of the 1992 general election is attributed to its limited mandate and lack of contingency planning. In defence of the UN, it might be argued that (1) the same minimalist approach had worked for the successful UNAVEM I and (2) the UN's peripheral approach was dictated by the conditions of the Bicesse Accords. However, there was always likely to be a crucial difference between the measure of cooperation provided by the concerned parties.

UNAVEM I's mandate – verification of the withdrawal of Cuban troops – had posed no problems for the UN personnel since it involved no concession or undertaking on the part of UNITA. The Cubans were totally cooperative and troops and equipment were ready for departure long before the appointed date.[46] In contrast, the confused nature of UN involvement in the implementation of the Bicesse Accords, although essentially peripheral, became, in the words of the SRSG, 'one of the fraught issues that bade fair to prevent agreement being reached at all'.[47] UNITA, suspicious of the government, had wanted the UN to be entrusted with a major role of direct supervision of all aspects of the process, supported by adequate resources including contingents of armed UN personnel. 'The Government on the other hand, despite its request to the Secretary-General, was reluctant to see the UN playing any part at all and insisted that its role be minimal on the grounds that a major UN presence with mandated supervisory powers would trespass on Angolan sovereignty.'[48] The government, in Anstee's opinion, wanted it both ways – a minimal UN presence with maximum responsibility, thus making it a 'toothless but handy scapegoat'.[49]

The Angolan president was prepared to do a remarkable volte-face when the situation deteriorated in late 1992. He wanted a more active mandate, suggesting that the UN take on not only the task of verification, but also those of mediation, establishing conditions of security and defending legality. These would have involved a sizeable presence of blue helmets. But UN Headquarters, while responding sympathetically, pointed to financial constraints arising from many other operations at this time.[50] SC Resolution 696 of 30 May 1991 made no reference to any perceived threat to international peace and security. The Accords had specified that overall political supervision of the ceasefire process would be the responsibility of the Angolan parties and that verification would be the only responsibility of the international monitoring groups alone. The CCPM (the Portuguese acronym for the Joint Political Military Commission) was to be the apex of a network of joint monitoring mechanisms and the only full members were to be the government and UNITA.[51] However, the CCPM was considering a list of tasks for UNAVEM II to perform which were not part of its original mandate. Thus, the observer body became involved in 'mission creep' as it gradually undertook tasks for which it did not have the resources and had only questionable authority.

The Bicesse Accords had set forth a straightforward proposition. Within 60 days, government and UNITA forces were to be confined to 50 assembly areas dotted in remote areas all over Angola, together with their weapons and materials. Demobilisation could then start. However, both parties were slow in establishing joint monitoring groups deploying their troops in assembly areas and granting UNAVEM II authority to conduct reconnaissance in those areas. The SRSG, conscious of the time limit, sought to push the process forward. UNAVEM planes and helicopters were made available to transport surrendered weapons to regional bases and to permit joint reconnaissance. These tasks were essential to the peace process but in performing them, UNAVEM was, as the SRSG accepted, 'going far beyond our mandate'.[52]

UNAVEM II's role in relation to the election was to be one of adviser and catalyst. But again, a high profile involvement by UNAVEM carried distinct risks. If the government lost, it could claim that UNAVEM's verification was faulty. If it won, UNAVEM was open to accusations that its intervention had helped dos Santos. Predictably, when UNITA lost, it declared that irregularities in the election had occurred with the knowledge and connivance of the SRSG.[53] Anstee, for her part, was sceptical about the merits of holding an election, noting the tendency in Western international policies after the Cold War to advance universal remedies in black and white terms. In theory, the road to liberty and prosperity lay in reliance on market forces; embracing democracy, and carrying out as quickly as possible free and fair elections. But, democracy could not be created overnight in a place with a long history of authoritarian rule or civil war. The Government had, since independence, been involved in the monolithic Marxist tradition while democracy was alien to the UNITA organisation.[54] UNITA was a guerrilla/peasant movement which would not easily adapt to the rigours of democratic politics; above all, it suffered from being controlled by a leader unwilling to play by the rules of the democratic game.[55] Moreover, there was substantial evidence that Savimbi was determined to reject any electoral outcome that did not bring him power.[56] Anstee's remark in relation to 'western international policies' was also to be given special irony by the refusal of the US to accept the election result.

When fighting broke out in late 1992, both sides showed total disregard for the UN's authority and personnel. In an incident in the north, a grenade was thrown into the UNAVEM II compound killing a Brazilian observer. In the southern city of Lubango, government forces entered the UNAVEM compound and seized three UNITA members of the joint monitoring mechanism. One was shot on the spot in front of the protesting UN observers, the other two were led away to certain death despite the efforts and appeals of the Regional Commander.[57] The resumption of hostilities in 1992 highlighted UNAVEM II's dilemma and the sense of frustration among personnel. UN observers were frequently accosted in public places and berated for the UN's failure to 'do something about the war'. But pointing out that responsibility for ending hostilities rested with the Angolans themselves was both futile and dangerous.[58]

With the original mandate now irrelevant but the UN unwilling to withdraw, it became necessary to find some task to justify the observers' presence. In an attempt to salvage something from the operation, Security Council Resolution 811 of 12 March 1993 encouraged the SRSG to coordinate the provision of humanitarian assistance to the population. That vast numbers were in need of assistance was certain, but this attempt to change UNAVEM II from an observer to a humanitarian mission was highly problematic. The UN in Luanda had no policy for humanitarian operations and there was little or no institutional discussion on an overall agency response to the crisis. The government and UNITA were persuaded to agree to safe road and air corridors on specific days, but UNITA cited difficulties in reaching some destinations because of logistical and security constraints. (UN aircraft were fired upon 'by accident', sometimes with fatal consequences.) Notably, of the cities that could not be reached, Kuito, Malange and Menongue harboured the worst humanitarian situations.[59]

Anstee also interpreted the resolution as authority for ordering UNAVEM observers to accompany all relief flights. This raised protests from the observers, uncertain as to their exact role and authority. Moreover, the relief agencies did not want UNAVEM observers aboard. WFP who planned programmes weeks in advance, were also dissatisfied with UNAVEM's inability to get clearance to land from the warring factions other than on a day-to-day basis. Some humanitarian workers preferred to 'go it alone' for other reasons. (One MSF doctor spoke of the great excitement of flying into troubled areas without UN clearance.) Equally, UNAVEM personnel found working with the relief agencies extremely frustrating – on two separate occasions in April 1993, two large aircraft were made available to transport relief supplies in the southern region. On the appointed dates, the agency workers could not trace the supplies and the aircraft flew round trips of over 1,200 miles to deliver 1,500 plastic buckets.[60] Tensions arising from UNAVEM's 'humanitarian' role came to a head when on 26 April 1993 a UN relief plane was brought down in a minefield by a Stinger missile fired from UNITA lines. Two of the crew were badly wounded by the mines and without any medical back-up, one bled to death. UNAVEM's failure to mount a rescue operation was criticised over BBC radio by a senior representative of WFP. UNAVEM pilots were also angry that their request to be allowed to attempt to 'lift out' the wounded without clearance was rejected by the SRSG. Tensions created by UNAVEM's 'new' mandate were exacerbated by involvement of observers in incidents in which they were humiliated by undisciplined soldiers and by lawless elements.[61]

It is difficult to regard UNAVEM II's humanitarian mandate as other than a face-saving device and an excuse to extend the mandate while the peace talks in the Ivory Coast continued. Were the UN seriously committed to a humanitarian operation, it would arguably have provided greater resources in terms of material and personnel. It could plead lack of resources: the UN appealed for 226 million dollars in assistance to the war victims but received only 60 million dollars because most international attention had been focused on the high profile crises in Bosnia and Somalia.[62] Its lack of commitment was however, underlined by its renewal of mandates (in 1993) by weeks rather than months.[63] These extensions of mandate were accompanied by a succession of Security Council Resolutions, one of which, SC Resolution 811 (March 1993), indicated the readiness of the Council to expand the UN presence in the event of significant progress in the peace process. In terms of their importance, Anstee described these resolutions as having 'no more effect on UNITA than water off a duck's back'.[64] SC Resolution 834 of 1 June 1993 referred to UNAVEM's function of providing 'mediation'. This new mediatory role was problematic, however, given that the resolution praised the disposition of the government in relation to peaceful settlement, while effectively condemning UNITA for its actions. In alluding to the perceived mediation role, the Council could only be seen as referring solely to the efforts of the SRSG to bring about a peaceful settlement. There was nothing that UNAVEM military or police personnel could do to improve relations since all remaining UNAVEM posts were in government-held territory. Apart from its extremely limited 'humanitarian' role, UNAVEM as represented by its observers had no useful function.

Political manoeuvres of the Great Powers

In 1992, the US and Russia had many concerns of apparently greater importance than Angola, but old allegiances died hard and both powers continued to have an influence on developments. When, directly following the 1992 elections Savimbi alleged fraud, the US (which had earlier expressed confidence in the UN verification) tried to excuse the UNITA leader's outburst by suggesting rather strangely that his remarks were 'aimed at calming down the situation'.[65] Savimbi had meanwhile told US Assistant Secretary of State, Herman Cohen, to 'go to hell' for urging him to respect the conditions of the Peace Accord.[66] When President Clinton on 20 May 1993 announced his government's recognition of the dos Santos regime, he explained that he had tried to use the possibility of recognition as 'a means of influence' to promote the end of the civil war.[67] But given US acceptance of the UN verification of the election results, this explanation sounded hollow.

The change in US attitude could be attributed to American concern for its commercial interests in Angola. When in early 1993 UNITA operations in northern Angola threatened Cabinda which produced two-thirds of Angola's oil,[68] the Americans warned of the gravest implications of a raid on the US-owned Chevron complex. It threatened not only to close UNITA's office in Washington, but to provide the Angolan government with military information including satellite technology concerning UNITA bases and movements on the ground.[69] The Russians also were not entirely blameless for the ongoing destruction and loss of life. The lifting of the arms embargo against the Angolan government in 1993 resulted in the immediate importation of arms from Russia which had, from the outset, opposed an arms embargo.[70] Right up to June 1993, aircraft flew in weekly from Russia bringing spares for the many Mig jet-fighters based in Lubango. The availability of these jets to the government and the absence of South African air support for UNITA troops was to be a major reason for UNITA's failure to achieve outright military success in 1993.[71]

A crucial factor in the perpetuation of the conflict had been the use of the country's natural resource potential to acquire arms. Angola's wealth in relation to commodities valued by the industrial powers enabled both sides to purchase large amounts of weaponry from international arms dealers. The government cashed in on its oil reserves: UNITA benefited from access to diamond reserves. In 1993, diamonds valued at an estimated 250 million US dollars went to Zaire and on to illegal markets. In 1992, De Beers admitted paying 500 million dollars for diamonds, a good proportion coming from areas controlled by UNITA.[72]

The Security Council's decision to impose sanctions on UNITA in September 1993 was too little too late. By that time, UNITA had control of 70–80 per cent of a country with porous frontiers. The tide turned against Savimbi and a resumption of peace talks became possible, not because of any positive action by the Council, but for other reasons. By late 1993, the lifting of the arms embargo against the government and a successful conscription campaign had led to greater military success against the rebels. UNITA having lost the support of the US was further weakened by the election of the ANC government in South Africa (1994).[73]

The Security Council's failure to take a more positive role in Angola following the resumption of hostilities in 1992 might be defended on the basis that it had done all that it was originally required to do and had stuck rigidly to the letter of the UN Charter. Angolans had been given an opportunity to decide who should rule through free and fair elections: What more responsibility had the Council in Angola's internal affairs? However, it could equally be argued that in accepting the tasks of monitoring and verifying, the UN had accepted the role of ultimate arbitrator. The failure of the Security Council to show greater concern had to be seen within the expanded role which the UN assumed in the post-Cold War international environment. The new interventionism, as Malaguias notes, induced severe budgetary strains which resulted in prioritisation of UN missions. The UN could be mobilised to act decisively and forcefully in the Gulf to defend Western interests. Equally, a major operation could be mounted in Yugoslavia because of the location of the conflict.[74] Television cameras had prompted action in Somalia, a 'far-away' country with a long-running civil war. But efforts by the SRSG to promote greater Council interest in Angola raised no meaningful response. Parsons describes the Council as adopting the 'Arab/Israeli posture, namely pumping out resolutions of which the offending party takes no notice'.[75]

Operational base

Boutros-Ghali's choice of Special Representative in Angola said much about the Secretary-General's view of the UNAVEM mission. Boutros-Ghali chose to appoint as his representative: (1) a woman, Margaret Anstee, (February 1991 to June 1993) and (2) an African, Blondin Beye of Mali (July 1993–), who spoke no Portuguese or English. The ability or commitment of either of these persons was not an issue, but their suitability for this particular role certainly was questionable. The appointment of these Special Representatives raised questions about the Secretary-General's judgement and his attitude to the operation. According to Anstee, Boutros-Ghali's predecessor, Pérez de Cuéllar, had been advised by an ambassador from a Western country that no woman could ever occupy such a post because it involved dealing with the military.[76] The problem with Anstee's appointment, however, was not just her acceptability to the military, but to Africans. Whether a male SRSG would have succeeded where Anstee failed would remain uncertain but many, including personnel serving on the mission, believed that neither the Angolan government nor Savimbi was prepared to take seriously a female Special Representative. Beye's appointment, particularly given the problems which Anstee had encountered in dealing with both sides in Angola, was also remarkable. Anstee states that she 'nearly fell off the sofa' when told by the Secretary-General that her successor spoke only French. 'Not speaking either of the two languages that would permit direct understanding of what was being said ... was one thing, but having no English would add a further complication when communicating with Headquarters.'[77]

It is clear from Anstee's writings that the Secretary-General, preoccupied with the major missions in Yugoslavia and Cambodia, was not disposed to giving much attention or resources to UNAVEM. In reply to a request from Anstee for an increase in resources, Boutros-Ghali, whom she describes as 'opinionated and argumentative',[78] responded sharply that problems were the same in all missions whether it was Yugoslavia or Cambodia. This ignored the fact that the budget for Angola was only 118 million US dollars for the year, compared to an initial bill of 2 billion dollars for Cambodia.[79] Anstee was instructed to discourage the Angolan government about the degree of logistical support that it could expect from the donor community and attempts by the SRSG to plead a case for assistance in organising the election went largely unheeded because the Secretary-General was reputedly 'too busy'.[80] But despite a less than harmonious relationship between the Secretary-General and his representative, Boutros-Ghali responded quickly to verbal attacks on Anstee from the Angolan parties and after one such attack in October 1992, indicated his impatience with the Angolans. Angolans must first help themselves if they wanted the continuing involvement of the international community, he reminded them. Responding to government suggestions that 'blue helmets' be sent to the country, he replied that given the acute fatigue among contributing countries, such an idea was fanciful. If there was no visible progress he warned, the UN would quickly transfer its attention and resources to other situations, and Angola would be in danger of becoming another Lebanon.[81] Boutros-Ghali's attitude is particularly interesting given his criticism of the Security Council for its failure to give the same attention to African states as was given to Yugoslavia.

Despite numerous indications to Anstee of his intention to visit the mission, the Secretary-General failed to arrive. When fighting broke out in the wake of the 1992 elections, it was left to the SRSG to work relentlessly to get the peace process back on track, but her efforts were hampered by several factors, not least being, according to Toby Lanzer (then stationed in Luanda), that UN Headquarters 'did not know what to do'.[82] Anstee was, in her own words, 'running a virtual one-woman show'.[83]

SRSG

Margaret Anstee (UK) had, before taking up her appointment in Angola, served for almost forty years with the UN in a variety of appointments ranging from working with UNDP to dealing with burning oil wells in Kuwait.[84] She was, therefore, experienced and enthusiastic. Frustrated by anodyne statements and reports emanating from the Security Council, she enthusiastically pursued a policy of pushing mandates to the limit and beyond with the finite resources at her disposal. She accepted that neither the Bicesse Accords nor UNAVEM II's mandate afforded any means of direct intervention.[85] And in contemplating measures which exceeded the mandate, she was between a rock and a hard place. Once involved, the UN was certain to be blamed for all that went wrong. She accepts that the perceived failure of the mission was seen by some as a consequence of sending a woman into a 'particularly macho-dominated area of black Africa'[86] and sexual slur became a weapon in the armoury of both parties. In December 1992, the *Jornal de Angola* (published in Luanda and expressing the government line), alleged that the purpose of Anstee's visit to New York was not to brief the Security Council, but to have an abortion, the progenitor of the baby, allegedly Savimbi.[87] Radio Vorgan, the mouthpiece of UNITA, broadcast a similar type message in May 1993.[88] However, the major problems of the SRSG did not arise directly from the gender of the office holder, but rather from the inadequacy of support from New York and the intransigence of the Angolans. Promised (in resolutions) assistance only when the situation settled or improved, the SRSG was required to become both leader and motivator. In his dealings with the Angolans, Beye, who favoured an approach based low on rhetoric and high on discretion was to find, like Anstee, that whichever side was militarily weaker would wish to negotiate, while the other would wish to fight for maximum advantage on the ground.

Force Commander (CMO)

The Chief Military Observer (CMO) under the authority of the SRSG was empowered with the responsibility of the military/police component of UNAVEM II. In the execution of his responsibilities, he was assisted by a deputy and he delegated his authority to the Regional Commanders. The CMO had full and exclusive authority with respect to the assignment of military and police members of the Headquarters Staff and in the deployment of both military and police observers of UNAVEM. In the particularly difficult conditions encountered by the personnel in the field, it was important that the CMO demonstrated both concern and understanding. The manner of deployment and the unsympathetic attitude of the CMO (General Edward Unimna of Nigeria, October 1991–December 1992) was to create major problems for personnel and was to have lasting effects on the efficiency and morale of UNAVEM II. The 70 military observers of UNAVEM I had been located in coastal cities. Location was not a problem. However, deployment of the 350 military and 126 police observers who formed UNAVEM II, was a major problem. Scattered over 84 locations, most UNAVEM personnel were required to live in what the SRSG described as 'harsh conditions' and what the Secretary General acknowledged were: 'in some respects the most difficult that have ever been faced by UN peacekeeping personnel' (see Plate 1).[89] Observers were exposed to many diseases, most especially malaria, and had no proper medical backup. There was also a serious threat to life from venomous snakes and wild animals. In one week in Muccuio, an observer killed three cobras which entered the compound.[90] A further problem for those in the outstations was that created by the wide variety of languages: in some cases, members of the groups were unable to converse with each other. All of these problems and the acute sense of isolation had a devastating effect on morale throughout the Force since even those in the better stations empathised with their compatriots/colleagues in the bush.[91] However, rather than seeking to alleviate the situation or to show understanding, the CMO adopted a totally unsympathetic and hard-line attitude. Personnel were refused permission to leave their posts for even a short break until they had completed a three-month stint in the post. Even then they could not be assured of release. Those in the HQ who questioned this policy were threatened with banishment to the bush. The office holder of the appointment of Chief Military Personnel Officer (CMPO) was changed four times in six months, a quite extraordinary turnover for such a key appointment. Regional commanders who attempted to make a case for better treatment of their subordinates were accused of disloyalty.[92]

The CMO looked upon malaria in the same light as a bad cold and one CMPO received instructions to regard those going down with the disease as malingerers. One Zimbabwean officer, it was widely believed, died of malaria; a Hungarian officer suffering from the same sickness survived only after being airlifted to South Africa.[93] The behaviour and sometimes violent attitude of the Nigerian CMO (observed more than once striking his driver) had several serious consequences.[94] It depressed already low morale even further: personnel became interested purely in survival and devoted less attention to the task in hand: it also created racial and cultural divisions within the mission. Since it was only the white contingents which dared to challenge the CMO's decisions, the mission split largely along 'African' and 'other' lines. Inevitably, contingents pursued, as far as possible, their own agenda. An Indian Chief of Staff who attempted to organise UNAVEM Headquarters along conventional lines failed because of the resistance of the large African element on the HQ staff.[95] He, in turn, reacted by dealing almost exclusively with the Indian officers in the various outposts. Conventional military procedures were thus largely ignored causing considerable frustration to those, particularly the European officers, accustomed to a proper chain of command.

Anstee notes that upon the outbreak of violence in Luanda in early November, during which time she was forced to remain in the British Embassy, General Uninma

Plate 1 UN outpost in Cafunfo, Angola

Source: Hennie Keeris (Ministry of Defence, NL); collection Institute of Military History RNLA

'simply disappeared off the radio waves and never answered any of my repeated calls'.[96] He later reappeared without explanation for his inaccessibility during the fighting and having been reprimanded by Under-Secretary Marrack Goulding, relinquished his post in December 1992. Anstee discreetly describes Unimna's departure as providing 'relief all round'.[97] What is revealing, however, is her apparent failure to do anything to have the CMO removed. She does note that Unimna's departure 'had to be handled with delicacy because Nigeria was an important African member state and a very sensitive one at that'.[98] Had he not 'disappeared' for a period, it is almost certain that he would have been allowed to serve out his term. The case of this CMO highlighted one of UN peacekeeping's greatest weaknesses, namely official unwillingness to risk offending a member state, even when it is clear that the morale and efficiency of the mission is jeopardised by the behaviour and attitude of one individual.

Tactical capabilities, contingents

UNAVEM II was described by Joseph Perkins, U.S. Permanent Representative to the UN, as 'a mission done on the cheap, a totally false economy on the part of the international community'.[99] When Anstee on a visit to New York in early 1992, suggested comparison between UNAVEM II's strength (432 military and police observers, 200 civilian staff) with UNTAG where 1,758 UN electoral and 1,035 UN police observers operated in a country with a population one-eighth that of Angola, she was told that UNTAG was a totally different and unique operation.[100] UNAVEM II was impressive only in terms of representation, being composed of observers from Europe (Ireland, Sweden, Norway, Spain, Hungary, Netherlands, Yugoslavia), North America (Canada), South America (Brazil, Argentina), Asia (India, Malaysia), Africa (Egypt, Morocco, Guinea, Congo, Algeria, Guinea-Bissau, Zimbabwe, Nigeria), and also New Zealand and Jordan.[101] It was plagued from the start by problems arising from differences in culture and military training. Arguably, the only thing members shared was a susceptibility to sickness. Whatever their country of origin, large numbers quickly succumbed not only to malaria, but amoebic dysentery and a variety of sicknesses caused by lack of proper food, clean water and general hygiene. Even in the best equipped posts, numbers were seriously depleted through personnel being laid low for lengthy periods.

The depletion of numbers exacerbated tensions created by the ill-conceived policy of lumping together individuals from vastly different cultures. The obvious lack of hygiene among certain contingents offended the Europeans, making communal cooking unacceptable in certain situations.[102] The Islamic ritual killing of a goat (although this was often the only form of fresh meat), caused considerable distress to many unused to Islamic practices. Some African observers obviously accustomed to harsh methods of discipline were wont to inflict extreme violence upon locals caught scavenging around the camps. This treatment of what were in many cases starving Angolans, greatly offended other observers. Expressions of disapproval created friction but did nothing to change such behaviour.

Racial tension was fuelled by the perception among European observers that the mission was controlled by a so-called 'African Mafia'. The suggestion that particular contingents, for example the Swedes in the Congo, the Irish in Lebanon, enjoyed special favour because the Force Commander was a compatriot, was and is a feature of most UN operations. What made UNAVEM II different was that it was not a contingent but a group from a particular continent that was perceived to be 'running the show'. Criticism of the perceived 'African Mafia' related to perceptions that individuals who were incapable of performing their duties or who were insubordinate were left untouched purely because they were African. This perception was given substance when one African officer was grossly insubordinate to a senior officer from the Netherlands. The African officer was reported to higher authority but rather than being admonished, he was posted to a senior appointment at the Ivory Coast Peace Talks.[103]

A major social and disciplinary problem arose from the over-close relationship of many observers with the local, particularly female, population. This was highly problematic because, (1) observers were known to carry what were, by local standards, very large amounts of money making them liable to attack, (2) the ability of observers to 'buy' local women created resentment and sometimes open hostility to UNAVEM, and (3) 60 per cent of the population was believed to be infected with HIV. In a Force with such a wide range of cultures and values, establishing a line between what was in the best interests of the mission, the force and the individual was extremely difficult.[104]

Some of the professional shortcomings of UNAVEM II personnel are referred to in an official UN report which in suitably diplomatic language observed: 'while UNAVEM had a generally high standard of military observers, there were lapses. Some countries sent observers with no military background or field experience and thus unsuitable for the task. A large number had poor driving skills, no exposure to staff work or computers, and little knowledge of English'.[105] Lack of language skills was a major problem. Fluency in the local language was an obvious advantage when dealing with the local population but few of the Portuguese or Spanish-speaking observers had any knowledge of English, effectively the lingua franca of the operation. One-third of the 15–20 observers on the staff of the Southern Region in 1993 spoke only Portuguese and daily conferences required the services of an interpreter. Obtaining an accurate picture of the situation was consequently extremely difficult.[106] (One officer from Guinea Bissau had only four words of English: 'yes', 'no', 'very' and 'problem'. Calm situations were 'very no problem', a killing or explosion was described as 'very very problem'). Brazilian observers were generally highly professional, had no shortage of field experience and a number had undergone courses in the US. However, remarkably few were fluent in English. This was particularly unfortunate since the Brazilians formed the Force's largest contingent.

Observers with poor or in some cases negligible driving skills were a double liability because (1) their unavailability for reconnaissance work threw an extra burden on the other members of the generally small teams, (2) because of climate and poor medical backup any accident involving injury was potentially fatal, and (3) accidents involving locals created unwelcome tensions and great hostility in many cases. One of the essential weaknesses of UN peacekeeping is revealed in the UN Report which suggested that a more stringent condition on selection procedures be put in place by DPKO (Department of Peacekeeping Operations). The Report observed that some staff officers 'had no clue as to what was required on the intended appointment'.[107] This was a problem that the UN had, for reasons of 'political correctness' failed to address on previous operations. UNAVEM revealed that despite hopes for more efficient operations post-Cold War, nothing had changed.

Communications

Within UNAVEM I, communications, whether between points or individuals, were a minor problem. Posts were in the readily accessible cities and towns on the coast; the UN body was small and the party with whom it was dealing was cooperative. UNAVEM II however, was for a large part of its life, distributed over an area twice the size of Texas, and was dealing with two parties, neither of which was particularly willing to trade information with it. Within the mission, there were major differences created by cultural and linguistic factors. Communication by land was at the best of times unsatisfactory. The three main railway lines ran east–west and were not interlinking; of the 75,000 kilometres of roads, 85 per cent were little better than dirt tracks and bridges, because of flash flooding, needed constant maintenance. By 1990, the destruction caused by bombing and the dangers created by mines meant that few roads could be travelled in safety.[108] Plane or helicopter was the only effective or secure means of travel. The telephone system was totally unpredictable, being subject to damage caused by a variety of factors.

UNAVEM II's communication problems thus arose in some measure from the inadequacies of equipment and the difficulties of terrain. However, the major problems were created by the chasm in communication between those in the headquarters in Luanda and those in the field, and in particular by the reluctance of the Angolans to establish a working relationship with the UNAVEM II teams. Problems for many observers were evident within days of their arrival. Of the observers who arrived in July 1991, 120 were detained in Luanda for two weeks without being briefed as to the exact nature of their task. They were then dropped by plane or helicopter across the country at 'posts' in cities, towns or simple clearings in the jungle, and left to fend for themselves. Their only communication with headquarters for at least three months was by way of radio. Aircraft delivered mail and occasionally supplies, at intervals of between a week and a fortnight.[109]

There was no telephone communication between most posts and the 'outside world', and radio contact was largely with regional headquarters. No two observers from the same state were permitted in any one observer team and since a team could be composed of individuals who spoke no language but their own, communication in some instances was confined to that made by means of sign.[110] In 1993, Dutch personnel were provided with INMARSAT equipment by their government enabling them to communicate with their compatriots in other posts and with The Hague. However, their good fortune merely created resentment and increased the sense of isolation amongst other nationals.[111]

Efforts by UN observers to keep abreast of developments (in 1993) through contacting government forces or authorities were largely ineffective. On the few occasions on which the military Commander of the Lubango region (General Kuanda) made himself available to the UN Regional Commander (T. O'Neill), the former provided little information and what was provided was generally found in the light of subsequent developments to be inaccurate. Reliable information on the extent of the fighting had to be gathered from Irish missionaries (Frs. Courtney and

Mullen) who were nightly called to attended wounded soldiers or civilians admitted to the local hospital, or from humanitarian workers who gathered information from locals. The UN Commander Southern Region UNAVEM II in early 1993, arranged several meetings with the local governor but on each occasion, the latter failed to appear. The Angolan authorities would however communicate with UNAVEM when needs required. For instance, when a train was attacked on 28 May 1993 by UNITA forces some 60 kilometres from Lubango resulting in the death of over 225 passengers, the governor sought the use of the two locally based UNAVEM helicopters. Clearly afraid that the government helicopters might be attacked, he requested that UNAVEM air lift the wounded and over two days, 65 badly wounded casualties were evacuated by UN craft. But apart from a 'thank you' note, the governor continued to ignore UNAVEM. In the absence of reliable information from government sources, senior officers of UNAVEM II were regularly faced with the problem of deciding upon whether to risk the lives of observers on questionable humanitarian operations in potentially dangerous areas and situations. The temptation, often succumbed to, was to err on the side of caution.[112]

Equipment

Within UNAVEM, logistics were important to different people for different reasons. To Anstee, logistics were a 'political factor'. Without aircraft and communications, the elections could, she maintained, never have been free and fair.[113] To the Regional Commander Southern Region in 1992, an improvement in the logistics system meant more regular supply flights with food and fuel and a somewhat less acute sense of isolation.[114] The 120 observers who arrived in July 1991 in a foretaste of things to come found themselves billeted in hotels in Luanda where no food was available and the supply of water erratic. Once in the outposts, the food supply system varied from the very bad to adequate. With no stocks provided by mission HQ, observers were required to purchase what they could, where they could. Between July and September 1991, observers were reporting weight losses of between 20 and 30 pounds. Water, where available, had to be treated with extreme caution. (A commonly displayed sign read: 'The water in Angola unless well-diluted with whiskey is very dangerous – NO WHISKEY).'[115]

The station-wagon type vehicles used by observers were in adequate supply but of limited value in a country whose roads were impassable because of mines. The mission was as a result utterly dependent upon aircraft of all kinds. UNAVEM II was equipped with one small fixed-wing aircraft and this provided a lifeline between Luanda and the remoter outstations. But it could never meet the demands put upon it. The arrival in September of 17 Russian and Bulgarian helicopters provided a means of re-supply to the more inaccessible outstations. However, these craft were frequently operating to the limit of their range and could not fly after dark (4.30 p.m.) They provided a very useful service in terms of establishing communication between posts, but because of their vulnerability to even small-arms fire, their value was limited overall. Aircraft were critical to plans for medical evacuation

(MEDEVAC). Personnel requiring urgent treatment for malaria or other serious complaints could avail on occasion of local medical treatment. But even in situations where a local hospital was available, treatment was uncertain and the possibility of contracting HIV from contaminated needles was considered high.[116] Provision existed for the lifting of seriously ill personnel from southern posts to hospital in Namibia; plans also existed for the airlifting of 'selected' personnel should any of the major towns in the south fall to the rebels. However, given distances involved and resources available, such evacuation would have posed major problems. UNAVEM was a totally disorganised and in the opinion of most observers, a highly unsatisfactory operation.

Analysis

Mandate performance

UNAVEM I fulfilled its mandate. Whether UNAVEM II succeeded or failed cannot be stated with certainty since the operation's primary task was to monitor activities over which it had no control. UNAVEM I and II highlighted the 'aspirational' nature of UN mandates. UNAVEM I worked because the parties concerned were co-operative. UNAVEM II and III failed or was perceived to do so because cooperation was not forthcoming. The Bicesse Accords provided grounds for optimism and when the mandates were being framed, the UN could not have known what the reactions of the parties would be. By the time the parties demonstrated their unwillingness to settle their differences amicably, there was arguably little the UN could do.

In examining UNAVEM's performance, it has to be recognised that the sheer size of Angola and the destruction of much of the country's infrastructure presented a huge challenge to the implementation of any UN mandate. How could the UN be involved in disarmament, for example finding arms caches and ensuring that soldiers returned to civilian life, when it lacked intelligence, numbers and the cooperation of the parties in dispute. There was the 'human' problem in relation to demobilisation. Angola had, between the opposing forces, the largest standing army in Africa. For generations, many Angolan men knew only army service as their source of income and had known only soldiers for comrades. Any path to peace would, therefore, require another form of employment. The Lusaka Agreement paid significant attention to the process of integrating UNITA troops into the 'national' army, but this development would require the building of trust between the military leaders, a process which after years of fighting was bound to take a considerable time. Also, the UNITA troops who had invested so much of their lives in the struggle, were never likely to meekly accept defeat.[117]

Facilitating conflict resolution

UNAVEM I appeared to have brought an end to conflict and in relation to the external parties, it had succeeded. However, the reopening of hostilities showed how illusory 'success' in general terms could be. To have had any influence on the Angolan parties, UNAVEM II would have required to start from a position of strength in terms of numbers and mandate. It would also have needed the respect of the parties. It had neither. Its personnel were forced to shelter within government-controlled territory and were, therefore, powerless to influence UNITA or to negotiate ceasefires. Even at Force Command level, it could not persuade Savimbi to attend peace talks in Addis Ababa in 1992.

Conflict containment

The departure of the Cubans and South Africans effectively reduced what had been a regional conflict to one within Angola's borders. But while UNAVEM I had been involved in this process, its role had been peripheral and had come after the process of de-escalation had run its course. UNAVEM II was powerless to control developments but the war-weariness in adjoining states which had led to the ending of regional conflict ensured that from 1992 onwards, the threat of overspill into neighbouring states was effectively nil. The problems faced by UNAVEM II were a painful reminder of the consequences of powerful governments' use of proxies to fight for their interests. These proxies had become what Goulding called 'malevolent genies' who could not be put back in the bottle when no longer needed.[118]

Assessment

A lesson that should be learnt from Angola, according to Anstee, is that the UN should be prepared to say 'No' when it is being assigned an inadequate mandate and inadequate resources.[119] Her remark highlighted the general confusion surrounding the UN, its nature and its role. It invites the questions; who is to give 'the UN' adequate mandate and resources?; whom precisely is 'the UN'?

The ready answer to the first question is 'The Security Council' and its performance had merited criticism. But the failure of the Council to show greater concern had to be seen within the expanded role which the UN assumed in the post-Cold War environment. The new interventionism induced severe budgetary strains which resulted in prioritisation of missions. The UN could be mobilised to act decisively and forcefully in the Gulf to defend Western interests. Equally, a major operation could be mounted in Yugoslavia because of the location of the conflict, while efforts by the SRSG to promote greater Council interest in Angola raised no meaningful response. But was not the Security Council a convenient scapegoat for 'the UN's' failure to do more in Angola? Would 'the UN's' member states have been willing to provide the resources for a more significant presence and would the 'non-interventionists, for example China, have been willing to see the organisation take more decisive action to end the civil war? Could 'the UN' have done more given the behaviour and attitude of the parties?

Noting the difference between the resources allocated to UNAVEM and UNTAC (16,000 men including engineers, military police and logistical units), Parsons advances the theory that Cambodia was favoured because of a deeper sense of guilt about the destruction wrought by the Vietnam war and about global indifference to Pol Pot's massacres.[120] But was this guilt real or perceived? Exactly how many member states felt guilty about what had happened in Cambodia? And if the international community was genuinely concerned about large scale loss of life, why was there so little response to the subsequent massacres in Rwanda? Perhaps those with influence within the UN and members generally regarded Africa as a hopeless case. Certainly, this view is supported by the report of Kofi Annan that when in 2000 he sought aid for the famine arising from the war between Eritrea and Ethiopia, potential donors responded: 'How do you expect us to put up money when they are using their money for war'?[121]

Describing Angola as 'a tragedy not to be forgotten', Anstee maintains that the UN should never become involved in any peace accord where it has not taken part in the negotiations and placing the onus of responsibility for implementing a complex peace agreement exclusively on the parties to the conflict is to court disaster. She also speaks of the policy of relying on the spirit of 'boy scout honour' among the parties and the need for 'a strong referee'.[122] In the light of what happened in Angola, her remarks are understandable but they also raise obvious questions. Could the UN refuse to become involved in the implementation of any peace accords where it would not be allowed to 'call the shots'? If it had refused the request of the Angolan government, would it not have been blamed for the re-commencement of hostilities? Given the insistence of states on respect for sovereignty, who is to decide that 'boy scout honour' should not prevail and on what criteria should judgement be based? If a referee is to be given strong powers, is it not likely that one or both parties will refuse to accept him? She further argues that the indifference shown by the international community to UNAVEM II contributed to the failure to demilitarise. She accepts however, that demilitarisation is a highly complex operation, requiring a commitment to peace by both sides and that the psychological barriers to creating the commitment are significant.[123]

It was this lack of commitment to peace by both sides which made the task of UNAVEM II virtually impossible. In contrast to the Angolans, Cambodians desperately wanted UNTAC to arrive.[124] In Angola as in the Congo and Cyprus, the parties had been willing to avail of the UN presence but only insofar as it suited their purposes. Once they refused to demilitarise and UNITA rejected the outcome of the elections, there was arguably nothing that UNAVEM could do to restore peace: even a large force of 'blue helmets' assuming such was available, could not guarantee 'success'. The failure to introduce peace through the medium of Western-style democracy indicated the need for a re-examination of the appropriate nature of politics in a decolonised country. But who would initiate the search for such a solution and how acceptable would it be? UNAVEM II and UNAVEM III once again demonstrated the limitations of the United Nations in the area of civil conflict while the pathetic efforts to salvage 'something' through UNAVEM II's 'humanitarian' role did nothing to enhance the UN's image. Perhaps the outstanding lesson for UNAVEM had been that once initial efforts at assistance have been rejected, the UN should withdraw. The experience appears to support the contention of Roberts and Kingsbury that establishing democratic structures in the face of severe continual division involves much more than the UN and other international agencies can realistically provide.[125]

Notes

1 For reasons that will become apparent, the title UNAVEM is used to cover UNAVEM 1, UNAVEM II and UNAVEM III
2 Keith Sommerville, 'Angola – Groping Towards Peace or Slipping Back Towards War?', *Terrorism and Political Violence*, Vol. 8, No. 4, 1996, pp. 15–17
3 Fathers Conor Courtney and Michael Mullen, Irish Missionaries in Angola, interviewed by Terry O'Neill, May 1993, Lubango, Angola
4 The meeting was held on the Algarve in Portugal. Martin Meredith, *The First Dance of Freedom* London, Sphere, 1985, p. 258
5 At the meeting between the three parties, it was agreed that elections for a constitutional assembly be held in October 1975. Ibid.
6 Sommerville, 'Angola', p. 20
7 David Birmingham and Phyllis Martin, *History of Central Africa*, Vol. 2, New York, Longman, 1983, p. 359
8 The battle of Cuito Cuanavale involved an entire Cuban combat division, the biggest tank battle in Africa since World War II and massive loss of life. (For details see Helmoed-Rohmer Heitman, *War in Angola: The Final South African Phase*, Gibraltar, Ashanti Publishing, 1990, pp. 186–273
9 An African Watch Report, *Angola Violations of the Law of War by Both Sides*, London, Human Rights Watch, April 1989, p. 40
10 UN, *The Blue Helmets*, p. 338
11 In the Museum de la Revelucion in Havana, the total death toll is given as 3,700. However, veterans of the war interviewed by the Terry O'Neill in Havana, August 1999, put the figure at 7,000 plus
12 Fortna, 'United Nations Angola Verification Mission in Angola I', in William J. Durch *The Evolution of UN Peacekeeping*, London, Macmillan, pp. 378–9
13 Toby Lanzer, *The UN Department of African Affairs – Angola Report*, No. 5, Uppsala, 1996, p. 10
14 Fortna, 'United Nations', p. 380
15 Ibid., p. 380
16 Ibid., p. 378
17 Ibid., p. 384
18 The meeting of 18 African Heads of State held in Zaire was presided over by General Mobutu. Ibid., p. 388
19 Ibid., p. 390
20 Vladmir Krska, 'Peacekeeping in Angola (UNAVEM I and II)', *International Peacekeeping*, Vol. 4, No. 1, September 1997, p. 83
21 Ibid., p. 85
22 Sommerville, 'Angola', p. 27

23 Ibid., p. 28
24 MPLA gained 53.74 per cent of the vote and UNITA 34.10 per cent. President Dos Santos beat Savimbi by 49.57 per cent to 40.07 per cent. Krska, 'Peacekeeping in Angola (UNAVEM I and II)', *International Peacekeeping*, Vol. 4, No. 1, 1997, p. 89
25 Ibid.
26 Sommerville, 'Angola – Groping Towards Peace or Slipping Back to War', *Terrorism and Political Violence*, Winter 1996, p. 29
27 Andrew Meldrum, 'Angola: Two Steps Back', *Africa Report*, March/April 1993, p. 45
28 Krska, 'Peacekeeping', p. 90
29 Sommerville, 'Angola', p. 30
30 Toby Lanzer, *The UN Department of Humanitarian Affairs in Angola*, Report No. 5, 1996, p. 53
31 Sommerville, 'Angola', p. 31
32 Ibid., p. 32
33 The numbers of mines were estimated at between 10–15 million. 80,000 Angolans had been maimed by land mines. Ibid., p. 32
34 Ibid.
35 Ibid., p. 33
36 Krska, 'Peacekeeping', p. 94
37 Crawford Young, *Ideology and Development in Africa*, New Haven, Yale University, 1982, pp. 290–1
38 Ibid., pp. 262–3
39 Anstee, *Orphan of the Cold War*, London, Macmillan Press Ltd, 1996, p. 9
40 William Feltz and Henry S. Bienn, *Arms and the Africans*, Military Influences on Africa's International Relations, London, Yale University Press, 1985, p. 15
41 Birmingham and Martin, *History*, pp. 358–9
42 Parsons, *From Cold War to Hot Peace*, p. 118
43 Helmoed-Rohmer, Heitman, *War in Angola*, Gibraltar, Ashanti Publishing, 1990, p. 338
44 Parsons, *From Cold War*, pp. 142–3
45 Sommerville, 'Angola', p. 27
46 Col. Arvid Geirulf, Norwegian Observer, UNAVEM I, interviewed by Terry O'Neill , May 1995, Oslo
47 Margaret Anstee, *Orphan*, p. 13
48 Ibid.
49 Ibid., p. 340
50 Ibid., p. 303
51 Ibid., p. 12
52 Ibid., p. 56
53 Ibid., p. 248
54 Ibid., p. 127
55 Meldrum, 'Angola: Two Steps Back', *Africa Report*, March/April 1993, p. 50
56 Before the elections, Savimbi told international journalists that if he and UNITA lost the elections, they would claim the polls were rigged and return to war. Andrew Meldrum, 'Lessons from Angola', *Africa Report*, January/February 1993, p. 23
57 Major Ashok Sharma, Indian Observer, interviewed by Terry O'Neill, 24 March 1993, Lubango, Angola
58 UNAVEM II observers in Lubango and Luanda, interviewed by Terry O'Neill, June 1993
59 Lanzer, *The UN Department*, p. 13
60 UNAVEM II Observers, interviewed by Terry O'Neill, March–June 1993, Lubango
61 Ibid.

62 Cindy Shiner, 'Angola: The World's Worst War', *African Report*, January/February 1994, p. 16
63 Anstee, *Orphan*, p. 468
64 Ibid., p. 424
65 Ibid., p. 205
66 Meldrum, 'Angola', p. 46
67 *Jornal de Angola*, (Luanda), 20 May 1993
68 Meldrum, 'Angola', p. 46
69 *Jornal de Angola*, 1 June 1993
70 Joanna Lewis, 'Angola 1995: The Road to Peace', *International Relations*, Vol. 13, No. 1, 1996, p. 87
71 UNAVEM II Observers, interviewed by Terry O'Neill, March–June, 1993
72 Joanna Lewis, 'Angola 1995', p. 86
73 Sommerville, 'Angola', pp. 31–32
74 Assis Malaquias, 'The UN in Mozambique and Angola: Lessons Learned', *International Peacekeeping*, Vol. 3, No. 2, 1996, p. 94
75 Parsons, *From Cold War*, p. 144
76 Anstee, *Orphan*, p. 5
77 Ibid., p. 501
78 Ibid., p. 40
79 Ibid., p. 38
80 Ibid., p. 38
81 Ibid., p. 249
82 Lanzer, *The UN Department*, p. 11
83 Anstee, *Orphan*, p. 38
84 Ibid., p. 4
85 Ibid., pp. 532–5
86 Ibid., p. 530
87 Ibid., p. 348
88 Major Ashok Sharma (Indian Observer) interviewed by Terry O'Neill, 24 April 1993, Lubango, Angola
89 Anstee, *Orphan*, p. 18
90 Comdt. L. Bracken, (Irish Contingent), interviewed by Terry O'Neill, 4 June 1994, Cork
91 Col. Thomas Dunne, (Irish Contingent), interviewed by Terry O'Neill, 26 May 1995, Dublin
92 Col. Bernard Howard, (Irish Contingent), interviewed by Terry O'Neill, 26 May 1995, Dublin
93 Ibid.
94 Marrak Goulding, *Peacemonger*, London, John Murray, 2002, p. 194
95 Col. Bernard Howard, interviewed by Terry O'Neill, 26 May 1995, Dublin
96 Anstee, *Orphan*, p. 285
97 Ibid.
98 Ibid., p. 337
99 Ibid., p. 223
100 Ibid., p. 25
101 Ibid., p. 18
102 Col. Howard, (Irish Contingent), interviewed by Terry O'Neill, 26 May 1995, Dublin
103 Lt Col. Lene Noordsij (Netherlands), interviewed by Terry O'Neill, 8 April 1993, Lubango, Angola
104 Reports of perceived misbehaviour were subsequently the subject of investigation and disciplinary action in the Netherlands, and publicity by the media in Norway. Warrant

Officer Ben Ortsen (Netherlands) and Major Alf Gervin (Norway) interviewed by Terry O'Neill in Holland (October 1994) and Norway (August 1996)

105 UN Dept. of Public Information, *UNAVEM Experience, Lessons Learned*, p. 2
106 Terry O'Neill was at this time Regional Commander
107 *UNAVEM Experience*, p. 2
108 Col. Michael Morriarty, 'A Challenge for Peace', in *An Cosantoir*, Dublin, Irish Defence Forces, p. 86
109 Col. Howard, (Irish Contingent), interviewed by Terry O'Neill, 26 May 1995, Dublin
110 Col. Dunne, (Irish Contingent) interviewed by Terry O'Neill, October 1994, Cork
111 Major Ashok Sharma (India), interviewed by Terry O'Neill, April 1993, Lubango
112 Major Alf Gervin, (Norway), interviewed by Terry O'Neill, May 1993, Luanda
113 Anstee, *Orphan*, p. 191
114 Col. Dunne, interviewed by Terry O'Neill, Cork, October, 1994
115 Ibid.
116 Ibid.
117 Joanna Lewis, 'Angola 1995', p. 92
118 Goulding, *Peacemonger*, p. 197
119 Anstee, 'Angola: The Forgotten Tragedy: A Test Case for UN Peacekeeping', *International Relations*, Vol. 11, No. 6, 1993, p. 497
120 Parsons, *From Cold War*, p. 166
121 Kofi Annan, '*UN Chief Faults Reluctance of US to Help in Africa*', p. 1
122 Anstee, 'Angola: A Tragedy not to be Forgotten', *The World Today*, Vol. 52, No. 7, July 1996, p. 2
123 Ibid.
124 Steven Ratner, *The New UN Peacekeeping*, London, Macmillan, 1997, p. 167
125 Adam Roberts and Benedict Kingsbury, *United Nations, Divided World*, Oxford, Oxford University Press, 1989, p. 52

7

UN PEACEKEEPING

Lessons learnt?

In the last four chapters we have focused on case studies of different peacekeeping operations in the Cold War and post-Cold War periods: the Congo, Cyprus, Somalia and Angola. In examining these cases the focus has been on looking at the nature of the conflict, the political base and involvement and interests of the Great Powers, the mandate given to the peacekeepers, the political manoeuvres of the Great Powers, as well as the operational base (the role of the Secretary-General, Force Commander and tactical capabilities). In each instance we have looked at the mandate performance, and particularly, the part of UN peacekeepers in maintaining peace and facilitating conflict containment, the underlying objectives of peacekeeping, and have drawn some preliminary conclusions about the success or failure of the operations.

It is, of course, difficult to make simple comparisons across the cases, as each conflict and operation is unique in its own way, and all yield different lessons for the UN in its involvement in peacekeeping. Nevertheless, in all of the cases the importance of decisions made in the Security Council and the role of the Secretary General in establishing what the mandate should be, provide a key element in understanding how the operations progressed on the ground. Understandably, the nature of the international environment and the conflict being examined is also critical in the likely success of any operation, but equally important are the reasoning, rationale and motives for UN involvement.

In this chapter we seek to understand the role of the UN in peacekeeping operations in the post-Cold War environment by looking at how and in what ways that environment has changed and in what ways that may have shaped the overall approach of UN peacekeeping operations in the 1990s. What, if anything changed at the international level, and what have been the implications of those changes for post-Cold War peacekeeping? We look at some early test cases, the Gulf War and Somalia, at the expectations and reality of peacekeeping, as well as whether the UN has learnt lessons from involvement in such operations.

The end of the Cold War and the shape of the future

The end of superpower rivalry and bipolarity raised the prospect of collective security replacing peacekeeping as one means of dealing with violent conflict within the international system. With improved relations between the US and Russia, there existed the possibility of agreement between these states to enforce the will of the Security Council on a state that had broken the peace. The new world order envisioned by President Bush and Gorbachev would be founded on the rule of law and on the principles of collective security.[1] New political thinking in the crumbling Soviet Union suggested that East and West had some basic interests in common. The most obvious of these was human survival, which was threatened either directly or indirectly by modern weaponry, pollution and poverty. These problems, Gorbachev argued, could best be settled through East–West cooperation using organisations such as the UN.[2] Evidence of the radical change in Gorbachev's foreign policy was the reaction to the Iraqi invasion of Kuwait in 1990. Moscow condemned the invasion and despite some wavering before the UN attack on Saddam Hussein's forces, Russia supported all the UN resolutions against its former ally.[3]

When the Cold War ended, the era of struggle was, in the opinion of some Western academics, supposed to have ended with it, and the period of peace and prosperity was to begin. 'In the 1990s, Cold War acrimony between the super powers is giving way to a new world order harmony' wrote one;[4] 'old enemies are new friends' wrote another.[5] Peace, Charles Maynes suggested, had broken out in Central America, South East Asia, Southern Africa, and even the Middle East. Culturally, the world was apparently coming together and other countries wanted to embrace American ways.[6] The UN had played a positive role in the late 1980s in ending the Iran–Iraq war, the Soviet withdrawal from Afghanistan, the crises in Angola and Namibia, establishing a government in Cambodia, and civil war in El Salvador; thus expectations as to its future role were high. Such hopes were fuelled by Boutros-Ghali's, *An Agenda for Peace* (1992) which assumed a willingness on the part of the member states to contribute to the preventive deployment of peacekeeping forces.

The mood of the time appeared to have been captured by Francis Fukuyama who argued that with the ending of the East–West ideological battle, liberal democracy combined with open market economics would become the only model a state could follow and would prevail everywhere.[7] With no other country now able to present a military challenge, the US could entrench its pre-eminence, or possible dominance in global politics. Fukuyama's scenario appeared to gain credibility when in 1990 President Bush proclaimed his hope for a new world order in classically liberal terms. He spoke of a new partnership based on consultation, cooperation and collective action, especially through international and regional organisations.[8] In his 1991 State of the Union address, George H. Bush stated:

It is a big idea – a new world order, where diverse nations are drawn together in common cause to achieve the universal aspirations of mankind:

peace and security, freedom, and the rule of law. Such is a world worthy
of our struggle, and worthy of our children's future.

In many ways the scenario being painted supported a liberal international
interpretation of international relations.[9] Old rivalries were to be put aside and
enhanced cooperation between America and Russia was likely to underpin the new
world order; one that was predicated on the triumph of capitalism at a global level.
Implicit in these perceptions of the changing world was the notion that a new and
better regulated international system was not only possible but that the international
community was ready and anxious to embrace it. But was there any valid reason to
assume that the scenario presented was what the peoples of the world desired? In
much less dangerous times was it reasonable to expect states to readily submit
themselves to some vague new US-dominated authority? Throughout the Cold War,
the superpowers had limited the autonomy of their allies and puppets, often, but
not always, preventing them from engaging in wars with their neighbours and
placing limits on other hostile acts. But no longer held in check by their former
masters, such states might be free to pursue their own agendas in whatever way they
saw fit without appearing to threaten world peace. There was also the question
of the perceived new peace. Certainly the threat of world war had receded, but
for many millions, the struggles on which they had embarked during the Cold War
looked likely to continue.

The reality of this new era also ignored the national interests of the US, Russia,
China, as well as many of the larger European states, such as Germany, France, UK
and Spain, and regional powers in Asia, Africa and elsewhere. In conceiving of the
international system from a liberal perspective, with an underlying assumption that
there existed a new moral order, based on fundamentally western values, many of
these commentators ignored the realities of the situation, namely that state interests might differ. US interests might not always be shared by the European Union,
and non-Western states might find the newly emergent system deleterious to their
own interests. While there was an initial period of multilateralism in the early 1990s,
the reality was that the permanent members of the Security Council were committed
to pursuing their own particular interests. Notably in 1994 the US adopted new
guidelines that restricted its possible support and participation in UN peace operations.[10] It also ignored the changed international map and growth of strong
nationalist and ethnic tendencies in the former Soviet Union and Yugoslavia.

The disintegration of the former Soviet Union and Yugoslavia created special
problems. One basis for a new order was the previous regime's official nationalities
policy. This had emphasised nationality as a key basis of political units and had
supported ethnic cultures. With the break up of the old Communist order, what
Roberts describes as 'its only half-real sub-order of republics and of ethnic groups'
suddenly had become the basis for a new order.[11] The theoretical right to secession
had become actual and the steadying hand of the old Communist order was no
longer there to hold centrifugal tendencies in check. Also, in at least some of the
new successor republics, there was an absence of legitimate parties, regimes,

political systems, civil societies, working economies, and laws. All of this reinforced the tendency towards ethnic politics.[12]

Most importantly, there was the issue of the US role in the expected New Order. The ending of the Cold War had produced a temptation in the West to recast the international environment in America's image, but not every state wanted this to be so. In Asia, even within democratic states, the emphasis was on national interests. There was no pretence of collective security or that cooperation should be based on shared domestic values.[13] The term 'world order' and Bush's reference to collective action might suggest the possibility of greater recourse to Chapter VII of the Charter, but China (in 1990) remained opposed to military involvement by big powers and opposed use of force in the name of the UN.[14] Russia insisted that political and diplomatic methods be employed to the maximum degree possible. Such fundamental disagreements thus defied efforts to develop guiding principles in relation to the introduction of world order. The triumphant 'Wilsonianism' vision of new world order might need US leadership but it required international support as well.[15] The US might envision as normal a global international order based on democracy, capitalism and international law, but since no such system had ever existed, its evocation, as Henry Kissinger notes, would appear to other societies as utopian.[16]

The arguments advocating the formation of a unipolar world could, Alfo Rusi observed, be reduced to two primary theses: (1) It was in the interests of the US to keep its leading position to safeguard its own interests; (2) US leadership was essential because it was the only country capable of acting as guardian of universal values and keeper of international order. These theses he regarded as flawed.[17] The US would no doubt protect its own interests but to what extent would it provide leadership and resources where its interests were not involved? There were also major question marks over the issues of whether US Presidents could guarantee the commitment of their domestic constituency and whether all the members of the international community could agree on universal values and norms. The US commitment to democracy, capitalism and collective security had never been absolute. It had at one time or another compromised on all these principles.[18] After World War I, Wilson's main preoccupation had involved imposing a structure derived principally from the US constitutional example upon the post-war international system. But America's enthusiasm for seeking stability through democratisation proved sporadic and his countrymen's ardour for the League had quickly cooled.[19] Seventy-odd years on and with Vietnam a vivid memory, the US would continue to be sensitive about sustaining casualties in conflicts where no vital or national interests were at stake and there was no obvious reason why they should now risk lives merely to promote democracy and liberal ideas.

The collapse of communism appeared to vindicate US ideals and to represent a triumph for liberalism and democracy but the theory that the emergence of democracy would necessarily promote peace remained unproved. Many Third World, particularly Africa states, while in theory democracies, had during the Cold War existed in a state of instability or turmoil. In contrast, Yugoslavia, where multiparty democracy was not allowed, had, during the same period, experienced its greatest period of stability. Developments in that country had exposed other weaknesses in liberal theory. The assumption of classical liberalism that the more extensive the contacts that took place between nations the greater the chances of peace[20] had been shown to be faulty in the Middle East and elsewhere, but most particularly in the Balkans. Also a central premise of liberal theory was the belief that if people had the right to choose, they would always choose peace.[21] But what, John Gaddis rightly asks, was to prevent a people from deciding by perfectly democratic means that they would rather hate than love their neighbours and want to cleanse their surroundings?[22] Aggression and civil violence could arise from the people rather than their authoritarian leaders and the ongoing creation of new states could encourage such tendencies. And what if the formation of new states unsettled previously stable arrangements? There had been no clear evidence that a proliferation of sovereignties provided any guarantee of a more orderly world, arguably it could do just the opposite.[23]

The creation of a more orderly world would require not only the exercise of authority but also the establishment of trust and understanding between the powerful and the deprived. Creation of these conditions would not easily be achieved as evidenced by the views expressed by the 1990 Southern Commission (a body chaired by Tanzania's President Julius Nyerere and consisting of leading Third World economists, government planners, religious leaders and others). The Commission called for a New World Order that would respond to the South's pleas for justice, equity and democracy in the global society.[24] This plea arising from the perceived institutionalisation of the South's second class status during the 1980s, raised again the problem of differing views of justice and democracy, and how these were to be introduced.

Under the UN Charter, human rights, justice and social progress were all affirmed as fundamental norms. But though it was the General Assembly which was charged with the progressive development of international law,[25] Third World members would inevitably impede implementation through their continuing sensitivities on the question of sovereignty. While all states had signed the Universal Declaration of Human Rights, (with the exception of South Africa whose apartheid policy was singled out for international criticism), it was governments which decided how they should implement their commitments. From 1960 onwards, governments had not been accountable for their human rights record.[26] The wealthier powerful states, invariably the initiators of humanitarian intervention, would remain liable to charges that their activities were prompted by ulterior motives such as financial interests, and since for many justice was synonymous with retribution, pursuit of the former could become an endless process.

There was also the major problem of how democracy was understood and how it was to be introduced. As evidenced by the case of Northern Ireland, the introduction of Anglo-Saxon democracy with its winner-takes-all character could in certain circumstances prove not an answer but a provocation. Equally, if the theory that democratic states did not wage war on each other[27] were true, then surely strenuous efforts should be made to ensure that all states become democracies. Yet, how far could this endeavour be taken? Was democracy both a reason for peace and justification for war? Did it make sense for states to wage war or use force to compel others to be democratic?

In the emerging international system, global communication would become one of the most important manifestations of Western power leading to the prospect of US-led humanitarian intervention. But equally, domestic support for intervention might become more difficult in the absence of a Communist threat with intervention being a matter of choice rather than compulsion. However, many commentators would perceive the so-called 'CNN (Cable News Network) effect' as constituting a sufficient condition for intervention. The causal mechanism of the 'CNN effect' was that television images of atrocities prompted journalists and leaders of opinion to put pressure on governments to do something, this pressure eventually leading to a response by one or more states.[28] Domestic pressure for intervention also had its advantages. By indicating concern for troubled areas, politicians, for example, lame-duck President Bush, could attempt to bolster their image both domestically and internationally.

But if the 'CNN effect' provoked legitimate humanitarian emotion and appeals for something to be done, once operations were seen to go wrong, appeals for withdrawal were just as likely. Public expectations and the influence exercised on the conduct of operations could also be affected by media presentation of events. Equally, by reacting to situations in relation to the latest atrocity, it would be all too easy to present one of the parties as the clear villain,[29] thereby making the crushing of that party the obvious objective of an international operation. In such circumstances, the outcome could be an unjust settlement which would merely create the basis for future conflict.

Greater media coverage had become possible not only because the Cold War was no longer held centre stage, but because the true nature of repressive regimes which the US had for decades supported, could now be exposed. Also, there was greater access to the former Eastern bloc. But if greater coverage brought distant events nearer, the extent of the international community's response remained to be resolved. While distressing news pictures might stimulate reaction in the West, there would be little evidence to support the assumption that the emergence of global communication produced a significant convergence of attitudes and beliefs. The same visual images transmitted simultaneously into living rooms across the globe, Kishore Mahbubani observed, triggered opposing perceptions. 'Western living rooms applaud when cruise missiles strike Baghdad. Most living outside, see that the West will deliver swift retribution to non-white Iraqi or Somalis, but not to white Serbians, a dangerous signal by any standard'.[30]

Early test cases: the Gulf War and Somalia

The immediate post-Cold War period was marked by a significant increase in the number of peacekeeping operations being authorised by the Security Council between 1988 and 1993. This seemed to reflect less a rise in the number of conflicts than a willingness of the permanent members of the Security Council to work together. It was also noticeable that a number of these operations departed from traditional peacekeeping operations in that they were focused on internal conflicts in states rather than war between states.[31] The nature of these operations also changed with a move away from peacekeeping (traditional military operations as well as more complex operations) to a greater emphasis on peace-building (see Table 7.1). In *An Agenda for Peace* Boutros Boutros-Ghali defined these operations as 'the creation of a new environment to forestall the recurrence of conflict'. Operationally, this meant that the role of the Special Representative of the Secretary-General (SRSG) grew in importance relative to the Force Commander, who usually reported to the SRSG, with a greater emphasis being placed on political mediation. Closely linked to this was the growing importance of civilian elements in such operations, including police, election monitoring, humanitarian relief and development work.[32]

A further noticeable trend during the 1990s was the move to sub-contract out UN operations to regional organisations (such as NATO, the Economic Community of West African States) and 'coalitions of the willing', thereby avoiding directly managing large-scale operations, which were likely to be costly and problematic to manage. Examples of this included NATO in Bosnia (IFOR and SFOR) and the International Force in East Timor (INTERFET) led by Australia. The number of UN delegated Chapter VII operations grew from one in the Cold War period to twelve by 2001. However, the growth of UN intervention in internal conflicts, justified on humanitarian grounds, was not seen as acceptable by some UN member states, who argued that there was a risk that the UN would stray into the grey area between humanitarian intervention and interference in the domestic affairs of a state. Notably the UN Security Council refused to authorise and support the NATO-led actions in Kosovo (1999) and the American-led coalition attack on Iraq; but the UN was also unable to stop these armed interventions.

The war in the Persian Gulf in 1991 was the first test for the grand new order. The world had a third chance to give Wilson's plan the test it had never received and there seemed no more appropriate occasion than by acting, not through US unilateral action, but rather through the 'reinvigorated' UN to restore the independence of Kuwait.[33] In responding to the Iraqi invasion of Kuwait, Resolution 678 was adopted by the Council under Chapter VII of the UN Charter. The resolution authorised the use of force by the member states against Iraq. The resolution 'authorises member states cooperating with the Government of Kuwait . . . to use all necessary means to uphold and implement resolution 660 (1990) and all the subsequent resolutions and to restore international peace and security in the area'.[34] The delegation of such powers to member states was not a new phenomenon, having been first used in Korea in 1950, and most recently in Somalia and Bosnia. In the Gulf case, former rivals, the US and the Soviet Union, united against a common enemy, Saddam Hussein. Significantly, the fact that the US had waited to gain UN approval before going to war and the fact that the Bush administration proceeded

Table 7.1 Examples of different roles played by UN peacekeepers

Operation	Examples of some UN Roles
UNTAG (Namibia) UNTAC (Cambodia) ONUMOZ (Mozambique) ONUSAL (El Salvador)	Elections
UNMIK (Kosovo)	Elections and democratisation
UNTAET (East Timor)	Elections, good governance and public administration
UNOSOM I (Somalia) UNOMUR (Rwanda)	Coordination/escort humanitarian aid
UNMIK (Kosovo) UNTAET (East Timor) MONUC (Rep of Congo)	Peacekeepers used for humanitarian tasks
ONUSAL (El Salvador) MINUGUA (Guatamala) UNTAC (Cambodia) UNMIH (Haiti) UNAMIR (Rwanda)	Promotion and monitoring of human rights
ONUC (Congo), West New Guinea UNFICYP (Cyprus) UNTAG (Namibia) UNTAC (Cambodia) UNPROFOR (Bosnia) UNMIH (Haiti) UNMIK (Kosovo) UNTAET (East Timor)	Police (monitoring and supervision) Police (move into law enforcement)

Source: Compiled from Malone and Wermester (2000)

Note: Some of these operations involved multiple roles and the above provides only selected examples of these roles.

in this way, suggested that it had come to see important advantages in the collective approach in such matters.

In terms of world order and the usefulness of the UN, Iraq's attack on Kuwait served to reanimate the mechanisms of the organisation. But it also exposed its weaknesses. The military forces engaged in the war against Iraq were not under UN command or under the UN flag, but remained under US leadership. Resolution 678 had effectively delegated to the member states the command and control of the coalition forces. The member states forming the coalition agreed that the US would exercise overall control over the armed forces. The world organisation played only a marginal role during the most critical phases of the conflict, although ultimately it did play an important part in ending the military role by ensuring a recognition of the ceasefire in Resolution 687.[35] There seemed, however, no realistic alternative to such a major venture.

While the operation reflected a certain measure of consensus, it was not of itself proof that similar ventures would be undertaken in the future. The international community was largely united against a commonly perceived enemy to world peace, but its interests could not always be guaranteed to be so clear-cut. Saddam Hussein was the ideal enemy and oil-rich Kuwait a victim whose rescue was in the interests of all industrial states. For America and George Bush, the Gulf War was a significant challenge to US interests in a new order and could not be tolerated. If oil was a factor it was perhaps less important than the role of American hegemony in this new world order. Future situations might not present such neat players and clean scenarios for intervention in this manner. Most significantly, even in this situation so seemingly conducive to unanimously agreed action, there was dissent. When the Security Council adopted the enabling resolution – 678 of 30 November 1991 – China abstained while Cuba and Yemen voted against.[36] Moreover, the war's conclusion provided no grounds for rejoicing among Arabs. Instead, the prevailing atmosphere was of disappointment, humiliation and resentment. Once again, the West had won.[37] The Gulf War was fought for the UN but not by it. And while the ending of hostilities could be linked to a wish to avoid further casualties, the UN/US failure to overthrow Saddam Hussein reflected an unwillingness to breach the norm of non-intervention. Implementation of collective security as originally conceived was, it appeared, still an impossibility.

The multinational military action in Somalia was supposed to be the second chapter in global enforcement.[38] The case proved far more problematic, as discussed in Chapter 5, and whilst a further example of the UN seeking an interventionist role, it was marked by failure. It was particularly daunting for the US, with the loss of US military personnel in combat (18 US Army Rangers), leading the US to announce that it would withdraw from the operation by March 1994. European governments followed the US in announcing that they would also withdraw their forces, leading ultimately to the collapse of the military enforcement operation. The failure of peacekeeping operations in Rwanda and Bosnia added to a further decline in the early post-Cold War enthusiasm for deploying UN peacekeepers.[39]

Expectations and reality

The high expectations following the end of the Cold War were rapidly being re-evaluated in light of the reality of the mid-1990s and operational failures in Somalia and Bosnia. In *A Supplement to an Agenda for Peace*, Boutros-Ghali noted the limited ability of the Security Council and the Secretary-General to deploy operations in support of enforcement, as well as the limited resources of the UN and of its existing capacity to meet traditional peacekeeping operations.

Reacting to the disappointing performance of post-Cold War operations, Kofi Annan in 1996 acknowledged that the UN faced challenges that did not fit into a neat peacekeeping package: the so-called grey-area operations. Meeting new challenges would require first, the development of a serious capacity for the lawful gathering of intelligence 'so that we can understand the crisis in which we are about to intervene, and are able to anticipate how it is likely to develop'. Second, UN operations would require appropriate capabilities upon deployment and the right force structure to be able to carry out the mandate and to be able to protect the operations. If the UN failed to do so, as was the case in Bosnia and Somalia, credibility would be further eroded and it would be increasingly difficult to find troop contributors.[40] In July 1997 Kofi Annan noted in *Renewing the United Nations: Programme for Reform*, that the UN did not have the institutional capacity to conduct military enforcement measures under Chapter VII, thus the UN must depend on coalitions of the willing to undertake such operations.

His words were significant in that they identified the problems which had long plagued UN operations. The UN had ventured into the Congo without any clear understanding of what it was trying to do, and therefore of how to do it. It had stumbled into conflict with an enemy that theoretically did not exist and in the absence of a proper plan of action the tenuous command and control system had broken down. 'Peacekeepers' had died in a military action for which they were not prepared. Ignoring the lessons of that venture, the UN had intervened in Somalia and engaged in armed confrontation with a party whose resistance to UN designs and whose military capability had been totally underestimated. Again, at a critical moment, the operation's command and control system had been found wanting. UNFICYP's mandate – restoration of normal conditions – assumed the compliance of the parties in a return to what was a manifestly unsatisfactory situation. The UN had employed inadequate resources, and the parties, when in pursuit of their objectives, had shown scant regard for the peacekeepers. The post-Cold War UN had failed to make a proper estimate of the situation in Angola and through this neglect had, just as in Cyprus, allowed the parties to dictate developments. In both the Congo and Somalia, the UN force was composed of contingents, many of which were inadequately equipped and hence operationally inefficient. The fact that something needed to be done to improve operations had been recognised by the creation of the various new bodies within the Secretariat.

In this context, other operational problems that have been identified by practitioners and academics include:[41] the multinational nature of the forces (member states' concerns for safety of personnel), the slow deployment of forces, a lack of pre-deployment planning, mobility limitations, restrictions on the use of force, limited military intelligence from member states, the chain of command (under the control of the Force Commander), the relationship of the SPRG and Force Commander, logistics and funding. It has also been suggested that an overall level of coordination and cohesion is required between the Department of Political Affairs, the Office of Human Resources, the Department of Peacekeeping Operations, the Office for Humanitarian Affairs (changed to the Office of the Emergency Relief Coordination in 1997) and Office of Legal Affairs. Does the continuance of such operational problems suggest that lessons have not been learnt and applied?

Lessons learned?

The failings and weaknesses of the UN system and of UN peacekeeping are known to most observers, yet the UN has seemed unable to learn lessons from its past endeavours, both at the political level of the Security Council and Secretary General and at the operational level in the field. Attempts at reform have sometimes smacked of tinkering and more ambitious proposals have tended to be whittled down by self-interested parties. Reforms proposed by two recent Secretary-Generals have addressed some, but not all, the issues and problems that surround day-to-day peace operation, and have left the UN susceptible to repeating its past failures without learning how to avoid such mistakes. For example, as Malone and Thakur[42] note of the UN Mission in Sierra Leone in 2000 (UNAMSIL), it seemed to repeat some of the mistakes of earlier missions: it was poorly planned, under equipped, with poorly trained military personnel all from the developing world, inadequate communication, weak command and control, and fractious local parties.[43] While the operation was authorised under Chapter VII, the mandate was restricted, limiting an all out enforcement operation. Moreover, the seizure of 500 Kenyan and Zambian peacekeepers as hostages in May 2000 highlighted the problems of the operation and required the deployment by the UK government of 700 military personnel to bolster the UN peace operation. It exemplified many of the problems that have been identified in the case studies, and yet past mistakes seem to have been repeated and lessons not learned. How has the UN responded to such incidents of clear failure (as was also the case in Rwanda and Bosnia) and what changes have been proposed and made to the manner in which UN peace operations are conducted?

In response to a mix of criticism and particular failures, Kofi Annan convened a high-level panel of nine experts under the chair of Lakhdar Brahimi (former Algerian Foreign Minister) to assess the shortcomings of the existing system and to make frank, specific and realistic recommendations for change in the way peace operations were conducted. The panel reported on 21 August 2000. The so-called 'Brahimi Report'[44] revealed that despite Annan's earlier assessment and proposals, nothing had really changed by way of planning or availability of resources. It highlighted the diffusion of responsibility at the UN and suggested that this led to further difficulties in the field.

The 'The Lessons Report' proposed among other things, that mandates and goals should be clear, realistic and practicable,[45] planning for an operation should begin with the collection of all information about the country and region of deployment,[46] and coordination between the Security Council and troop-contributing countries should be strengthened.[47] It noted that intelligence could greatly assist operations and recommended that individual contingents respond consistently to the directions of the Force Commander and not to national imperatives and agendas.[48] It also suggested that military and financial resources should be of a sufficient nature to undertake the mandate. It also noted that CIVPOL should be trained in human rights monitoring, and be aware of internationally approved norms and guidelines on crime prevention and criminal justice.[49] This effectively recognised the ongoing great disparity in values and attitudes between member states. The UN HQ's own shortcomings were recognised in the report's statement that equipment at the logistics base in Brindisi to which Annan had referred so optimistically in 1996, 'should be in a serviceable condition before being dispatched to missions'.[50] But officials in the UN as far back as ONUC had known all of these lessons, so what has now happened and have changes occurred?

Implementation of the Brahimi Report was contingent on the support of the Security Council, the Secretary-General and the General Assembly. Moreover, the problem of resources was likely to remain a core issue of concern, as the changes proposed in the report not only needed political support but financial assistance. The findings of the report were largely supported by the US, UK and other Western states, with the main opposition coming from India, Russia and China. The Security Council adopted the report in November 2000 and in December the Special Committee on Peacekeeping (General Assembly) also endorsed it. Deputy Secretary-General Frechette was designated to oversee the implementation of the report. Proposals for implementation included (October Report 2000):

- enhancing the effectiveness of key peace and security instruments;
- new mechanisms for improving system-wide integration;
- enhancing rapid and effective deployment capacities;
- funding of HQ support to peacekeeping operations;
- restructuring of DKPO;
- strengthening areas of the UN system.

In seeking to implement these recommendations the Department of Peacekeeping Operations was to receive additional resources to support the planning, deployment and management of traditional and multifunctional peacekeeping operations.

This was followed in March 2002 by the Report of the Special Committee on Peacekeeping Operation, the 'Comprehensive Review of United Nations Peace-keeping Operations',[51] whose recommendations, Annan described as 'far-reaching, sensible, and practical'.[52] It began by acknowledging that over the last decade, the UN had failed to meet its original challenge of saving succeeding generations from the scourge of war and accepted that it 'could do no better today'.[53] Implementation of the recommendations was, he declared, essential if the UN were to be credible. However, the review, while presenting more detailed recommendations, largely covered by now well-trodden ground. It recommended that brigade-size forces be made available,[54] that field intelligence be afforded:[55] and that member states make available a pool of civilian police.[56] It also spoke of a doctrinal shift in the use of civilian police.

The 'Comprehensive Review' reflected a feeling of frustration at the failure of operations and went through the problems and dilemmas encountered in the tortuous search for an effective and acceptable response to the problem of conflict. It accepted that the UN did not wage war but entrusted that task to coalitions of willing member states.[57] The UN's problem, the review recognised, was in finding a form of activity that adhered to the principles of peacekeeping, but 'not quite'. The 'not quite' arose in the area of impartiality. The 'Comprehensive Review' accepted that consent, impartiality and use of force in self-defence should remain the bedrock principles of peacekeeping, but also declared that in a situation where one party to a peace agreement clearly and uncontrovertibly violated its terms, continued equal treatment of all parties by the UN could 'at best result in ineffectiveness, and at worst amount to complicity with evil'.[58] The implication that the UN should now contemplate action against the 'bad guy' appeared consistent with Annan's proposal in 1996 that 'operations possess both the mandate and capacity to conduct, if necessary, offensive operations against recalcitrants'.[59]

However, having identified the UN's dilemma, the 'Comprehensive Review' skirted around a solution, referring only to the need for UN forces to be able to protect themselves. It declared, quite understandably, that peacekeepers, once deployed, must be able to carry out their mandate professionally and successfully. This meant that UN military units must be capable of defending themselves, other mission components, and the mission's mandate. Rules of engagement should be sufficiently robust and not force UN contingents to cede the initiative to their attackers. This meant that mandates should specify an operation's authority to use force. This, in turn, would involve bigger forces, better equipped and able to provide an effective deterrent. In particular, UN forces for complex operations should have field intelligence and the capabilities needed to mount an effective defence against violent challenges.[60] These were all very sound and reasonable recommendations, particularly in the light of the UNPROFOR and UNAMSIL experiences, but there remained a number of unanswered questions. Was it proposing that further action against perceived 'bad guys' be taken in the guise of self-defence? If so, would it be possible to frame a mandate that specified when, and how much, force would be employed to deal with 'evil', particularly when as in Sierra Leone, there was more than one 'evil' party? What would be the limits of action taken in self-defence?

The 'Comprehensive Review' expressed the belief that until the Secretary General was able to obtain solid commitments from member states for the forces believed necessary to carry out the operation, it should not go forward at all. This made considerable sense when and where large-scale opposition could be expected, but what of situations such as Rwanda where even a small well-armed force might prove effective?[61] The review also recommended that the Security Council should also leave its authorising resolution in draft form until the Secretary-General had confirmed that he had received necessary troops and other contingents from member states, sufficient to meet their requirements.[62] But would potential troop-contributors be willing to volunteer forces without knowing the risks involved? The review noted the reluctance of member states to accept the risk of casualties since the difficult missions of the mid-1990s. To gain the support of member states, the Security Council and Secretariat would have to be able to win the confidence of troop-contributors that the strategy and concept of operations for a new mission were sound and that they would be sending troops or police to serve under a competent mission with effective leadership.[63] This move, however sensible, would take a lot of time and effort.

A further recommendation was that the Secretary-General send a team 'to confirm the readiness of each potential troop-contributor to meet the requisite UN training and equipment required for peacekeeping operations. 'Units that did not meet requirements must not be deployed.'[64] This raised the questions – what training? What equipment? Such questions merely highlighted once again the confusion and general 'wooliness' sourrounding perceptions of peacekeeping.

With regard to training, was this to be geared towards traditional-type peace-keeping or some other still to be clarified form of activity? For many years, some members, notably the Nordic states and Ireland, had introduced their troops to certain traditional peacekeeping practices and techniques, including crowd control, manning of road-blocks, and mediation of local disputes. However, this training, while extremely useful, was of limited value only in the kind of conflicts with which peacekeepers of the 1990s found themselves involved. The experience of UNPROFOR and UNAMSIL demonstrated, and the context of the review's proposals implied, that modern-day peacekeepers needed training for direct con-frontation with large, well-armed forces. To be 'properly' trained, peacekeepers would require 'proper' equipment.

In an era when aircraft, tanks and sophisticated infantry weapons were common features of peacekeeping operations, the capacity or willingness of governments to provide for their peacekeepers now constituted a major problem. The armies of many 'regular' troop-contributing states clearly lacked current combat-type equipment, either because the states in question were too poor or, as in the case of Ireland, because a combat role was never seriously contemplated. Such troops would, therefore, be unable to train for such a role. Besides, any proposal to over-come this problem by using borrowed equipment would be effectively meaningless since contingents would still be expected to arrive on missions fully equipped.

While training might lead to more effective participation by troops from weaker/lesser states, any such development would not necessarily result in uniform performance by contingents or ensure more effective operations. An ongoing feature of operations would inevitably be the widely differing approaches of participating states to the task in hand. Such approaches, shaped by culture, combat ethos, or a determination not to be 'pushed around' would, as ever, range from patient pursuit of the perceived objective, to 'firm action' or outright confrontation. In Somalia as in Lebanon (MNF), the patient Italians had gained the confidence and cooperation of the local population. In contrast, the heavy-handedness of US forces in those theatres had proved disastrous, both for the Americans and the missions. Certainly the attitude of some states could, over the years, be seen to have changed. The readiness of the Indians to resort to force in the Congo had precipitated conflict: yet they had exercised restraint in Somalia and insisted that UNAMSIL, despite its Chapter VII mandate, was a peacekeeping not a combat force. However, there was no evidence to suggest that powerful states such as the US and Russia would ever be concerned with 'winning hearts and minds'.

The question of training and the problems created by lack of uniformity, assumed a particular importance when linked to proposed greater involvement of CIVPOL. In Cyprus, well-trained CIVPOL from Ireland and the Antipodes had for many years provided a useful liaison service between the island's factions. Employed as election monitors and observers in Namibia and Angola, many CIVPOL contingents also performed well in a brief and limited capacity. It was the role in 'peace-building' which raised greatest doubts about increased CIVPOL employment.

The new multifunctional peacekeeping operations required the UN to acquire a range of civilian personnel to assist in fulfilling the much-expanded peacekeeping mandate. To restore and nurture confidence and well-being among people in divided communities, the UN needed trained, responsible, and committed personnel. However, despite the existence of a clear precedent in the Namibia operation, UN, in the case of Cambodia, failed to attract an efficient, knowledgeable body of police. Many contributing states lacked any tradition of police respect for citizens and did not send their best. Some, including an entire group from Bulgaria, were corrupt, even criminal in their behaviour.[65] The Japanese police contingent was viewed as extremely ineffective in the performance of its duties and excessively concerned about the domestic impact of sustaining casualties.[66] A majority of complaints from Cambodians stemmed from bad behaviour by CIVPOL members, including harassment and rudeness, and their behaviour tarnished the UN's image.

A major problem is that amongst member states, a significant number possess police forces which bolster and maintain in power repressive and arbitrary regimes. In the context of peacekeeping, regimes of this kind may be among those to which a CIVPOL contingent may be deployed or be contingent contributors. Overall, it had to be recognised that severe disparities in the skill levels of personnel, coupled with disparities in policing styles and values, made the delivery of a good service by an international police force an illusionary goal. A greater reliance on CIVPOL would therefore not solve the UN's problems.

In its attempts to 'get it right' during the 1990s, the UN had employed a variety of military options. At one extreme, it had entrusted the problem of Sierra Leone to a regional organisation. But this solution was a failure with the UN having eventually to take over, only to endure subsequent humiliation. In the 'middle', it had, in Somalia, tried a mixture of traditional peacekeeping, the use of the US 'big stick' and invocation of Chapter VII, but with disastrous results. At the other extreme, it had availed of NATO's power to assist its efforts in former Yugoslavia but even this solution proved less than satisfactory. This 'solution' not only exposed the organisation's military weakness, but left it open to claims that it was becoming 'marginalised'.[67]

However, if the UN's performance in the 1990s was generally regarded as disappointing, it was relevant to ask: upon what basis had expectations been raised and by whom? Did states and peoples the world over really want the UN to undertake a more assertive role in international affairs or was this something which only 'UN watchers', academics and the media believed could and should happen. Were expectations pitched too high relative to past performance? Given that from its inception, the UN had, in political conflicts, been paralysed by East–West confrontations, it was understandable that when this situation changed, there would be hope in some quarters that the organisation might become a truly global security institution. These hopes were however always misplaced. The ideological confrontation of the past had only hidden more subtle and enduring divisions within the general body. One factor which had led to the UN's paralysis was differing definitions of national sovereignty. Many European states had become accustomed to pooling their actions; for them, sovereignty was not a matter of major importance. However, sovereignty remained sacred to African and Asian states. There were still serious divisions within the Security Council. So long as China remained under control of a hard-line Communist party, a global order which respected human rights would continue to be a dream. And while Russia had formally accepted democracy, its politicians would show little enthusiasm for human rights reform. In theory, weak states might desire a strong UN, but many developing countries would remain fearful that a more powerful and effective UN might at some stage seek to intervene in their essentially private wars.[68] There was also the question of what form UN action was expected to take.

In the early 1990s, the academic and scholarly literature was, as Diehl observes, brimming with suggestions for new kinds of peacekeeping.[69] But Cold War strategists and battlefield analysts who had for years maintained at best contemptuous disregard for the UN in general, and the concept of peacekeeping in particular, were poorly qualified to master its complexities. As a result, their attention focused on the effects of changes on the military element without understanding the 'UN element' that had become such an essential factor. Like the Cold War strategists, the UN experts and the peace-studies institutions were poorly qualified to react to the approaching doctrinal void. Although the 'UN experts' had developed a valuable understanding of the political and institutional components of the UN, many were ignorant of the prevailing military requirements and techniques.[70] Much of the academic literature on the UN after the Cold War had been the product of aspiration focusing largely on what was theoretically desirable rather than on what was politically or practicably feasible.[71] The token Cold War era peacekeepers could, many believed, cope in internal conflicts. But this was to ignore the vast difference between the relatively straightforward task of maintaining a buffer zone and confronting large armed forces engaged in bitter internal disputes. There were also significant changes in circumstances surrounding operations.

The ending of the Cold War had encouraged the view that future developments in the principles and practices of peacekeeping would allow the UN to serve as an effective instrument to reduce violent conflict within the international system.[72] But the change in circumstances also impacted on operational effectiveness. A driving force behind peacekeeping during the Cold War was the superpowers' mutual interest in bringing an end to proxy wars before these powers were dragged into direct confrontation. Hence, the superpowers were in a position to dramatically reduce military and economic assistance to their allies and induce them to consent to a peacekeeping operation and to cooperate with it.[73] This important 'prop' to peacekeeping efforts was now removed. There was also the issue of 'consent'. The UN now found itself dealing with insurgent forces that were distinctly different from those of the past. In the earlier UN operations, consent and cooperation could be pledged with a degree of assurance by leaders involved in negotiation who could, if they were disposed to doing so, also control the violence. However, in states such as Somalia or Cambodia, there were no government structures and insurgent leaders had no concept of statesmanship or the law.[74]

A major source of raised expectations had been Boutros-Ghali's *An Agenda for Peace* which energised the search for a new concept but lacked essential conceptual detail. Boutros-Ghali's reference to peace-enforcement encouraged expectations of robust action to introduce, if not impose, international values and norms. Pressure for action was further boosted by the emergence of a concerned global community which, while relatively small in numbers, was motivated by sentiments of empathy and moral obligation to respond to human suffering wherever it occurred. But the simplistic solution to a problem as perceived by well-intentioned observers might, as shown in Somalia, prove unacceptable to those whom the UN was attempting to help. Also implicit in the use-of-force approach, was the naïve belief that UN forces could deliver just the precise amount of force required to 'take out' the 'evil' party. However, the clean clinical strike, which observers might see as desirable, was something which a UN force was because of its nature, totally incapable of delivering. Ultimately, these were the simple realities of peacekeeping operations.

Whatever the academic assessment of the prospects for improved peacekeeping post-Cold War, each new operation would, for those involved 'on the ground', be a totally new and uncertain venture into the unknown. Each operation would, just as during the Cold War, involve entirely different circumstances and different 'players'. There would be the same lack of clear objectives and direction. There would be the same problems of communication and resources, and the same problems of command and control. Forces would, as before, be composed of disparate elements, each ultimately responsive to the concerns and dictates of their home governments. The soldier at the check-point or facing an angry mob would draw little comfort or support from the knowledge that the Security Council which had given him his mandate, was now perceived to be functioning more harmoniously than in earlier decades. Those engaged in, or threatening, violence would probably know or care little about the contents of Chapter VII of the UN Charter. Operations would still tend towards a freezing of what one or more of the parties regarded as an unsatisfactory status quo.

Expectations that post-1989 UN peacekeeping operations could be adapted to the changed international circumstances were totally unrealistic. To entertain such expectations was to ignore the nature and experience of Cold War operations. At all times, 'doing something' by way of military intervention presented the UN with a choice between peacekeeping and going to war. Choosing the former meant adherence to the three principles and the engagement of the parties in a common effort to achieve peace. Choosing the latter meant commitment of the necessary political will and military and financial resources to achieve victory. During the

Cold War, peacekeeping had been the UN's method of 'doing something' and the cooperation of the parties had been crucial to the work of all peacekeepers prior to and including 1989. Peacekeepers by definition and experience could not impose their will on those who did not wish to keep the peace. However, in the heady days post-Cold War, this obvious truth tended to be overlooked.[75] The media and opinion leaders clamouring for UN intervention wanted action that involved peacekeepers being more assertive and confrontational with recalcitrants: it was now not so much a matter of 'doing something' but 'doing something more'. But 'doing something more' implied less reliance on consent, 'less' impartiality and less restraint in the use of force. However, any such attempted modification of the rules of peacekeeping was destined to lead to confusion as to objectives and the method of intervention. It could only lead to hybrid and ultimately disastrous operations as demonstrated most notably in UNOSOM.

Hopes for a new invigorated, more effective UN had all but evaporated by early 2000. The Security Council practice of delegating Chapter VII operations to regional organisations and coalitions-of-the-willing plus the delegation of the operation in East Timor to an Australian-led force in September 1999 indicated a trend that was likely to continue.[76] The 'delegation' process confirmed not only the UN's limitations, but the divisions which had always prevented a common approach to conflict resolution.

After Somalia, Western powers with the capacity to intervene proved reluctant to support complex operations in Africa. The reluctance of Western permanent members of the Security Council to lead or support operations outside their spheres of influence was perceived to have weakened UN legitimacy in the Third World, African elites feeling that Western powers were applying double standards by supporting strong measures in former Yugoslavia while refusing to do so in Africa.[77] However, this perceived unequal treatment was a reminder of stark realities. Africa did not have at its disposal an equivalent to NATO in terms of power and Sierra Leone had shown that a largely African force could not restore peace when faced by formidable opposition. But then, even a strong Western-dominated force, assuming such was available and acceptable, might be no more successful than UNOSOM in addressing Africa's problems.

The chaotic situation in the Congo in 2000 and the failure in Sierra Leone appeared to confirm the UN's impotence as an instrument for introducing peace. Conventional wisdom would suggest that the UN do less peacekeeping either by not getting involved at all, or by working only on the margins. But such a course of action is, as Annan argued in 1996, an illusionary option. Inaction in the face of massive violence is, he argues, morally indefensible. Equally 'doing nothing to respond to violent upheavals invites those affected in whatever way to take matters into their own hands'.[78]

The record of peacekeeping operations as detailed in the case studies and the sense of helplessness evident in Annan's comments and in the 'Lessons Report' and 'Comprehensive Review', serve as a reminder of the extraordinary character of the UN. It is not a security company competing with other organisations for 'business' and concerned about its performance and image. Neither is it a government elected by and answerable to, constituents. It cannot compel its members to engage in peacekeeping operations, and even those who do may opt out at any stage. It cannot be held to account for its actions or omissions. There is no responsible body required to implement recommendations or to respond to criticism. Critics of the UN, particularly those in the media, may expect or demand more from the larger powerful members, but those members may argue that if they exercise their 'muscle' they risk being accused by 'the UN' of the smaller states of neo-imperialism or of imposing alien values. 'The UN' of the powerful states may well perceive 'the UN' of the weaker states with its insistence on respect for sovereignty, as the creator of its own problems.

Inaction during the 1994 massacres in Rwanda might be widely regarded as the UN's greatest failure, but who really was to blame? Was it the Secretary-General; the Security Council; the West; or the many African and other states which could have, but failed to provide contingents? And who then was entitled to level accusations or apportion blame? The reason for the UN's perceived ineffectiveness in maintaining peace is, Ciechaski notes, that 'the doctrine of collective security embodied in the Charter is based on assumptions which are invalid in a world where states are not prepared to defend the existing order in situations where their national interests are not directly affected'.[79]

However, if the record of peacekeeping in the 1990s presents a mixed picture, one recently launched operation provides some measure of hope in the twenty-first century. The UN's efforts to nation-build in East Timor represent an enormous challenge in which the credibility of the UN is at stake. However, if it succeeds, it could become a model for future ventures and help restore faith in the organisation. In East Timor, the UN faces the problem that its operation is in effect an exercise in benevolent colonialism[80] in an age when colonialism is no longer acceptable. Unlike other operations such as ONUC, the UN is not just helping the government, it is the government.[81] A major task has been that of establishing a Timorese legal system and helping devise a body of laws for this embryonic country.[82] UNTAET (UN Transitional Administration for East Timor) could not pay its Timorese employees until it devised a banking law and settled on a currency. It could not punish law-breakers without a body of criminal law; the alternative would be to rule by decree, but this would violate the spirit of the mission and the UN's larger goals of fostering democratic values. As a result, the first statute that the UN Transitional Administration passed was one that delineated its own authority and stipulated that Indonesian law (Indonesia having been the previous ruling power) would remain, unless it conflicted with UN human rights standards or with the UNTAET mandate.[83] The second new law set up a National Consultative Council to give the Timorese a say in the legislation process. However, a major stumbling block to effective implementation of law and the creation of a normal society is the marked absence of qualified personnel. Thanks to a twenty-five year diaspora, there are Timorese doctors and academics in Portugal and Australia but it will be a long time before a sufficient number of these are persuaded to return.[84]

UN efforts in East Timor have been commendable insofar as it provided a high-class team of international technocrats and 8,500 well-armed and trained soldiers.[85] However, there have been expressions of dissatisfaction and discontent with the operation. Part of the problem is that the only people with jobs are those working with the UN. Also, Ramos Hortha complained about the incompetence of the UN police: 'Our people are supposed to be assisting some policemen from Gambia – we have some very senior people and the idea that they should be assisting the CIVPOL is stupid and insulting', Asked if he could think of anything good that UNTAET had done, he replied: 'In terms of anything visible so far? Nothing.'[86] An international response to the problems of East Timor had been long overdue. However, when it came it was not only one of the swiftest in the history of UN operations but was the first time post-Rwanda that the Security Council met a crisis head on.[87] The UN force has rebuilt bridges and repaired roads and spent time reassuring the Timorese. Apart from harassing refugees at the border, the two Indonesian militaries have posed little threat. The UN commitment appears broad and serious and while the goal might appear almost utopian, the venture provides grounds for optimism about UN intent in the new century.

Notes

1 Bruce Russett and James Sutterlin, 'The UN in the New World Order', in *Foreign Affairs*, Vol. 70, No. 2, 1991, p. 69
2 Mike Bowker and Robin Brown (eds), *From Cold War to Collapse: Theory and World Politics in the 1980s*, New York Press Syndicate of the University of Cambridge, 1993, pp. 89–90
3 Ibid., p. 95
4 Ramesh Thakur, 'The United Nations in a Changing World', *Security Dialogue*, 1993, Vol. 24, No. 1, 1993, p. 7
5 G. Till, 'Maritime Strategy and the Twenty-First Century', Strategic Studies, Vol. 17, No. 1, 1994, p. 166, quoted in Andrew Dorman, Mike Laurence Smith and Matthew Uttley, 'Jointery and Combined Operations in an Expeditionary Era: Defining the Issues', *Defence Analysis*, Vol. 14, No. 1, 1998, p. 2
6 Charles William Maynes, 'Squandering Triumph: The West Botched the Post-Cold War World', *Foreign Affairs*, January/February 1999, p. 15
7 Francis Fukuyama, 'The End of History', *The National Interest*, quoted in Charles Maynes, 'Squandering Triumph', *Foreign Affairs*, summer 1989, p. 15
8 Henry Kissinger, *Diplomacy*, New York, Simon and Schuster, p. 804
9 Roland Paris 'Peacebuilding and the Limits of Liberal Internationalism', *International Security*, Vol. 22, No. 2, 1997, pp. 54–89
10 Michèlle Griffin 'Blue Helmets: Assessing the Trend Towards "Subcontracting" UN Peace Operations', *Security Dialogue* Vol. 30, No. 1, 1999, pp. 43–60
11 Roberts, 'Ethnic Conflict: Threats and Challenges to the UN', in Anthony McDermott (ed.), *Ethnic Conflict and International Security*, Oslo, Norsk Utenrikspolitisk Institutt, June 1994, pp. 12–13
12 Ibid., pp. 12–13
13 Kissinger, *Diplomacy*, p. 826
14 Christopher Brady and Sam Daws, 'UN Operations: The Political-Military Interface', *International Peacekeeping*, Vol. 1, No. 1, 1994, p. 76

15 Alpo Rusi, *Dangerous Peace*, Boulder Colorado, Westview Press, 1997, pp. 30–1. Note: after World War I, US President Woodrow Wilson wanted to use US power to direct international relations in support of a more 'liberal order'
16 Kissinger, *Diplomacy*, p. 18
17 Rusi, *Dangerous Peace*, Boulder, Colorado: Westview Press, 1997, p. 32
18 John Lewis Gaddis, *The United States and the End of the Cold War*, Oxford, Oxford University Press, 1992, p. 195
19 John Lewis Gaddis, 'The Post-War International System', in Oyvind Osterud (ed.), *The Reform of the International System: Studies of War and Peace*, Oslo, Norwegian University Press, 1986, p. 135
20 Ibid., p. 197
21 Timothy Dunne, 'Liberalism', in John Baylis and Steve Smith (eds), *The Globalisation of World Politics*, Oxford, Oxford University Press, 1997, p. 161
22 John Lewis Gaddis, 'The Post Cold War World: Finding a Theme', *New Zealand International Review*, March/April 1996, p. 6
23 Ibid.
24 Naom Chomsky, *Year 501, The Quest Continues*, London, Verso, 1993, pp. 44–5
25 David Armstrong, 'Law, Justice and the Idea of a World Society', *International Affairs*, Vol. 75, No. 3, 1999, p. 549
26 James Mayall, *The New Interventionism 1991–1994*, New York, Press Syndicate of the University of Cambridge, 1996, p. 5
27 Marc Peceny, 'A Constructivist Interpretation of the Liberal Peace: The Ambiguous Case of the Spanish–American War', *Journal of Peace Research*, Vol. 34, No. 4, 1997, p. 415
28 Peter Jakobsen, 'National Interest, Humanitarianism or CNN: What Triggers UN Peace Enforcement After the Cold War?', *Journal of Peace Research*, Vol. 33, No. 2, 1996, p. 206
29 From the outset of the crisis in former Yugoslavia, the Serbs would be presented by the media as the clear villains. Yet military personnel from Ireland, Norway, Sweden, and the Netherlands would unsolicitedly echo the sentiments of Danish Lt Col. Sohnemann: 'They're all bastards out there, but the Serbs are the best of them.' Lt Col. Sohnemann, interviewed by author, Karup, Denmark, in September 1994
30 Kishore Mahbubani, 'The Dangers of Decadence: What the Rest Can Teach the West', *Foreign Affairs*, September/October 1993, p. 12
31 David Malone and Karen Wermester, 'Boom and Burst? The Changing Nature of UN Peacekeeping', *International Peacekeeping*, Vol. 7, No. 4, 2000, pp. 37–54
32 Ibid., p. 40
33 Gaddis, *The United States*, p. 212
34 Danesh, Sarooshi, *The United Nations and the Development of Collective Security*, Oxford: Oxford University Press, 1999, p. 174
35 Dimitris Bourantonis and Panayotis Tsakonas, 'The United Nations and Collective Security in the Gulf Crisis: A Missed Opportunity', *New Zealand International Review*, Vol. 18, No. 4, 1994, p. 32
36 Parsons, *From Cold War to Hot Peace*, London, Michael Joseph, 1995, p. 63
37 Samuel P. Huntington, *The Clash of Civilisations and the Remaking of World Order*, London, Touchstone Books, 1998, p. 251
38 Saraooshi, *The United Nations*, 187–91, also Nicholas Wheeler, *Saving Strangers: Humanitarian Intervention in International Society*, New York, 2000
39 Malone and Wermester, 'Boom and Burst?', pp. 37–54
40 Kofi Annan, 'Challenges of the New Peacekeeping', in Otara Otunnu and Michael Doyle (ed.), *Peacemaking and Peacekeeping in the New Century*, Maryland, Littleford Inc., 1996, p. 172

41 James, 1995. Emel Osmancavusogla, 'Challenges to United Nations Peacekeeping Operations in the Post-Cold War Era', *Perceptions*, December 1999/February 2000, p. 140
42 David Malone and Ramesh Thakur, 'UN Peacekeeping: Lessons Learned', *Global Governance*, Vol. 7, No. 1, 2002, p. 11
43 John L. Hirsch, 'War in Sierra Leone', *Survival*, Vol. 43, No. 2, 2001, p. 147
44 Report of the Panel on United Nations Peace Operations, UN General Assembly, A/55/305#S/2000/809, August 2000, p. 809. For a recent account of the Brahini Report, see William Durch *et al.*, *The Brahimi Report and the Future of UN Peacekeeping Operations*, Washington, DC, The Henry Stimson Centre, 2003; Trevor Findlay *The Use of Force in UN Peace Operations*, Oxford, SIPRI, Oxford University Press, 2002; Christine Gray, 'Peacekeeping after the Brahimi Report: Is There a Crisis of Credibility for the UN?', *Journal of Conflict and Security Law*, Vol. 6, No. 2, pp. 267–88
45 Multidisciplinary Peacekeeping: Lessons from Recent Experience, UNDPKO, 9 August, 2000, p. 2
46 Ibid., p. 3
47 Ibid., p. 4
48 Ibid., pp. 5–6
49 Ibid., p. 7
50 Ibid., p. 8
51 Report of Special Committee on Peacekeeping Operations, UN General Assembly, A/56/732, December 2001
52 Ibid.
53 Ibid., p. xii
54 Ibid., p.12
55 Ibid., p. 20
56 Ibid., p. viii
57 Ibid., p. 10
58 Ibid., p. ix
59 Annan, 'Challenges', p. 174
60 '*The Comprehensive Review*', p. x
61 Annan quotes the Commander of the UN Force in Rwanda as stating that a brigade-size force quickly available could have saved hundreds of thousands of lives. Annan, (n. 40 above), p. 174
62 United Nations, *Comprehensive Review*, p. 11
63 Ibid., p. 10
64 Ibid., p. xi
65 Steven R. Ratner, *The New UN Peacekeeping*, London, Macmillan, 1997, p. 171
66 Mats Berdal, 'Whither UN Peacekeeping'?, Adelphi Paper No. 281, Spring 1993, p. 46
67 Peter Viggo Jakobsen, 'Overload Not Marginalisation Threatens UN Peacekeeping', *Security Dialogue*, Vol. 31, No. 2, 2000, p. 167
68 John Mackinlay, 'Improving Multifunctional Operations', *Survival*, Vol. 36, No. 3, 1994, p. 170
69 Paul Diehl, 'Forks in the Road: Theoretical and Policy Concerns for 21st Century Peacekeeping', *Global Security*, Vol. 14, No. 3, 2000, p. 353
70 Mackinlay, 'Improving Multifunctional Operations', p. 152
71 Berdal, 'Whither UN Peacekeeping', p. 9
72 Ibid., p. 3
73 Annan, 'Challenges', p. 173
74 Mackinlay, 'Improving Multifunctional Forces', p. 150
75 Shashi Tharoor, 'Should UN Peacekeeping Go "Back to Basics"'?, *Survival*, Vol. 37, No. 4, 1995–6, p. 57

76 Peter Jakobsen, 'Overload Not Marginalisation Threatens US Peacekeeping'; also see Cotton, James, 'Against the Grain: The East Timor Intervention', *Survival*, Vol. 43, No. 1, 2001, pp. 127–42
77 Ibid., p. 175
78 Annan, 'Challenges', p. 169
79 Ciechanski, 'Enforcement Measures Under Chapter VII of the UN Charter' in Michael Pugh *The UN Peace and War*, London, Frank Cass and Co. Ltd, 1997, p. 83
80 James Traub, 'Inventing East Timor', *Foreign Affairs*, July/August 2000, p. 75
81 Ibid., p. 74
82 Ibid., p. 82
83 Ibid., p. 82
84 Ibid., p. 83
85 Ibid., p. 80
86 Ibid., p. 85
87 Ibid.

8

THE FUTURE OF UN
PEACEKEEPING

The UN is often accused by journalists and seasoned commentators of having failed to act to resolve crises, of having not done enough, or indeed in some instances of having done too much. In the Iraqi crisis of 2003, the UN was perceived as having 'failed' to agree, thus leaving America, along with Britain and Spain, to pursue independent military action against Iraq. Of course, claims of failure may have some justification, as in the Rwandan case, where some suggest that the UN might have prevented genocide, or possibly UN peacekeepers could have stopped the murder of people in the UN safe haven of Srebrenica. In levelling such accusations at the UN, it is interesting to note that many commentators see the UN as a highly purposeful actor, rather than a complex organisation reflective of its members' own interests and concerns. In effect, this means that their expectations are often unrealistic and greater than what might be reasonably expected of the UN in many crises.

The UN does not exist in a vacuum and its ability to act is very much affected by the international environment and its dependence on its member states to agree on action and to provide the resources to successfully accomplish its missions. As the Brahimi Report (p. viii) noted:

> Without renewed political commitment on the part of the Member States, significant institutional change and increased financial support, the United Nations will not be capable of executing the critical peacekeeping and peace-building tasks that the Member States assign to it.

Again, the role of the international environment and the great powers has been highlighted in this study. The UN, then, exists as part of the international system, as well as being a product of that system. It also faces a range of crises, some of which may not be soluble through the UN, and which may be ultimately resolved through violence, sometimes as part of new state building processes. The nature of political conflict needs to be understood, if the UN is to determine what possible courses of action it may pursue, if it is to play a role in such situations, as opposed to falling into the trap of having to be seen to do something. Secretary-General Kofi Annan argued at the Millennium Summit that the UN had to look at the underlying causes of such conflicts, which he suggested reflected broader human needs. The Millennium Declaration defined the priorities for the new century as:

> The fight for development for all the peoples of the world; the fight against poverty, ignorance and disease; the fight against injustice; the fight against violence, terror and crime; and the fight against the degradation of our common home.

In order to pursue these priorities, emphasis was placed on making the United Nations a more effective instrument.

The UN as a learning organisation

In looking at the UN as an organisation, it is important to recognise that officials are very aware of the lessons that can be learnt from past peacekeeping operations. The issue is whether lessons learnt can be applied in new contexts and this is far more difficult to assess. For example, UN officials stress that they are clear on what they think should not be done by the UN in future peacekeeping and it is unlikely that the UN will become involved in as many operations as those undertaken in the 1990s.[1] Most officials are of the view that the UN has learnt lessons from intervening in situations in which there was little hope of conflict resolution and where the numbers of peacekeepers were insufficient to keep or enforce peace. The problem remains, however, as to whether the UN is largely still reactive to crises, and does not act quickly enough. For example, will the crisis in the Congo in 2003 follow a similar pattern to that in Rwanda? As a crisis it has been ongoing for some time, but it would appear only as media attention has focused on the situation, that the UN had been prompted into action, leading to a French-led coalition.

The capacity of the Department of Peacekeeping Operations (DPKO) to plan and manage operations has grown and improved, reflecting lessons learnt. However, the limitations of the DPKO must also be recognised, as it remains a relatively small department. Staff numbers have grown since the 1990s from fifty officials to in excess of six hundred personnel, but this remains small by comparison with the Foreign Ministries of even most small states (see Table 8.1).

The DPKO has, through the Peacekeeping Best Practices Unit, established in 2001, focused on the task of evaluating and assessing UN peacekeeping experiences and results. The objective of the unit has been to use the lessons learnt and the best practices to improve future peacekeeping. The unit has undertaken a number of studies of past peacekeeping operations and has organised seminars, in conjunction with NGOs such as the International Peace Academy and the UN University. It has also produced a *Handbook of UN Multinational Peacekeeping Operations* (UN 2003). It has provided a useful forum for considering what lessons can be learnt from past peacekeeping operations, although whether these lessons inform future operations is a matter for debate.[2] The lessons highlighted in the seminars point to the following types of challenge for future UN peacekeeping:

Table 8.1 Personnel, DPKO, January 2003

Office	Staff numbers
Office of the Under-Secretary General	18
Best Practices Unit	14
Executive Office	13
Office of Operations	79
Situation Centre	21
Office of Mission Support	357
Military Division	83
Civilian Police Division	24
Mine Action Service	5
Total	614

Source: Department of Peacekeeping Operations, 2003

• the need for clear and achievable mandates;
• unity of objectives and command and control over operation;
• the need for increased coordination between HQ and missions;
• the objective of promoting peace building processes (civil-military cooperation, rule of law and transitional authority);
• the requirement of public awareness and local ownership;
• the UN and the greater use of regional organisations.[3]

The need for a clear and achievable mandate for those charged with undertaking the operations in the field remains a key concern of many peacekeepers. The SRSGs and force commanders highlight the importance of being clear as to what an operation is about. Yet, in many of the cases examined, there is an absence of such clarity reflecting mixed political signals from the Security Council, sometimes a poor understanding of the conflict and in some instances inadequate planning. Again, the motives and the political willingness of the member states that make up the Security Council to authorise actions are important determinants in explaining UN actions. For example, the US role in world affairs post-September 11 has become increasingly problematic for the UN, with US foreign policy pursuing an increasingly unilateralist approach. There is a risk that the Security Council will act with great haste, as in the Congo in the 1960s, where the operation was authorised in two days, but without adequately thinking through the mandate. There is also the risk of the UN not acting, given that states such as China and Russia have often been reluctant to agree to intervention. Some mandates appear to exhibit mission creep, with Chapter VI operations becoming Chapter VII over time, as the UN becomes entrapped in a conflict situation. In some cases, the UN has lacked the resources to match the demands of the mandate and, at an operational level, promises and commitments fail to materialise, are sometimes withdrawn or found to be inadequate.

Command and control has also been highlighted as a continuing challenge for the UN in its operations. The growing role of the SRSGs has been noted in our case studies and the need to ensure that these individuals have overall control of the operation, without which there is a risk of poor coordination and confusion, is considered important to the success of a mandate. Arising out of the case studies considered herein, as well as more generally suggested, there is a need to empower the SRSGs to deal with issues of conduct in a timely manner, as past breaches or poor conduct on the part of military and civilian personnel have not always been treated with due concern and have led to much adverse comments.

A related issue concerns the make-up of forces and their appropriateness to the missions. It is clear that some states are more willing than others to contribute forces to UN operations and that these may not always be the ones most appropriate or trained to handle the mission (see Table 8.2). It is notable that developing states have contributed far more troops to missions in recent years than developed states. It would also seem that US, Russia, some European states and China have been more reluctant to commit forces where there is a risk of casualties. For example, in the case of Somalia, the US decided to withdraw its forces from the UN mission after it suffered casualties, leading others to withdraw their troops. Notably, there was no such public outcry and response from the Pakistani government following the death of a number of Pakistani peacekeepers.

In noting the significant role that developing countries play in peacekeeping operations, it hardly surprising that they also suffer the most casualties, as in 2002 the largest number of claims for deaths on missions came from Bangladesh (7), Kenya (6), Nigeria (3), Thailand (3), Ukraine (4) and Zambia (6).[4] A total of 42 such claims led to a total payment of $2,045,449 in compensation.

What role the UN should play in the future is evident in the remaining three challenges (highlighted above) in that they raise questions about the willingness of the member states, and the ability and capacity of the UN to undertake complex missions that promote peace-building, and that are dependent on a mix of military and civilian personnel, and that involve regional organisations. In instances where the UN has become involved in such operations, as in Kosovo (UNMIK), East Timor (UNTAET) and Afghanistan (UNAMA), there has been an increased onus on the DPKO to work in tandem with other departments in the UN Secretariat to achieve a much more integrated approach to the operation on the ground.[5] In the case of UNTAET the peace-building mandate was to restore stability and to establish administrative and political structures for an independent East Timor. The mission included military personnel from 29 states and police officers from a further 39 states. In total there were some 737 international civilian personnel and 1,745 local civilian officials. The operation also involved a large number of UN agencies, including the Office of the High Commissioner of Human Rights, UNHCR, UNFPA, UNDP, UNICEF, as well as many others. While the operation has been seen as successful, the Director of the Asia and Middle East Division (DPKO), has commented, that the operation was far from smooth with difficulties in finding the required personnel to undertake some of the specialised tasks required.[6]

Table 8.2 Military and civilian police on UN operations, April 2003

Rank	Member country	Numbers
1	Pakistan	4,245
2	Nigeria	3,316
3	India	2,735
4	Bangladesh	2,658
5	Ghana	2,060
6	Kenya	1,806
7	Uruguay	1,690
8	Jordan	1,611
9	Ukraine	1,046
10	Nepal	921
11	Zambia	890
12	Australia	860
13	Guinea	797
14	Poland	732
15	Portugal	711
16	Morocco	658
17	Slovakia	609
18	United Kingdom	593
19	Argentina	565
20	USA	558
21	Thailand	546
22	Senegal	529
23	Japan	526
24	Austria	435
25	Germany	389
26	Russia	337
27	China	329
28	France	328
29	Tunisia	293
30	Republic of Korea	292
31	Ireland	271
32	Canada	262
33	Singapore	259
34	Fiji	240
35	Romania	220
36	Bolivia	216
37	South Africa	194

Source: Department of Peacekeeping Operations, www.un.org/Depts/dpko

The problem remains that the UN is still limited in what it can achieve as an organisation, and whilst the reforms introduced since the Brahimi Report may have brought about positive changes in the DPKO's management culture and the way in which operations are planned, established and conducted, there are still limitations in personnel and budgets. There are also organisational problems with the different departments having overlapping responsibilities that can make it difficult to undertake operations. For example, in the area of preventive diplomacy the

Executive Office of the Secretary-General is responsible for early action when a crisis appears on the horizon, but the Department of Public Affairs is responsible for collection and analysis of information.[7] Such overlapping responsibilities may cause problems unless there is significant inter-departmental cooperation and procedures to make sure this happens. Past reforms have also led to some staff reductions and redeployments limiting what is possible in the early detection of crises.

The implementation of the Brahimi Report and the realities of the UN system

There has been some incremental progress since the Brahimi Report was published with the DPKO receiving additional resources and being involved in internal reforms. In particular, the department has espoused a number of strategic goals, which provide it with a much clearer sense of purpose and direction. These are to:

- enhance the rapid deployment capability for peacekeeping operations;
- strengthen the relationship with Member States and legislative bodies;
- reform the department's management culture;
- reorientate the department's relationship with field missions;
- strengthen the relationship with other parts of the UN system.

In assessing the implementation of the recommendations of the Brahimi Report, the Under-Secretary-General for Peacekeeping Operations,[8] has noted that resource base had been strengthened, but that peacekeeping needs to be further professionalised.[9] The Special Committee on Peacekeeping has supported the changes arising out of the Brahimi Report, including providing enhanced resources, but has also suggested that the department needs to conduct regular self-evaluations and systematic reviews to ensure that the additional resources are having a tangible effect. The committee reiterated its support for creating a post of Director of Management in the Under-Secretary's Office. Other proposals and recommendations have included:

- *Strategic planning*: strategic manual on multi-dimensional peacekeeping operations and emphasis on utilising lessons learnt for future peacekeeping, including the intention to introduce a validation mechanism for lessons learnt;
- *Need for system-wide information* and analysis;
- *Mission support*: enhanced role for situation centre in preparation of reports and fact sheets;
- *Rapid deployment*: enhance capacity to deploy within 30 days (or 90 for complex missions), including the need to improve the standby arrangements system with pledges of specific expertise, material readiness (strategic deployment stocks at the UN logistics base at Brindisi), funding (pre-mandate commitment authority), and improved strategic air- and sea-lift capabilities;

- *Training*: increased emphasis on training and capacity development, including lessons learnt, as well as on national and regional training centres;
- *Civilian police*: increasing use of the Civilian Police Division;
- *Mission leadership*: avoid statements on any allegations or charges;
- *Need for disarmament*, demobilisation and reintegration programmes
- *Gender*: mainstreaming a gender perspective in DPKO activities;
- *Importance of public information* in peacekeeping operations.

The emphasis in the Special Committee on Peacekeeping and in the General Assembly has been on wanting to ensure that additional resources make a tangible contribution to peacekeeping operations. Such an emphasis is hardly surprising given the UN's budget and the high assessment levels for peacekeeping in the mid-1990s and again in 2000 and 2001 ($3 billion in 2001).[10] While in 2002 the assessment levels were lower, $2,281 million, only approximately one-third of the monies had been paid by October 2002, with the US owing the largest sum ($866 million).[11] The total budget cost in 2002 was $2.8 billion. In practice this has tended to lead to the slow payment of monies to states participating in peacekeeping. The cost of operations, July 2002–June 2003, is highlighted in Table 8.3.

The implications of the budget raise questions as to whether and where the UN should intervene, given the difficulties encountered in managing complex and expensive operations in Kosovo, East Timor, the Democratic Republic of Congo and Sierra Leone. Nevertheless, the recommendations of the Brahimi Report, following detailed examination by the Advisory Committee on Administrative and Budgetary Questions, has been acted on and the General Assembly has provided additional posts and budgetary resources. For example, it approved the allocation

Table 8.3 Peacekeeping budget and numbers, by mission, 2002–03

Mission	Budget US$	Total international personnel
UNOMIG (Georgia)	33,143,700	208
UNMIBH (Bosnia/Herzegovina)	82,106,000	2,062*
UNMIK (Kosovo)	344,966,100	5,507
UNFICYP (Cyprus)	45,632,400	1,288
UNDOF (Observer Force)	40,760,200	1,082
UNIFIL (Lebanon)	117,123,800	2,193
UNIKOM (Iraq–Kuwait)	52,866,800	1,168
UNMISET (East Timor)	305,242,700	5,478
MINURSO (Western Sahara)	43,412,900	409
UNAMSIL (Sierra Leone)	699,838,300	16,384
MONUC (Congo)	608,325,264	4,979
UNMEE (Ethiopia/Eritrea)	230,845,300	4,261

Source: UN General Assembly (A/C.5/57/22), 13 November 2002

Notes: This table excludes UNTSO and UNMOGIP, which are financed from the UN regular budget.
*The UNMIBH mission concluded in December 2002.

of $140 million for the creation of the Strategic Deployment Stocks, thereby enhancing the UN's rapid deployment capacity to undertake a complex mission.

Are further reforms of the UN system needed and are they likely to be possible? Secretary-General Kofi Annan has been committed to reforming the UN, seeking to adapt its internal structures and change its culture to meet new expectations and challenges. These changes began in 1997,[12] and were reinforced in the UN's Millennium Declaration, and have been reiterated and reinforced in the Secretary-General's report, *Strengthening of the United Nations: An Agenda for Further Change*, presented to the General Assembly in 2002.[13] In this document the Secretary-General highlights the need for a stronger General Assembly, the enhancement of the Economic and Social Council, the need for Security Council reform, the problem of too many meetings in the UN system and a programme of action. In reality the proposed actions focus on achieving the goals outlined in the Millennium Declaration rather than on the reform of the UN system, reflecting the limits of what the Secretary-General can do and the lack of agreement on institutional reform among the Member States. There is also little in the proposals relating specifically to peacekeeping, except for a commitment to present peacekeeping budgets in a new format with an emphasis on the strategic use of resources (Action 23). Nevertheless, Annan's actions have been perceived positively by the US and Russia, with the view that he has done much to reform the UN's management and budgetary system, thereby restoring confidence in the UN system.

At a practical level, the demand for peacekeeping remains high, with a surge in requests for peacekeeping since 2000, especially in relation to intrastate or internal conflicts. Peacekeeping is also 'healthy' in terms of the numbers of people on missions, with some 44,000 military personnel and civilian police deployed in 2002, with a greater mix of military and civilian personnel than in the Cold War era.[14] The demand for traditional peacekeeping (Chapter VI) operations was very high during the 1990s with 39 such operations.[15] The involvement in Chapter VII operations necessitated a move away from use of forces under UN command to an increasing dependence on coalitions of the willing, often led by a single state, and the greater reliance on regional organisations. Examples have included the US-led force in Haiti, the Italians in Albania, Gabon/France in the Central African Republic, France in Rwanda, Russia (CIS) in Georgia, Nigeria (as well as ECOWAS) in Liberia, Sierra Leone, and Guinea-Bissau. The greater reliance on these types of arrangements reflects the limited capacity of the UN, as well as a change in attitude dating back to the former Secretary General Boutros-Ghali's discussion of the modes of cooperation in a *Supplement to An Agenda for Peace*.

In order to cope with these type of arrangements the Security Council has had to develop a number of new measures to monitor these delegated operations, including:[16]

- specific rules of engagement and time limits to the mandates;
- inclusion of civilian elements in delegated operations;
- attachment of UN liaison officers to delegated operations;

- regular submission of reports to the Security Council;
- regular briefing meetings between the Security Council and those states conducting the operations;
- co-deployment of UN observers and other personnel with delegated operations;
- joint operations conducted with other regional organisations;
- handover to the UN as soon as the conditions for a consent based operation has been created.

Whether such arrangements are effective and desirable depends in part on who is leading the operation, be it an individual state or regional organisation, as well as the nature of the conflict and the context in which the force is operating. Under such arrangements there may be a risk of Great Powers abusing their positions, as some allege was the case with the French in Rwanda, the US in Haiti, and Australia in East Timor. States such as Russia and China, as well as many developing nations, jealously guard their sovereignty and remain cautious about such direct intervention.[17] There is also a risk that the Great Powers will not intervene, fearing casualties and thus preferring to subcontract such operations to other, often developing states and regional organisations. Notably, the US from 1994 onwards took a more limited view of peacekeeping, refusing to put US lives in jeopardy where danger was evident. The pursuit of such a unilateralist policy is problematic for the UN, which is financially dependent on the US, as well as needing US logistical and technical support. There is also a risk that the US may pursue a 'go it alone' policy, outside of the UN, as in the case of the war on Iraq in 2003, potentially undermining the UN's role in peacekeeping.

Some commentators, suggest that, 'through its failure to exercise responsibility and restraint in authorising such 'subcontracted' operations, the Security Council is undermining its own legal and moral primacy'.[18] Alternatively, some claim that regional organisations may be less intrusive, know the region better than the UN and are likely to be closest to the problem. Again, reputations vary in this arena, with European organisations, such as the Organisation for Security and Cooperation in Europe (OSCE), the European Union (EU), and the North Atlantic Treaty Organisation (NATO) generally enjoying a better track record than entities such as the Organisation of African Unity (OAU), the Economic Community of West African States (ECOWAS), the Organisation of American States (OAS), or ASEAN. The difficulty lies in the fact that many of these weaker organisations lack resources and a capacity to respond to crises, and may be dominated by a single, powerful state. The Brahimi Report acknowledged these types of problems and suggested that the UN might seek to address some of the problems that regional organisations face by providing more training, equipment, logistical support and other resources to all such organisations. While this may address some of the operational problems that such organisations face, it does not take into account the weaknesses of such organisations, as well as their standing and legitimacy.

The emphasis throughout the DPKO on increased mid- and long-term planning, preparation and training of personnel suggests that many of the lessons of previous operations have been learnt and that the department is attempting to address many of the problems and issues identified in past operations.[19] The failures of past operations, as well as the successes, are well known, although applying the lessons may be somewhat more problematic. The DPKO has placed a greater emphasis on the preparation and planning of operations, seeking to assemble mission leadership at HQ and include them as part of an integrated mission task force prior to deployment. The importance of timelines for deployment have also been emphasised, with the objective being to try to ensure that equipment and personnel are ready as and when needed for a rapid deployment within 60 to 90 days (e.g. Standby Arrangements System for troops and police, rosters of available civilian staff, availability of material stocks in Brindisi, and financial commitment authority). As part of this process member states' governments were asked in 2001 to identify particular categories of experts (the on-call list system) to be available for missions. The military division has identified 155 on-call list positions, nine of which are part of the core-planning element. The response, however, from the member states has been slow, reflecting problems in making such commitments at a practical level, as well as some concerns among the states with this approach.

The emphasis on training and professionalisation has grown, with the UN developing its own training programmes (e.g. standard generic training modules), as well as working closely with member state peacekeeping training schools and facilities. The training and evaluation service (military division) has developed particular courses around such areas as gender and peacekeeping, as well as courses aimed at enhancing African peacekeeping capabilities. Such training is necessary to ensure those troops contributed to operations are sensitive to the cultural environments in which they are operating, but as suggested in the previous chapter, this can be problematic.

The department has improved its own management culture and there is a perceived improvement in the type of force personnel being assigned to work in the DPKO. Nevertheless, there remain some staffing problems, with the UN still seen as a sinecure by some developing states, as well as problems arising in terms of continuity owing to the rotation of military staff.

The political realities of the UN system, however, remain evident, with the Great Powers seeking to influence the overall direction and planning of operations, given their own particular interests. In practice, this means that the Great Powers may have a greater interest in undertaking operations in strategic areas, such as Europe, NIS or the Middle East, rather than in Africa or Asia. For example, in the case of UNAMSIL in Sierra Leone the operation was largely left to the regional organisation, the Economic Community of West African States (ECOWAS), led by Nigeria, until some five hundred Kenyan and Zambian peacekeepers were taken hostage, at which point the UK intervened. As Hayes notes the key distinction between the two forces was that the UK contingent were seen by the rebels as a credible combat force, whereas UNASMIL was seen as not being credible (it was a lightly armed force, that lacked combat power, was hampered by poor command and control, and a lack of political will among the contributing states[20]). Similarly, the long-term conflicts in the Sudan and the great lake region have never featured as a priority for many of the developed states, compared to the crises in East Timor and Kosovo, which received immediate and high priority. Many developing states perceive the Great Powers and the developed states as operating a double standard, being more interested in human rights violations in Kosovo and East Timor than in many parts of Africa. The example of Rwanda in 1993–4 is instructive, as it was simply not an important issue from the perspective of the Permanent Members of the Security Council, and as such without decisive leadership from the then Secretary-General, Boutros-Ghali, UNAMIR (UN Assistance Mission for Rwanda) was unable to sustain its operation in the country.[21]

In summary, peacekeeping in the post-Cold War era has changed, although not in the ways many commentators expected at the beginning of the 1990s, as the UN faces new challenges and complex issues. The challenges include internal reform and adaptation of the UN system to cope with new tasks, the continuing lack of political support and unity in the Security Council, as well as the challenge of an increasingly diverse range of inter- and intrastate conflicts (e.g. civil wars and ethnic violence), as well as international terrorism. The issue of whether, when and how the UN intervenes remains problematic, especially in the face of humanitarian crises, which seem to increasingly lead to direct intervention. The related issue of enforcement versus peacekeeping raises concerns about whether the UN should engage in direct intervention, as well as higher priority being placed on the need for preventive diplomacy and a greater understanding of conflict prevention. Many demands are being made of the UN, and its member states and the Secretary-General need to realistically decide what it is capable of doing and whether UN intervention is likely to be successful. There remains the dilemma of reconciling the spirit of the UN Charter with a more assertive approach to peace operations, whereby the UN intervenes in situations where no peace exists, sometimes in contexts where there is no agreement among the warring parties. There is always likely to be a demand by some member states for 'it' to do 'something', as in the case of Somalia, but reconciling this with what is likely to be possible and effective is a challenge.

Options for future operations

Given that prevention is better than cure, one possible option for the UN would be to engage in the kind of preventive deployment that appeared to have worked in Macedonia.[22] Deployment of peacekeepers in 'unstable areas' would appear to provide the possibility of helping to provide an environment in which problems could be nipped in the bud, or at least controlled. Such an approach would represent a departure for the UN from the traditional peacekeeping role that it undertook during the Cold War period. In the past the UN has not enjoyed a strong reputation in this regard and has on a number of occasions found itself facing conflict that it has not previously been aware of coming to the boil. For example, in the case of the war in the Falklands/Malvinas, it was rumoured that the UN lacked a map of the area.[23] Following this crisis the Office of Research and the Collection of Information was established to provide an early warning system to the Secretary-General.[24] There are, however, also many examples where the UN was not able to prevent conflict from occurring: Cambodia, Angola, Congo, Guinea, Rwanda, Somalia, Kosovo, Sierra Leone and East Timor, even if later intervention was successful.

However, the option of preventive diplomacy faces several problems. There would be the issue of deciding upon which situations to address. Also, it would be highly demanding upon resources given the likely open-ended nature of commitment. Furthermore, as Diehl notes, even with accurate early warning, there is the presumption of the international political will to act. Such political will seems to have been lacking in some instances and at best the UN Security Council has been reactive to events rather than taking a more pro-active stance. Secretary-General Annan has highlighted the root causes of conflict arising out of the Brahimi Report, but it requires political action to support his efforts to address such problems. Moreover, states may be offended by being named as sites for potential armed conflict; particularly intense conflict and recourse to this option would raise serious sovereignty issues.[25]

A second option is the creation of a permanent force as an organ of the UN. It would act as an integrated force specially trained in the requirement of peacekeeping operations and serve as the nucleus around which a larger force could be built. Such a force would, in theory, experience fewer command problems than the normal 'UN force', and would provide the Secretary-General with a rapid response capability for emergencies. However, the concept of such a force encounters major problems. There is the question of the precise role of such a force, particularly with regard to the circumstances in which it would be employed. Moreover, it would be extremely costly, has little backing from the permanent five and the Security Council, and is strongly opposed by the developing countries.[26]

A third option is the standby force composed of national contingents, which would be constituted for UN duties and available for deployment at the Secretary-General's request. Such a force would be an enhancement of the existing stand-by arrangements system, whereby states have agreed to a certain level of commitments. Again, the existence of the Rapidly Deployable Mission Headquarters (RDMHQ) and the Multinational Standby State of Forces High Readiness Brigade (SHIRBRIG) since 1997 (with troops from ten small and medium sized countries) has enhanced the existing capacity of the UN to support such operations. In practice, however, states may be unwilling or find it difficult to support such arrangements, given other commitments. It would require states to commit themselves to providing a known number of troops in a known formation, to known equipment scaling, and with a known timetable. This should, in theory, be acceptable to member states since it would leave forces under national command when not on duty. But this proposal, endorsed by the Security Council in 1992, has encountered problems. At a time of rapidly declining defence budgets, commitments have proved difficult to elicit. The US has been reluctant to provide binding assurances and the British government made it clear that it did not favour making specific commitments in advance: so too did India, a potentially significant contributor of personnel.[27] The idea is seen to suffer from the disadvantage that it would require a specific decision each time by participating states as to whether the unit it had pledged would, in fact, participate in the proposed operation. States might be willing to engage in traditional peacekeeping operations, but would they be prepared to risk their personnel in operations of an uncertain nature?

A fourth option is that of Kayser and Rathjens who present the idea of a standing UN force composed entirely of volunteers from member states – in effect an international Foreign Legion. A force of this kind, approximately 15,000 in number and backed up by larger forces remaining under national control, would, they argue, dramatically improve the world community's rapid response capability when faced with humanitarian crises and civil unrest.[28] They suggest that had such forces been employed in the Congo and Somalia, a more rapid solution would have been probable.[29] But would it? As shown in case study A, the UN forces, which arrived within a couple of days, were prevented by the UN Secretariat from disarming the ANC, whose activities triggered the disorder. Equally, it is far from certain that the Somali clans would have cooperated with such a force.

At a practical level, the Foreign Legion concept would encounter major problems. At the outset, it would be difficult to create a force with the right racial/international mix required to avoid friction within the force and make it acceptable to any potential host state. Supplementing standing forces with 'casuals' from member states would create perceptions of 'professionals' and 'others', first and second class elements, resulting inevitably in friction and disharmony. This disharmony would be exacerbated by the 'Legion' personnel being responsible only to New York, while the others would, as before, incline towards national government instructions. Who would command such a two-element force? There would also be the problem of numbers. If the mission required commitment of all 15,000 'Legionaires', absence of replacement/reserves would make rotation of personnel impossible. And what would happen in the event of further crises?

A standing force would do nothing to facilitate determination of objectives or manner of engagement. However ready such a force, a mandate would still be required and the consent of the host state a prerequisite. Framing a mandate for restoration of order would be as difficult as ever. Even the task of providing a buffer-zone in all but the smallest states, would be immensely difficult. Were a small 'standing force' body to attempt to interpose whilst awaiting reinforcement by 'casuals', the risk of confrontation with one or both parties would be extremely high. Kayser and Rathjens advance the theory that had a volunteer body been available for employment in former Yugoslavia, there would have been less sensitivity about casualties and it might have been possible to introduce the force earlier with salutary effect, particularly if it had a mandate to engage in some enforcement actions.[30] But this is pure speculation and appears to seriously underestimate the strength of potential opposition. The reference to casualties does however raise a fundamental point in the debate about whether the UN should establish such a force. A force of this kind would very likely be regarded as a mercenary body willing to, and capable of, performing any kind of military task. Since no member state would bear direct political responsibility for it, everyone would opt out of obligations and frivolously call for its deployment in any small conflict around the world. Far from being the answer to global concerns, a UN Foreign Legion would be another excuse for member states to do nothing.

Proposals

What is the future for UN peacekeeping and in what form? First, the basic distinction between peacekeeping and enforcement must be upheld. There is otherwise a risk of the type of operations becoming blurred and the UN failing to distinguish in what type of missions it is becoming engaged. Traditionally, the UN's involvement in peacekeeping has rested on it being seen as an impartial third party, although in practice this may not have always been the case. Will an association with a range of regional organisations compromise this position and is there a risk that the UN may opt for what appears to be easy options in peacekeeping by such an association with these organisations? Second, while the UN must eschew enforcement-type operations other than in the form employed in Korea and Kuwait, it must be willing to muster and display overwhelming military might, what Annan calls 'credible coercive capacity',[31] both as an indication of its authority and of its earnestness of its intent. While the operation in Somalia highlighted the dangers of trying to combine peacekeeping with enforcement, UNITAF demonstrated the value of employing numbers and firepower to overawe and impress. This represented a dramatic change in UN peacekeeping operations. From UNEF I to UNAMSIL, the numerical strength and equipment inadequacies of UN peacekeepers have been recognised and exploited by assorted elements in various disputes. Time and again, UN forces have been brushed aside and humiliated. The lesson of both UNITAF and Srebrenica was that to carry conviction, the UN has to 'go in strength'. It is upon this premise that proposals for future peacekeeping are based.

New peacekeeping forces, it is proposed, should be large, well equipped and serve for a period not to exceed two years. In terms of numbers, forces would be not less than 20,000 strong. This would demonstrate UN intent, create confidence amongst the parties and permit the force, if required, to establish an effective buffer. Size would also encourage potential contributors since as was shown in Somalia, states believe in 'safety in numbers'. Contingents would also come equipped with heavy weapons, tanks, APCs and helicopters; possession of such 'muscle' would generate confidence within the force and eliminate the problems arising from the presence of weak, dependent contingents. Each contingent would be capable of independent action while making a full contribution to the overall effort. Ideally, such a force would be spearheaded by a major power, one capable of providing a significant troop contribution and of inspiring confidence among a wide spectrum of states. Since the US, Russia or China (assuming it agreed to participate) would be seen to carry excessive 'political baggage', candidates for the task of the 'spearheading' role could include large states such as Britain, France, Canada, Australia, India, Brazil or the Scandinavian countries, that command the respect of other states and have the ability to lead. The difficulty with such a list of candidates is that it is likely to change over time in response to the international political climate and events, such as the war in Iraq (2003).

A force constructed on the above lines would arguably provide the desired rapid response capability, since participating states would be better aware of the conditions and terms of their involvement. Consultation between peacekeepers and home governments would inevitably continue, but since operations would likely be more efficient, there would be less need for such links. There would therefore be fewer problems of military command. With a powerful, efficient force in place, the Secretary General could concentrate efforts on the complementary diplomatic/political effort. The requirement for well-armed and independent contingents would obviously mean the exclusion of many developing states and regular contributors such as Ireland. There would inevitably be cries of 'elitism'. However, the ultimate choice for the UN would be between offending smaller states or risking more Srebrenicas, Rwandas, and Sierra Leones; between operations which enhanced the UN's image and further humiliating debacles.

But it is the proposal to limit the operations strictly to two years, which would represent the greatest challenge to the UN and the international community. For too long, problems of intrastate conflict have been passed to and left with the peacekeepers. Sending in international forces may help address the immediate crises but even the largest and best-equipped forces cannot solve underlying problems. This is a task requiring the full attention and efforts of the UN and international community and, most of all, the parties to the conflict. The history of peacekeeping however, has been one of hoping that the problems will somehow go away. In many cases, the crisis has gone from the headlines, but the problems still remain.

Two years would provide adequate time for a strong peacekeeping force to establish itself, create a 'cooling-off' period, and provide an opportunity for the parties to consider their options. It would also provide an opportunity for all those professing concern to exert pressure by diplomatic or other peaceful means. It would allow the UN time to consider and propose solutions, including elections. In situations where such was required, it would allow for the provision of adequate humanitarian assistance, for the return of refugees, for the reconstruction of infrastructure, for the retraining of security forces and where necessary for the commencement at least of a programme of mine-lifting. It would provide an opportunity for ensuring that everyone understood the purpose of the operation, why the peacekeepers were there, and what they were legally entitled to do. It would, therefore, reduce, if not totally remove, concerns about breaching sovereignty, thereby avoiding the possibility that an initial welcome might turn into a sullen resentment. Most of all, it would concentrate the minds of all concerned. It has to be accepted that one or more of the parties might avail of the two years to regroup for further hostilities. Equally, as demonstrated in Angola, the losers in any election may choose to ignore the democratic will. These are possibilities which the UN must be prepared to accept.

The cases of Cyprus, Angola, Somalia and the Congo show that there are problems which are to all intents and purposes insoluble. The UN, therefore, must be prepared to withdraw or abstain from intervening in conflicts where peacekeeping does not reinforce a broader political process for the resolution of conflict. To persist with open-ended operations will only reinforce the perception in the public mind of UN impotence and essential irrelevance. 'The UN of the Secretariat' may have examined in the 'Lessons Report', its system of planning and managing field operations. However, the question is whether the 'UN of the members', a body riven by racial and ideological differences, can engage in the necessary critical self-analysis and then agree on action. Only when there is evidence that the many positive proposals contained in the 'Comprehensive Review' are being taken to heart by the members can we hope for future well-organised and effective operations.

Notes

1 *'Challenges in Peacekeeping: Past, Present and Future'*, Seminar Report, Millennium Hotel, New York, 29 October 2002. Organised by the International Peace Academy and the Best Practice Unit (DPKO)

2 See the UN University project on Conflict Prevention. Carment, David and Albrecht Schnabel 'Building Conflict Prevention Capacity: Methods, Experience, Needs' *UNU Workshop Seminar Series Report*, February, 2001

3 Ibid., p. 2

4 United Nations, *'Death and Disability Claims: Note by the Secretary-General'* UN General Assembly (A/C.5/57/37), 14 March 2003

5 See Simon Chesterman, *Justice Under International Administration: Kosovo, East Timor and Afghanistan*, Project on Transitional Administrations, New York: International Peace Academy, September, 2002

6 Statement by Julian Harston, Director, Asia Division, DPKO 'Transformation of UN Peacekeeping: Role of the International Community in Peace-Building', JIIA-UNU Symposium, 18 September 2002

7 Connie Peck, *Sustainable Peace, The Role of the UN and Regional Organisations in Preventing Conflict*, New York, Ronman and Little, 1998, p. 74

8 Presentation to the General Assembly's Special Committee on Peacekeeping Operations, in February 2002

9 Report of the Special Committee on Peacekeeping Operations, *Comprehensive Review of the Whole Question of Peacekeeping Operations in All Their Aspects* (A/56/8653), 11 March 2002

10 Report of the Secretary-General *Improving the Financial Situation of the United Nations*, UN General Assembly (A/57/498), 23 October 2002

11 Between 1994 and 1999 the US Congress refused to pay US dues and arrears to the UN. In 1999 under the Helms-Biden agreement new legislation meant that the US authorised payment of arrears to the UN thereby lessening the UN's debt to Member States

12 A notable start was made in 1997 with the creation of the Senior Management Group. The objective of the group, which comprises the heads of all departments, funds and programmes (some 30 individuals), is to provide strategic coherence and direction to the organisation

13 See UN General Assembly (A/57/387), 9 September 2002
14 See UN Peace Operations: Year in Review 2002, UN Department of Public Information, http://www.un.org/Depts/dpko/yir/english/ (accessed 07/03/2003)
15 Peter Jakobsen 'Overload, Not Marginalisation, Threatens UN Peacekeeping' *Security Dialogue* Vol. 31 No. 2, 2000, p. 171
16 Ibid., p. 172
17 See Margaret Karns and Karen Mingst 'Peacekeeping and the changing role of the United Nations: four dilemmas', in Ramesh Thakur and Albrecht Schnabel (eds), *United Nations Peacekeeping Operations: Ad hoc Missions, Permanent Engagement*, Tokyo, UN University Press, 2001, pp. 215–37
18 See Michelle Griffin, 'Blue Helmets: Assessing the Trend Towards "Subcontracting" UN Peace Operations' *Security Dialogue* Vol. 30, No. 1, 1999, p. 43
19 Note that the Lessons Learned Unit was merged with the Policy and Analysis Unit in 2001 to form the Peacekeeping Best Practices Unit and operates under the Office of the Under-Secretary General for Peacekeeping
20 Vera Hayes, 'Establishing the credibility of a regional peacekeeping capability', in Ramesh Thakur and Albrecht Schnabel (eds), *United Nations Peacekeeping Operations: Ad hoc Missions, Permanent Engagement*, Tokyo: UN University Press, 2001, pp. 129–45
21 See Astri Suhrke and Bruce Jones (2000) 'Preventive Diplomacy in Rwanda: failure to act or failure of actions', in Bruce Jentleson (ed.), *Opportunities Seized, Opportunities Missed: Preventive Diplomacy in the Post-Cold War Period*, New York, Rowan and Littlefield, 2000, pp. 238–64
22 See the Carnegie Commission's Report on *Preventing Deadly Conflict*
23 Peck, *Sustainable Peace*, p. 72
24 It was abolished by Boutros-Ghali and absorbed into the Department of Political Affairs. At this time peace-making was assigned to the Department of Political Affairs, a new department was created to respond to humanitarian issues (Department of Humanitarian Affairs)
25 Paul Diehl, 'Forks in the Road: Policy Concerns for 21st Century Peacekeeping', *Global Security*, Vol. 14, No. 3, 2000, p. 343
26 Mats Berdal, 'Whither UN Peacekeeping', *Adelphi Paper*, No. 281, Spring 1993, p. 62
27 Ibid., p. 63
28 Carl Kaysen and George Rathjens, 'Send in the Troops: A UN Foreign Legion', *Washington Quarterly*, 1997, Vol. 20, No. 1, 1997, p. 208
29 Ibid.
30 Ibid., p. 213
31 Kofi Annan, 'Challenges of the New Peacekeeping', in Olunna and Doyle (eds), *Peacemaking and Peacekeeping in the New Century*, Maryland, Rowman and Littleford Inc., 1996, p. 174

BIBLIOGRAPHY

Abiew, Francis Kofi and Keating, Tom, 'Outside Agents and the Politics of Peace-Building and Reconciliation', *International Journal* (winter 1999–2000): 80–8

Akehurst, Michael, *A Modern Introduction to International Law* (3rd edition), London: Allen and Unwin, 1970

Akenson, Donald Harmon, *A Biography of Conor Cruise O'Brien*, Vol. II, Montreal: McGill, Queens University Press, 1994

An Africa Watch Report, Angola Violations of the Law of War by Both Sides, London: Human Rights Watch, April 1989

Anstee, Margaret J., 'Angola – The Forgotten Tragedy: A Test Case for UN Peacekeeping', *International Relations*, Vol. II, No. 6 (1993): 496–8

Anstee, Margaret J., 'Angola: A Tragedy Not To Be Forgotten', *The World Today* (1996): 190–1

Anstee, Margaret J., *Orphan of the Cold War*, London: Macmillan Press, 1996

Armstrong, David, 'Law, Justice and the Idea of a World Society', *International Affairs*, Vol. 75, No. 3 (1999): 548–61

Baehr, Peter R. and Gordenkor, Leon, *The United Nations in the 1990s* (2nd edition), London: Macmillan Press, 1994

Baev, Pavel K., *The Russian Army in a Time of Troubles*, Oslo: International Peace Research Institute, 1996

Bates, Gill, and Reilly, James, 'Sovereignty, Intervention, and Peacekeeping: The View from Beijing', *Survival* (autumn 2000): 41–59

Baylis, John and Smith, Steve (eds), *The Globalisation of World Politics: An Introduction to International Relations*, Oxford: Oxford University Press, 1997

Bennett, A. Leroy, *International Organisations: Principles and Issues*, Englewood Cliffs, New Jersey: Prentice-Hall International, 1988, 145

Berdal, Mats, '*UN at the Crossroads*', Oslo: Institutt for Forsvarstudier (Institute for Defence Studies), Norskutenriks Politisk Institutt, Info. No. 7, 1993.

Berdal, Mats, 'Whither UN Peacekeeping?', *Adelphi Paper*, No. 281, spring 1993

Berdal, Mats, 'Fateful Encounter: The United States and UN Peacekeeping', *Survival*, Vol. 36, No. 1 (1994): 30–50

Berdal, Mats, *The United Nations at Fifty: Its Role in Global Security*, Oslo: Institutt for Forsvarstudier (Institute for Defence Studies), Info. No. 3, 1995

Biermann, Wolfgang and Vadset, Martin (eds), *UN Peacekeeping in Trouble: Lessons Learned from the Former Yugoslavia*, Aldershot: Ashgate Publishing, 1998

Birmingham, David and Martin, Phyllis M., *History of Central Africa*, Vol. II, New York: Longman, 1983

Bolton, John R., 'Wrong Turn in Somalia', *Foreign Affairs* (January/February 1994): 57–66

Bourantonis, Dimitris and Panayollis, Tsakonas, 'The United Nations and Collective Security in the Gulf Crisis: A Missed Opportunity', *New Zealand International Review*, Vol. 18, No. 4 (1993): 20–2

Bourantonis, Dimitris and Wiener, Jarrod (eds), *The United Nations in the New World Order*, Basingstoke, Hants: Macmillan, 1995

Boutros-Ghali, Boutros, *An Agenda for Peace*, New York: UN Department of Public Information, 1992

Boutros-Ghali, Boutros, 'Empowering the United Nations', *Foreign Affairs*, Vol. 72, No. 5 (1992): 89–102

Bowker, Mile and Brown, Robin, *From Cold War to Collapse: Theory and World Politics in the 1980's*, Cambridge: Cambridge University Press, 1993

Boyd, Andrew, *United Nations: Piety, Myth and Truth*, Middlesex: Penguin Books, 1962

Boyd, Andrew, *Fifteen Men on a Powder Keg*, London: Macmillan, 1971

Boyd, Gavin and Pentland, Charles, *Issues in Global Politics*, London: Collier Macmillan, 1981

Boyd, James, *United Nations Peacekeeping Operations: A Military and Political Appraisal*, London: Anvil Books, 1972

Brady, Christopher and Daws, Samuel, 'UN Operations: The Political-Military Interface', *International Peacekeeping*, Vol. 1, No. 1 (1994): 59–79

(British) Army Field Manual, Wider Peacekeeping (3rd draft)

Calder, Richie, *Agony of the Congo*, London: Victor Gollanez, 1961

Calvocoressi, Peter, *World Politics Since 1945* (6th edition), London: Longman, 1991

Carment, David and James, Patrick, 'The United Nations at Fifty: Managing Ethnic Crises – Past and Present', *Journal of Peace Research*, Vol. 35, No 1, 1998: 61–82

Carment, David and Schnabel, Albrecht, 'Building Conflict Prevention Capacity: Methods, Experience, and Needs', *UNU Workshop Seminar Series Report* (February 2001)

Chesterman, Simon, 'Justice Under International Administration: Kosovo, East Timor and Afghanistan', Project on Transitional Administrations, New York: *International Peace Academy* (September 2002)

Chomsky, Naom, *Year 501: The Conquest Continues*, London: Verso, 1993

Chopra, Jarat, Aknes, Aage and Nordboe, Toralf, *Fighting for Hope in Somalia*, Oslo: Norsk Utenrikspolitisk Institutt, NUPI Report No. 6, 1995

Ciechanski, Jerzy, 'Restructuring of the UN Security Council', *International Peacekeeping*, Vol. 1, No. 4 (1994): 413–39

Clarke, William and Herbst, Jeffroy, 'Somalia and the Future of Humanitarian Peacekeeping', *Foreign Affairs* (March/April 1996): 49–56

Claude, Inis L., *Swords into Plowshares*, London: University of London Press, 1965

Claude, Inis L., 'The Management of Power in the Changing United Nations', *International Organisation*, Vol. 15 (1971): 12–24

Clements, Kevin and Ward, Robin, *Building an International Community*, Canberra: Allen and Unwin, 1994

Coleman, Christopher C. and Ginifer, Jeremy, *An Assessment of UNOSOM 1992–1995: A Seminar Report*, Oslo: Norsk Utenrikspolitisk Institutt, 1995

Cooper, Robert and Berdal, Mats, 'Outside Intervention in Ethnic Conflict', *Survival*, Vol. 35, No. 1 (1993): 118–42

Cotton, James, 'Against the Grain: The East Timor Intervention', *Survival*, Vol. 43, No. 1 (2001): 127–42

Crossette, Barbara, 'UN Chief Faults Reluctance of US to Help in Africa', *The New York Times*, 13 May 2000

Daalder, Ivo, Lindsay, James M. and Steinberg, James B. (eds), 'The Bush National Security Strategy: An Evaluation', *Policy Brief, Brookings Institution*, 4 October 2002 (www.brookings.edu)

Dayal, Rajeshwar, *Mission for Hammaerskjöld*, London: Oxford University Press, 1976

Deonanden, Kalowatie, 'Learning from Somalia', *Peace Review*, Vol. 6, No. 4 (1994): 453–9

DeWaal, Alex, 'African Encounters', *Index on Censorship*, London, Writers and Scholars International, (November/December 1994): 14–31

Diehl, Paul, 'Peacekeeping Operations and the Quest for Peace', *Political Science Quarterly*, Vol. 103, No. 3 (1988): 485–507

Diehl, Paul, *International Peacekeeping*, Baltimore/London, John Hopkins University Press, 1993

Diehl, Paul, Reifschneider, Jennifer and Hensel, Paul 'United Nations Intervention and Recurring Conflict', *International Organisation*, Vol. 40, No. 4 (1996): 683–700

Diehl, Paul, 'Forks in the Road: Theoretical and Policy Concerns for 21st Century Peacekeeping', *Global Society*, Vol. 14, No. 3 (2000): 337–60

Dorman, Andrew, Lawrence, Mike, and Uttley, Matthew, 'Joint and Combined Operations in an Expeditionary Era: Defining the Issues', *Defence Analysis*, Vol. 14, No. 1 (1998): 1–8

Dorr, Noel, *United Nations Seminar*, Institute of European Affairs, Dublin, 23 May, 1999

Durch, William J. (eds), *The Evolution of UN Peacekeeping*, London: Macmillan, 1993

Durch, William *et al.*, *The Brahimi Report and the Future of UN Peacekeeping Operations*, Washington, DC: The Henry Stimson Centre, 2003

Eide, Espen Barth, *Regionalising Intervention? The Case of Europe in the Balkans*, Oslo: Peace Research Institute, Report 2/99, February 1999: 61–86

Eknes, Aage and McDermott, Anthony, *Sovereignty, Humanitarian Intervention, and the Military*, Oslo: Norsk Utenrikspolitisk Institutt, NUPI Report No. 3, 1994

Evans, Gareth, *Co-operating for Peace*, St Leonard's, Australia: Allen and Unwin, 1993

Evriviades, Marios, and Dimitris, Bourantonis 'Peacekeeping and Peacemaking: Some Lessons from Cyprus', *International Peacekeeping*, Vol. 1, No. 4 (1994): 394–412

Farrell, Theo, 'Sliding Into War: The Somali Imbroglio and US Army Peace Operations Doctrine', *International Peacekeeping*, Vol. 2, No. 2 (1995): 192–214

Feltz, William J. and Bienen, Henry S., *Arms and the Africans: Military Influences on Africa's International Relations*, New Haven: Yale University Press, 1985

Findlay, Trevor, *The Use of Force in UN Peacekeeping Operations*, Oxford: SIPRI, Oxford University Press, 2002

Francis, David J., 'Torturous Path to Peace: The Lome Accords and Post-War Peace-Building in Sierra Leone', *Security Dialogue*, Vol. 3, No. 3 (2000): 357–73

French, Anthony, '*Peacekeeping and Impartiality*', paper delivered to Israeli National Defence College, Tel Aviv, 18 May, 1993

Fukuyama, Francis, 'The End of History', *The National Interest*, No. 16, (1989): 4–18

Gaddis, John Lewis, *The United States and the End of the Cold War*, Oxford: Oxford University Press, 1992

Gaddis, John Lewis, 'The Post-Cold War World: Finding a Theme', *New Zealand International Review* (March/April 1996): 3–9

Gann, L.H., and Duignan, P., *Colonialism in Africa 1870–1960, Vol.ume II: The History and Politics of Colonialism 1914–1960*, Cambridge: Cambridge University Press, 1970

Gibbs, David N., 'Secrecy and International Relations', *Journal of Peace Research*, Vol. 32, No. 2 (1995): 213–28

Ginifer, Jeremy and Eide, Espen Barth, *An Agenda for Preventive Diplomacy: Theory and Practice*, Oslo: Norsk Utenrikspolitisk Institutt, No. 215, March 1997

Gnesotto, Nicole, 'Reacting to America', *Survival*, Vol. 44, No. 4 (2002): 99–106

Goldsborough, James O, 'The Roots of Western Disunity', in *At Issue: Politics in the World Arena*, New York: St Martin's Press, 1984

Goulding, Marrack, 'The Evolution of United Nations Peacekeeping', *International Affairs*, Vol. 3, No. 69 (1993): 451–64

Goulding, Marrack, *Peacemonger*, London: John Murray, 2002

Gow, James and Dandeker, Christopher, 'Peace-Support Operations: The Problem of Legitimisation', *The World Today* (August–September 1995): 171–4

Gray, Christine, 'Peacekeeping after the Brahimi Report: Is There a Crisis of Credibility in the UN?', *Journal of Conflict and Security Law*, Vol. 15, No. 2 (2001): 267–88

Griffin, Michelle, 'Blue Helmets: Assessing the Trend Towards "Sub-Contracting" UN Peace Operations', *Security Dialogue*, Vol. 30, No. 1 (1999): 43–60

Gurr, Ted Robert, 'Ethnic Warfare on the Wane', *Foreign Affairs*, Vol. 79, No. 3 (2000): 52–62

Hansen, Birthe and Heurlin, Bertel, *The New World Order*, London: Macmillan, 2000

Harbottle, Michael, 'UN Peacekeeping: Past Lessons and Future Prospects', David Davies Lecture, 25 November, 1971

Harston, Julian, *Transformation of UN Peacekeeping: Role of the International Community in Peace-Building*, JIIA-UNU Symposium, 18 September, 2002

Hayes, Vera, 'Establishing the Regional Credibility of a Regional Peacekeeping Capability' in United Nations Peacekeeping Operations, New York: UN University Press, 2002, 129–145

Heiberg, Marianne, *Observations on UN Peacekeeping in Lebanon*, Oslo: Norsk Utenrikspolitisk Institutt, No. 305, September 1964

Heitman, Helmoed-Romer, *War in Angola: The Final South African Phase*, Gibraltar: Ashanti Publishing, 1990

Henn, Francis, 'The Nicosia Airport Incident of 1974: A Peacekeeping Gamble', *International Peacekeeping*, Vol. 1, No. 1 (1994): 80–98

Higgins, Rosalyn, *United Nations Peacekeeping 1946–1976: Documents and Commentary, Vol. III, Africa*, Oxford: Oxford University Press, 1980

Higgins, Rosalyn, *United Nations Peacekeeping: Documents and Commentary, Vol. 4, Europe*, Oxford: Oxford University Press, 1981

Higgins, Rosalyn, 'The New United Nations and Former Yugoslavia', *International Affairs*, Vol. 69, No. 3, 1993: 465–84

Hirsch, John L., 'War in Sierra Leone', *Survival*, Vol. 43, No. 3 (2002): 145–62

History of 33 Irish Battalion, Dublin: Irish Military Archives

Hitchens, Christopher, *The Trial of Henry Kissinger*, London: Verso, 2002

Hobsbawn, Eric, *Age of Extremes: The Short Twentieth Century 1914–1991*, London: Michael Joseph, 1994

Holst, Johan Jorgen, 'Enhancing Peacekeeping Operations', *Survival*, Vol. 32, No. 3 (1990): 264–75

Howe, Jonathan T., 'The United States and United Nations in Somalia: The Limits of Involvement', *The Washington Quarterly*, Vol. 18, No. 3 (1995): 49–62

Huntington, Samuel, *The Clash of Civilisations and the Remaking of World Order*, London: Touchstone Books, 1996

Inbar, Efraim and Sheffer, Gabriel, *The National Security of Small States in a Changing World*, London: Frank Cass, 1997

International Peace Academy, *Peacekeepers Handbook*, New York: International Peace Academy, 1984

International Peace Academy, 'Challenges in Peacekeeping: Past, Present and Future', seminar organised by the *International Peace Academy* and the Best Practice Unit (DPKO), Seminar Report, Millennium Hotel, New York, 29 October, 2002

Ito, Tetsuo, *UN Authorised Use of Force: Recent Changes in UN Practice*, Oslo: Institutt for Forsvarsstudier (Institute for Defence Studies), Info. No. 5, 1995

Jakobsen, Peter Viggo, 'Overload Not Marginalisation Threatens UN Peacekeeping', *Security Dialogue*, Vol. 31, No. 2 (2000): 167–77

Jakobsen, Peter Viggo, 'The Transformation of United Nations Peace Operations in the 1990's', *Co-operation and Conflict*, Vol. 37, No. 3 (2002): 267–82

James, Alan, *The Politics of Peacekeeping*, London: Chatto and Windus, 1969

James, Alan, 'The UN Force in Cyprus', *International Affairs*, Vol. 65, No. 3 (1969)

James, Alan, *The UN on Golan: Peacekeeping Paradox?*, Oslo: Norsk Utenrikspolitisk Institutt, No. 100, 1986

James, Alan, *Peacekeeping in International Politics*, London: Macmillan Academic and Professional, 1990

James, Alan, 'The Congo Controversies', *International Peacekeeping*, Vol. 1, No. 1 (1994): 44–58

James, Alan, 'UN Peacekeeping: Recent Developments and Current Problems', in Dimitris Bourantonis and Jarrod Wiener (eds), *The United Nations in the New World Order: The World Organisation at Fifty*, Basingstoke: Macmillan, 1995, pp. 105–123

James, Alan, *Britain and the Congo Crisis 1960–63*, London: Macmillan Press, 1996

Jentleson, Bruce, *Opportunities Missed, Opportunities Seized: Preventive Diplomacy in the Post-Cold War World*, New York: Rowman and Littlefield, 2000

Kalb, Madeleine, *The Congo Cables: The Cold War in Africa from Eisenhower to Kennedy*, New York: Macmillan, 1982

Karns, Margaret and Mingst, Karen, 'Peacekeeping and the Changing Role of the United Nations: Four Dilemmas', in Thakur, Ramesh and Albrecht Schnabel (eds), *United Nations Peacekeeping Operations*, New York: UN University Press, 2001: 215–37

Karsh, Efrain, 'Cold War Post-Cold War: Does It Make a Difference for The Middle East?', in Inbar Efraim and Sifeffon Gabriel (eds), *The National Security of Small States*, London: Frank Cass, 1997

Kaysen, Carl and Rathjens, George W., 'Send in the Troops: A UN Foreign Legion', *The Washington Quarterly*, Vol. 20, No. 1 (1997): 207–18

Keesings Contemporary Archives, Bristol: Keesing Publications, 1960–70

Kissinger, Henry, *The Necessity for Choice*, New York: Harper and Brothers, 1961

Kissinger, Henry, *Diplomacy*, New York: Simon and Schuster, 1994

Kramer, Heinz, 'The Cyprus Problem and European Security', *Survival*, Vol. 39, No. 3 (1997): 16–32

Krska, Vladimir, 'Peacekeeping in Angola (UNAVEM I and II)', *International Peacekeeping*, Vol. 4, No. 1 (1997): 75–97

Lake, David A. and Rothchild, Donald, 'Containing Fear: The Origins and Management of Ethnic Conflict', *International Security*, Vol. 21, No. 2 (1996): 41–75

Lanzer, Toby, *Angola Report No. 5*, Uppsala: UN Department of Humanitarian Affairs, 1996

Lefever, Earnest W., *Crisis in the Congo*, Washington, DC: Brookings, 1965

Lewis, Joanna, 'Angola 1995: The Road to Peace', *International Relations*, Vol. 13, No. 1 (1996): 81–98

Lumumba, Patrice, *Congo My Country*, London: Pall Mall Press, 1962

Lundestad, Geir and Westad, Arne, *Beyond the Cold War: New Dimensions in International Relations*, Oslo: Scandinavian University Press, 1993

McDermott, Anthony, *Ethnic Conflict and International Security*, Oslo: Norsk Utenrikspolitisk Institutt, June 1994

McDonald, Robert, 'The Problem of Cyprus', *Adelphi Paper No. 234* (Winter 1988/9)

McInnes, Colin, '9/11 and the Afghan War', *Review of International Studies*, Vol. 29, No. 2 (2003): 165–84

Mackenzie, Lewis, *Peacekeeper: The Road to Sarajevo*, Vancouver: Douglas and McIntyre, 1993

Mackinlay, John, *The Peacekeepers: An Assessment of Peacekeeping Operations at the Arab-Israeli Interface*, London: Unwin Hyman, 1989

Mackinlay, John, 'Improving Multifunctional Forces', *Survival*, Vol. 36, No. 3, (1994): 149–73

Mahbubani, Kishore, 'The Dangers of Decadence: What the Rest Can Teach the West', *Foreign Affairs* (September/October 1993): 10–18

Maier, Karl, 'A Fragile Peace', *Africa Report* (January/February 1995): 23–7

Makinda, Samuel M., *Seeking Peace from Chaos: Humanitarian Intervention in Somalia*, Boulder: Lynne Rienner Publishers, 1993

Makinda, Samuel M., 'Sovereignty and Global Security', *Security Dialogue*, Vol. 29, No. 3 (1998): 281–92

Malaguias, Assis, 'The UN in Mozambique and Angola: Lessons Learned', *International Peacekeeping*, Vol. 3, No. 2 (1996): 87–103

Malone, David, 'The UN Security Council in the Post-Cold War World: 1987–1997', *Security Dialogue*, Vol. 28, No. 4 (1997): 393–409

Malone, David and Thakur, Ramesh, 'UN Peacekeeping: Lessons Learned', *Global Governance*, Vol. 7, No. 1 (2002): 11–17

Malone, David and Wermester, Karin, 'Boom and Burst? The Changing Nature of UN Peacekeeping', *International Peacekeeping*, Vol. 7, No. 4 (2000): 37–54

Marten, Kimberly Zizk, 'Defending Against Anarchy: From War to Peacekeeping in Afghanistan', *The Washington Quarterly*, Vol. 26, No. 1 (2002): 35–52

Mayall, James, *The New Interventionism 1991–1994*, Cambridge: Cambridge University Press, 1996

Maynes, Charles William, 'Squandering Triumph: The West Botched the Post-Cold War World', *Foreign Affairs*, Vol. 78, No. 1 (1999): 15–22

Melakopides, Costas, 'Making Peace in Cyprus: Time for a Comprehensive Initiative', *Martello Papers*, Ontario: Centre for International Relations, 1996

Meldrum, Andrew, 'Lessons from Angola', *Africa Report* (January/February 1993)

Meldrum, Andrew, 'Angola: Two Steps Back', *Africa Report* (March/April 1994): 45–47

Meredith, Martin, *The First Dance of Freedom*, London: Sphere Books, 1985

Miller, Benjamin, 'Competing Realist Perspectives on Great Power Crisis Behaviour' *Security Studies*, Vol. 5, No. 3 (1996): 309–57

Misra, Amalendu, 'Afghanistan: The Politics of Post-War Reconstruction' *Conflict, Security and Development*, Vol. 2, No. 3 (2002): 5–23

Moriarty, Michael, 'A Challenge for Peace', *An Cosantóin*, The Defence (Irish) Forces Magazine (September 1991): 28–32

Morphet, Sally, 'UN Peacekeeping and Election Monitoring', in Adam Roberts and Benedict Kingsbury (eds), *United Nations, Divided World*, Oxford: Clarendon, 1993, 183–239

Moskos, Charles, *Peace Soldiers: The Sociology of a UN Military Force*, Chicago: Chicago University Press, 1976

Norton, Augustus R. and Weiss, Thomas G., 'Superpowers and Peacekeepers', *Survival*, Vol. 32, No. 3 (1990): 212–20

O'Brien, Conor Cruise, *To Katanga and Back*, London: Hutchinson, 1962

Oksenberg, Michael, 'A Decade of Sino-American Relations', in Steven L. Spiegel (ed.), *At Issue*, New York: St Martin's Press, 1984

Olonisakin, Funmi, 'Peace and Justice in Africa: Post-Cold War Issues', *International Relations*, Vol. 15, No. 1 (2000): 41–50

ONUC Force Commander Directive Sept. 1960, Dublin: Irish Military Archives

Osmancavusoglu, Emel, 'Challenges to United Nations Peacekeeping Operations in the Post-Cold War Era', *Perceptions* (December 1999–February 2000): 133–45

Osterud, Oyvind, *The Reform of the International System: Studies of War and Peace*, Oslo: Norwegian University Press, 1986

Otunnu, Olara and Doyle, Michael W. (eds), *Peacemaking and Peacekeeping in the New Century*, Maryland: Rowman and Littlefield, 1996

Paris, Roland, 'Peacebuilding and the Limits of Liberal Internationalism', *International Security*, Vol. 22, No. 22 (1997): 54–89

Parsons, Anthony, *From Cold War to Hot Peace: UN Interventions 1947–1994*, London: Michael Joseph, 1995

Peceny, Marc, 'A Constructivist Interpretation of the Liberal Peace: The Ambiguous Case of the Spanish–American War', *Journal of Peace Research*, Vol. 34, No. 4 (1997): 415–30

Peck, Connie, *Sustainable Peace: The Role of the UN and Regional Organisations in Preventing Conflict*, New York: Rowman and Littlefield, 1998

Pierson-Mathy, P., 'The Prospects for Consolidating the Peace in Angola', *The Courier*, No. 153 (September/October 1995): 53–5

Puchala, Donald J., 'The United Nations Today: Reflections on a Dangerous and Fragmented World', *At Issue, Politics in the World Arena*, New York: St Martin's Press, 1984

Puchala, Donald J., 'Some Non-Western Perspectives on International Relations' *Journal of Peace Research*, Vol. 34, No. 2 (1997): 129–34

Pugh, Michael, *From Mission Cringe to Mission Creep*, Oslo: Institutt for Forsvarsstudier (Institute for Defence Studies), No. 2, 1997

Pugh, Michael, *The UN, Peace and Force*, London: Frank Cass and Co., 1997

Ratner, Steven R., *The New UN Peacekeeping*, London: Macmillan Press, 1997

Reno, William, 'War and the Failure of Peacekeeping in Sierra Leone', *SIPRI Yearbook 2001*

Rikhye, Indar Jit, *The Theory and Practice of Peacekeeping*, London: C. Hurst and Co., 1984

Roberts, Adam and Kingsbury, Benedict, *United Nations, Divided World* (2nd edition), Oxford: Oxford University Press, 1993

Roberts, Adam, 'The United Nations and International Security', *Survival*, Vol. 35, No. 2 (1993): 3–30

Roberts, Adam 'The Crisis in UN Peacekeeping', *Survival*, Vol. 36, No. 3 (1994): 93

Roberts, Adam, 'From San Francisco to Sarajevo: The UN and the Use of Force', *Survival*, Vol. 37, No. 4 (1995–6): 7–28

Roper, John, Nishihara, Masashi Olaka, Ottuna, Olaka and Schoettle, Enis C.B., *Keeping the Peace in the Post-Cold War Era: Strengthening Multilateral Peacekeeping A Report to the Trilateral Commission*, New York: Trilateral Commission, 1993

Rusi, Alpo M., *Dangerous Peace: New Rivalry in World Politics*, Boulder: Westview Press, 1997

Russett, Bruce and Sutterlin, James S., 'The UN in a New World Order', *Foreign Affairs*, Vol. 70, No. 2, 1991: 69–83

Ruzie, David, 'Maintaining, Building and Enforcing Peace: A Legal Perspective', *UNIDIR Newsletter* (December 1993): 12–18

Sahnoun, Mohammed, 'Prevention in Conflict Resolution: The Case of Somalia', *Irish Studies in International Affairs*, Vol. 5, 1994: 5–13

Sarooshi, Danesh, *The United Nations and the Development of Collective Security*, Oxford: Oxford University Press, 1999

Schnabel, Albrecht and Thakur, Ramesh, 'From *An Agenda for Peace* to the Brahimi Report: Towards a New Era of Peacekeeping', *United Nations Peacekeeping Operations*: New York: UN University Press, 2001: 238–255

Semb, Anne Julie, 'The New Practice of UN-authorised Interventions: A Slippery Slope for Forcible Interference', *Journal of Peace Research*, Vol. 37, No. 4 (2000): 469–88

Shimura, Hisako, 'The Role of the UN Secretariat in Organising Peacekeeping', in Ramesh, Thakur and Albrecht Schnabel (eds), *United Nations Peacekeeping Operations*, New York: UN University Press, 2001: 46–56

Shiner, Cindy, 'Angola: The World's Worst War', *Africa Report*, (January/February 1994): 14–16

Siekmann, Robert C.R., *Basic Documents on United Nations and Related Peacekeeping Forces*, Dordrecht: Martinus Nijhoff Publishers, 1989

Simpson, Chris, 'Angola: Peace or War', *Africa Report* (March/April 1994)

Skjelsbaek, Kjell (ed.), *The Cyprus Conflict and the Role of the United Nations*, Oslo: Norsk Utenrikspolitisk Institutt, No. 122, November 1988

Skjold, Nils, *Med FN Kongo*, Stockholm: Probus, 1994

Smith, Michael Laurence, and Uttley, Matthew, 'Joint and Combined Operations in the Expeditionary Era, Defining the Issues', *Defence Analysis*, Vol. 14, No. 1 (1998): 1–8

Sommerville, Keith, 'Angola: Groping Towards Peace or Slipping Back Towards War?', *Terrorism and Political Violence*, Vol. 8, No. 4 (1996): 11–39

Spiegel, Steven L. (ed), *At Issue, Politics in the World Arena* (4th edition), New York: St Martin's Press, 1984

Stenenga, James, 'UN Peacekeeping in the Cyprus Venture', *Journal of Peace Research*, Vol. 7 (1970): 1–10

Stiles, Kendall W. and MacDonald, Mary Ellen, 'After Consensus, What? Performance Criteria for the UN in the Post-Cold War Era', *Journal of Peace Research*, Vol. 29, No. 3 (1992): 299–311

Stjernfelt, Bertil, *The Sinai Peace Front*, London: Hurst and Company, 1992

Suhrke, Astri and Jones, Bruce, 'Preventive Diplomacy in Rwanda: Failure to Act or Failure of Actions?', in Bruce W. Jentleson (ed.), *Opportunities Missed, Opportunities Seized:*

Preventive Diplomacy in the Post-Cold War World, New York: Rowman and Littlefield, 2000: 238–64

Thakur, Ramesh, 'The United Nations in a Changing World', *Security Dialogue*, Vol. 24, No. 1 (1993): 7–20

Thakur, Ramesh, 'A Second Term for Boutros Ghali?', *Pacific Research* (August 1996): 35–8

Thakur, Ramesh and Schnabel, Albrecht (eds), *United Nations Peacekeeping Operations*, New York: UN University Press, 2001

Tharoor, Shashi, 'Should UN Peacekeeping Go Back to Basics?', *Survival*, Vol. 37, No.4 (1995–6): 52–65

Traub, James, 'Inventing East Timor', *Foreign Affairs* (July/August 2000): 74–89

Trigeorgis, Lenos and Trigeorgis, Hadjipavlou Maria, 'Cyprus: An Evolutionary Approach to Conflict Resolution', *Journal of Conflict Resolution*, Vol. 37, No. 2 (1993): 340–60

United Nations Report on the Situation in Katanga, 15 December 1960, UN Records, Irish Military Archives, Dublin, 1960

United Nations, *The Blue Helmets, A Review of United Nations Peacekeeping* (2nd edition), New York: United Nations Department of Public Information, 1990

United Nations, *Further Report of the Secretary General on the United Nations Angola Verification Mission (UNAVEM II)*, Security Council, S24125, 24 June 1992

United Nations, *Report of the Commission of Inquiry Established Pursuant to Security Council Resolution 885 (1993) to Investigate Armed Attacks on UNOSOM II Personnel Which Led to Casualties Among Them*, Security Council, S/1994/653, 1 June 1994

United Nations, *Report of the Secretary General on the United Nations Angola Verification Mission (UNAVEM II)*, Security Council, S/1994/374, 31 March 1994

United Nations, *UNAVEM Experience, Lessons Learned*, UN Department of Public Information, 1995

United Nations, *Co-operation Between the United Nations and Regional Organisations/ Arrangements in a Peacekeeping Environment*, Department of Peacekeeping Operations (DPKO), March 1999

United Nations, *Eighth Report of the Secretary General on the United Nations Observer Mission in Sierra Leone*, 23 September 1999

United Nations, *Comprehensive Review of the Whole Question of Peacekeeping Operations in All Their Aspects*, DPKO, 21 August 2000

United Nations, *Fourth Report of the Secretary General on the United Nations Observer Mission in Sierra Leone*, 19 May 2000.

United Nations, *Multidisciplinary Peacekeeping: Lessons from Recent Experience*, Security Council, DPKO, 9 August 2000

United Nations, *Report of the Panel on Peacekeeping Operations*, New York: General Assembly, A/55/305#S/2000/809, August 2000

United Nations, *Report of the Secretary-General on the Implementation of the Report of the Panel on United Nations Peace Operations*, UN General Assembly, A/55/502, 20 October 2000

United Nations, *Implementation of the Special Committee on Peacekeeping Operations and the Panel on United Nations Peace Operations*, UN General Assembly, A/56/732, 21 December 2001

United Nations, *Approved Budgetary Levels for Peacekeeping Operations for the period from 1 July 2002 to 30 June 2003: Note by the Secretary General*, UN General Assembly, A/C.5/57/22, 13 November 2002

United Nations, *Comprehensive Review of the Whole Question of Peacekeeping Operations in all their Respects: Report of the Special Committee on Peacekeeping Operations*, UN General Assembly, A/56/863, 11 March 2002

United Nations, Report of Secretary-General, *Improving the Financial Situation of the United Nations*, UN General Assembly, (A/57/498), 23 October 2002.

United Nations, *Strengthening of the United Nations: An Agenda for Further Change*, UN General Assembly, A/57/387, 9 September 2002

United Nations, *Death and Disability Benefits: Note by the Secretary General*, UN General Assembly, A/C.5/57/37, 14 March 2003

United Nations, *Handbook of UN Multinational Peacekeeping Operations*, New York: Department of Peacekeeping Operations, December 2003: Presentation to the General Assembly's Special Committee on Peacekeeping Operations in February 2002

Urquhart, Brian, 'UN Peacekeeping in the Middle East', *The World Today*, (March 1980): 37–45

Vitalis, Vangelis, 'Cyprus: Divided People, Divided Land', *New Zealand International Review*, Vol. 38, No. 1, (1992): 12–17

Von Horn, Carl, *Soldiering for Peace*, London: Cassell & Co., 1966

Voronkov, Lev, 'International Peace and Security: New Challenges to the UN', in Dimitris Bourantonis and Jarrod Wiener (eds), *The United Nations in the New World Order: The World Organisation at Fifty*, Basingstoke, Hants: Macmillan, 1995: 1–18;

Waern, Jonas, *Experiences of a Brigade Commander in Katanga*, K. Krigsvet, Akad, Tidskript, 1962

Weiss, Thomas P., 'Humanitarian Shell Games: Whither UN Reform', *Security Dialogue*, Vol. 29, No. 1 (1998): 9–25

Weiss, Thomas P., 'Researching Humanitarian Intervention: Some Lessons', *Journal of Peace Research*, Vol. 38, No. 4 (2001): 419–28

Weiss, Thomas P., Forsythe, David P. and Coate, Roger A. *The United Nations and Changing World Politics*, Boulder: Westview Press, 1997

Weissman, Stephen, *American Foreign Policy Towards the Congo 1960–1964*, Ithaca, New York: Cornell University Press, 1974

Wheeler, Nicholas, 'Saving Strangers: Humanitarian Intervention', *International Society*, New York

White, Brian, and Little, Richard Michael, *Issues in World Politics*, London: Macmillan, 1997

Wiseman, Henry (ed.), *Peacekeeping: Appraisals and Proposals*, New York: Pergamon Press, 1983

Worsley, Peter, and Kitromilides, Paschalis, *Small States in the Modern World* (revised edition), Nicosia: New Cyprus Association, 1979

Wrightson, Patricia S., 'Morality, Realism and Foreign Affairs: A Normative Realist Approach', *Security Studies*, Vol. 5, No. 2 (1995): 356–7

Yannis, Alexandra, 'Kosovo Under International Administration', *Survival*, Vol. 43, No. 2 (2001): 31–48

Young, Crawford, *Ideology and Development in Africa*, New Haven: Yale University Press, 1982

Zanghi, Claudio, 'The Inter-Relationship Between The Cyprus Invasion and Human Rights', *New Cyprus*, Vol. 7, No. 1 (1992): 23–7

Interviews (undertaken by Terry O'Neill)

Irish military personnel

Bergin, Noel, Lt General (retired), Former Chief-of-Staff, Irish Permanent Defence Force, Interview, 25 May 1995, Kildare

Bracken, Laurence, Commandant, Staff Officer Southern Command, Interview, 4 June 1994, Cork

Buckley, Mortimer, Colonel (retired), Former General Officer Commanding Western Command, Interview, 14 May 1995, Athlone

Conway, Dermot, Lt Colonel, Staff Officer, Army Headquarters, Interview, 6 June 1995, Dublin

Dixon, Patrick, Brig. General (retired), Former General Officer Commanding Western Command, Interview, 24 May 1995, Athlone

Donnelly, Liam, Comdt (retired), Interview, 16 November 1994, Mullingar

Dunne, Thomas, Colonel (retired), Former Officer Commanding 1st Brigade, Interview, 3 July 1994, Cork

Flynn, James, Brig. General (retired), DSM (Distinguished Service Medal), Former General Officer Commanding Eastern Command, Interview, 3 June 1995, Dublin

Freeman, Patrick, Lt Colonel (retired), Former Staff Officer Western Command Headquarters, Interview, 21 November 1994, Athlone

Goggin, Colman, Lt Colonel, Psychologist, Irish Permanent Defence Forces, Interview, 29 November 1994, Dublin

Howard, Bernard, Colonel, Aide President of Ireland, Interview, 26 May 1995, Dublin

Kilbride, Sean, Lt Colonel O.C., 6th Inf. Btn, interview by the author, 1 September 2000, Athlone

Leech, Joseph, Colonel (retired), Former Officer Commanding 4th Brigade, Interview, 12 October 1995, Athlone

McKeown, Sean, Lt General (retired), Former Chief of Staff Irish Permanent Defence, Force, Force Commander ONUC 1961–2, Interview, 30 March 1995, Athlone

Molloy, Patrick, Lt Colonel (retired), Former Officer Western Command, Interview, 3 October 1995, Athlone

Murphy, Daniel, Commandant, Staff Officer Western Command, Interview, 8 November 1997, Athlone

Murphy, Michael J., Major General (retired), Former Quartermaster-General, Irish Permanent Defence Force, Interview, 24 February 1995, Athlone

O'Callaghan, William, Lt General (retired), DSM, Former Force Commander, UNIFIL, Interview, 6 July 1995, Dublin

O'Donoghue, Maurice, Commandant (retired), Former Staff Officer Southern Command, Interview, 6 December 1994, Cork

O'Hanlon, Eiver, Colonel (retired), Former Executive Officer Western Command, Interview, 30 May 1997, Athlone

O'Leary, Richard, Commandant, Staff Officer Western Command, Interview, 3 November 1996, Athlone

O'Neill, Eugene, Colonel (retired), Former Officer Commanding Command and Staff School, Military College, Interview, 14 May 1995, Dublin

O'Sullivan, Gerald, Lt General (retired), D.S.M., Former Chief of Staff, Irish Permanent Defence Force, Interview, 10 May 1995, Dublin

Rohan, Patrick, Colonel (retired), Army Headquarters, Irish Permanent Defence Forces, Interview, 10 September 1996, Athlone

Young, William, Colonel (retired), Former Director of Cavalry, Irish Permanent Defence Force, Interview, 10 March 1983, Tibnin, Lebanon

Irish civilian personnel

Courtney, Conor, Father – Holy Ghost Order Missionary in Angola, Interview, March 1993, Lubango, Angola

Dorr, Noel, Former Irish Ambassador to the United Nations, Former First Secretary, Department of Foreign Affairs, Interview, 3 April 1995, Dublin

Kavanagh, Paul, Civilian Advisor to Force Commander UNIFICYP, Interview, 16 March 1996, Nicosia

Mullen, Anthony, Father – Holy Ghost Order Missionary in Angola, Interview, March 1993, Lubango, Angola

Military personnel of other armies

Egge, Bjorn, Lt General (retired), Royal Norwegian Army in conversation with the author, 21 August 1997, Oslo and subsequent correspondence

Geirulf, Arvid, Colonel (retired), Royal Norwegian Army, Interview, 28 August 1996, Oslo

Gervin, Alf, Major (retired), Royal Norwegian Army, Interview, 30 August 1995, Oslo

Noel, Stefan, Lt Colonel, Royal Netherlands Army, Interview, 12 October 1994, Ossondrecht, Netherlands

Noordsij, Lene, Lt Colonel, Royal Netherlands Army, Interview, 18 April 1993, Lubango, Angola

Orsten, Ben, Warrant Officer, Royal Netherlands Army, Interview, 21 October 1995, Arnhem, Netherlands

Sharma, Ashok, Major Indian Army, Interview, 24 March 1993, Lubango, Angola

Sohnemann, Bengt, Lt Colonel, Royal Danish Army, Interview, 10 December 1994, Karup, Denmark

Stromberg, Sven, Colonel, UN School, Royal Norwegian Army, Interview, 28 August 1995, Akershus, Norway

Wadensjo, Sven, Lt Colonel, UN School, Royal Swedish Army, Interview, 18 September 1994, Sodertalje, Sweden

Wahlgren, Lans-Erik, Lt General Royal Swedish Army, Former Force Commander UNIFIL and UNPROFOR, Interview, September 1994, Halmstad, Sweden

INDEX

Page numbers in bold indicate a table or map.